EYEWITNE

DUBLIN

MAIN CONTRIBUTOR: TIM PERRY

OBEDIENTIA · FELICITAS · CIVIUM · URBIS

LONDON, NEW YORK,
MELBOURNE, MUNICH AND DELHI
www.dk.com

PROJECT EDITOR Claire Folkard
ART EDITOR Jo Doran
EDITOR Freddy Hamilton
DESIGNERS Paul Jackson, Nicola Rodway
EDITORIAL ASSISTANT Sophie Warne
DTP DESIGNERS Samantha Borland, Lee Redmond, Rachel Symons
PICTURE RESEARCH Victoria Peel

PHOTOGRAPHERS
Joe Cornish, Tim Daly, Magnus Rew, Antony Souter,
Alan Williams

ILLUSTRATORS
Stephen Conlin, Gary Cross, Claire Littlejohn,
Maltings Partnership, Robbie Polley, John Woodcock

Reproduced in Singapore by Colourscan
Printed and bound in Malaysia by Vivar Printing Sdn. Bhd

First published in Great Britain in 1999
by Dorling Kindersley Limited
80 Strand, London WC2R 0RL

12 13 14 15 10 9 8 7 6 5 4 3 2 1

Reprinted with revisions
2000, 2001, 2002, 2003, 2004, 2006, 2008, 2010, 2012

Copyright 1999, 2012 © Dorling Kindersley Limited, London
A Penguin Company

ALL RIGHTS RESERVED. NO PART OF THIS PUBLICATION MAY BE
REPRODUCED, STORED IN A RETRIEVAL SYSTEM, OR TRANSMITTED IN ANY
FORM OR BY ANY MEANS, ELECTRONIC, MECHANICAL, PHOTOCOPYING,
RECORDING OR OTHERWISE, WITHOUT THE PRIOR WRITTEN PERMISSION OF
THE COPYRIGHT OWNER.

A CIP CATALOGUE RECORD IS AVAILABLE FROM THE BRITISH LIBRARY.

ISBN 978-1-40536-864-3

*Front cover main image: Typical door of a Georgian ivy-covered
house, Pembroke Street, Dublin*

LIBRARIES NI

C700884429

RONDO	24/01/2012
914.18350483	£ 10.99
BME	

Every care has been taken to ensure that this book is as up-to-date as
possible at the time of going to press. Some details, however, such as
telephone numbers, opening hours, prices, gallery hanging
arrangements and travel information are liable to change. The
publishers cannot accept responsibility for any consequences arising
from the use of this book, nor for any material on third party websites,
and cannot guarantee that any website address in this
book will be a suitable source of travel information. We value the views
and suggestions of our readers very highly. Please write to: Publisher,
DK Eyewitness Travel Guides, Dorling Kindersley, 80 Strand,
London, WC2R 0RL, Great Britain, or email: travelguides@dk.com.

Façade of St Teresa's Church

CONTENTS

INTRODUCING DUBLIN

View across the tombstones of
Glasnevin Cemetery

◁ Government buildings at dusk

Interior of Avondale House, the
home of Charles Stewart Parnell

Bookcases of rare books in
Marsh's Library

Sheep on the farm at Newbridge
Demesne, north of Dublin

Castletown House

INTRODUCING DUBLIN

FOUR GREAT DAYS IN DUBLIN

Celtic bronze fitting

A trip to Dublin, with its vibrant, historic city centre and the dramatic landscapes of Dublin Bay and the Wicklow Mountains in close proximity, appeals to both urbanites and wilderness lovers. What makes the Irish capital unique is its culture – a lively mix of traditional Gaelic games, music and dance and the refined pleasures of art, literature and drama, not to mention a fascinating history. These itineraries are intended to give you a taste of what Dublin has to offer, and to whet your appetite for a more in-depth experience. Costs include travel, food and admission to sights and tours. Family prices are for two adults and two children.

Baily Lighthouse at Howth Head

CELTIC LEGENDS

- A taste of ancient history
- Hurling at Croke Park
- A traditional Irish music session

TWO ADULTS allow at least €80

Morning
Start the day at **Trinity College** *(see pp38–9)*, where the Old Library houses the famous **Book of Kells** *(see p40)*. It is also worth looking at the splendid Long Room, with its barrel-vaulted ceiling and earthy smell of old books.

An early start will leave plenty of time to walk across to the nearby **National Museum – Archaeology** *(see pp44–5)*, with its beautiful Bronze Age collection and Iron Age bog bodies. Allow yourself at least an hour to wander through the finest collection of prehistoric gold artifacts in western Europe.

For lunch, there are a number of eateries on and around Kildare Street and Grafton Street, including **Gotham Café** *(see p139)* and the tasty but pricey **La Cave** *(see p139)*, with its impressive wine selection.

Afternoon
Catch a bus to the suburb of Drumcondra to watch sports legends play a top-class hurling or Gaelic football match at **Croke Park** stadium *(see p28)*. (Book tickets in advance at www.ticket master.ie). Matches generally take place at weekends, usually at 2pm and 4pm. The season runs from May to October; at other times of year, you can visit the lively Croke Park **GAA Museum**, and take a shot yourself with a hurley.

In the evening, head back into the city centre and on to the regenerated area of **Smithfield** *(see pp74–5)*, where the cosy and popular **Cobblestone** pub *(see p146)*, hosts regular sessions of traditional Irish music.

HOWTH

- Around Howth Head
- Seafood lunch
- Boat trip to Ireland's Eye
- An evening in Temple Bar

TWO ADULTS allow at least €80

Morning
Spend the morning walking around gorgeous **Howth Head** *(see p90)*. Dramatic cliff paths lead around the coastline, through the fishing village of Howth and its ruined abbey, and past **Baily Lighthouse**. More than half of Ireland's plant species can be found here, and there is also an abundance of wildlife, particularly birds.

On a sunny day, Howth Head is ideal for a picnic; alternatively, you can return to the village for lunch at **King Sitric** *(see p145)* or any one of the many fine restaurants along the waterfront, serving freshly caught fish and seafood.

Afternoon
From the East Pier, take a boat trip out to **Ireland's Eye** to explore the uninhabited

A hurling match at Croke Park

◁ St Stephen's Green (1796) by James Malton

island, now taken over by wildlife. There are two buildings on the island: a 19th-century Martello tower and an 8th-century church ruin. The most spectacular natural feature is the huge freestanding rock called The Stack, teeming with bird life. Always stick to the paths to avoid walking on any birds' nests; great black-backed gulls will dive-bomb any intruders. It is possible to spot shags, razorbills, guillemots, kittiwakes, fulmars and even puffins.

If the weather turns bad, visit the **Howth Transport Museum**, just past the DART station. It is filled with every form of transport imaginable.

Spend the evening in one of Howth's many cosy pubs, or head back into Dublin to join the crowds and a more lively scene in vibrant **Temple Bar** *(see pp58–9)*.

CULTURED DUBLIN

- **Admiring the Irish Masters**
- **A lunchtime concert**
- **Dublin's literary heritage**
- **A play at the Abbey**

TWO ADULTS allow at least €150

Morning
Begin the day with a stroll through the excellent **National Gallery** *(see pp48–51)*, for which you should allow at least an hour. At weekends, you may exit the gallery to find more art displayed on the railings around **Merrion Square** *(see pp46–7)*.

Enjoy a lunchtime concert at the **National Concert Hall** *(see p157)*, just south of **St Stephen's Green** *(see p41)*. Concerts take place every Tuesday from early June to late August, and usually once a week (mostly Fridays) during the rest of the year. The music performed can be anything from classical to jazz. In summer, there are often outdoor concerts in the adjacent **Iveagh Gardens** *(see p42)*. Stop for lunch at the **Shelbourne Hotel** *(see p130)*.

An impressive room within the 19th-century National Gallery

Afternoon
After lunch, cross the river to the **Hugh Lane Gallery** *(see p73)* and the **Dublin Writers' Museum** *(see p73)* in Parnell Square. At weekends, the museum often offers one-man shows called Writers Entertain, on the works of Ireland's foremost writers, such as Beckett, Joyce, Wilde and Yeats *(see p23)*. In the evening, see a play at the nearby **Gate Theatre** *(see p72)* or at the **Abbey** *(see p70)*, Ireland's national theatre, a short stroll away. Alternatively, join the popular **Dublin Literary Pub Crawl** *(see p156)*, which starts at 7:30pm from the Duke pub on Duke Street.

FAMILY FUN

- **A Viking invasion**
- **Living history at Dublinia**
- **Animal magic at Dublin Zoo**

FAMILY allow at least €150

Morning
The **Viking Splash Tour** *(see p156)* offers one of the liveliest – and wettest – ways to learn about Dublin's Viking history in special amphibious vehicles. Tours take place every half-hour from 10am until 5:30pm and start from St Stephen's Green North. Tour groups are dropped back at the Green, from where it is a 10–15-minute walk to **Dublinia** *(see p63)*.

Exhibits here include life-size reconstructions of a Viking ship, medieval markets and the skeleton of a medieval woman found during excavations. Stop for fish and chips at **Leo Burdock's** *(see p141)*.

Afternoon
After lunch, visit **Dublin Zoo** *(see p81)*, in **Phoenix Park** *(see p80)*, the largest urban park in Europe. The zoo has created a safari-like experience in the Elephant Habitat, where visitors can meet a family of elephants. The zoo also has white rhinos, including one born in May 2008.

A wander through the zoo can last all afternoon, but it is also worth taking some time to explore Phoenix Park itself, which opens out into woodland the further away from the city you get. It is ideal for a picnic or games – and deer spotting.

Children petting the elephants at Dublin Zoo

Putting Dublin on the Map

Dublin is the capital of the Republic of Ireland,
which takes up 85 per cent of Ireland, an island
that lies in the far northwest of Europe. Dublin sits
on the eastern coast of Ireland, on the Irish Sea, which
separates Ireland from Great Britain. The Liffey is the
main river running through the city. Dublin and its
surrounding county have a population of just over
one million, and good international communications.

EUROPE

Europe

*Most visitors to Dublin come
either by air or on the ferry to
Dun Laoghaire or Dublin Port.
The main ferry routes are from
Wales, Scotland and England.
There are international flights
to Dublin airport. Many
European flights are routed via
Amsterdam or Great Britain,
but flight times are only around
an hour from British airports.*

| 0 kilometres | 100 |
| 0 miles | 50 |

KEY

✈	Airport
⛴	Ferry port
⛴	Fast ferry port
═	Motorway
═ ═	Motorway under construction
▬	Major road
—	Railway line

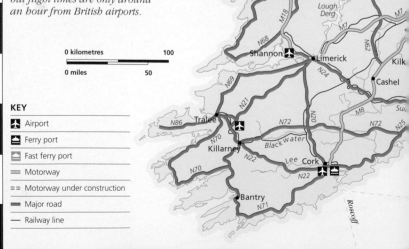

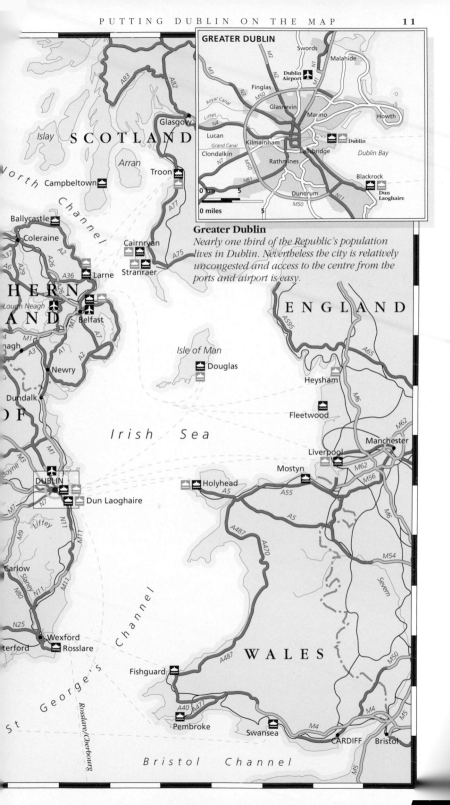

GREATER DUBLIN

Swords
Malahide
Dublin Airport
Finglas
Royal Canal
Glasnevin
Marino
Howth
Liffey
Lucan
Grand Canal
Kilmainham
Dublin
Clondalkin
Ballsbridge
Dublin Bay
Rathmines
Dundrum
Blackrock
Dun Laoghaire

0 km 5
0 miles 5

Greater Dublin
Nearly one third of the Republic's population lives in Dublin. Nevertheless the city is relatively uncongested and access to the centre from the ports and airport is easy.

Islay
SCOTLAND
Glasgow
Arran
Troon
Campbeltown
North Channel
Ballycastle
Coleraine
Larne
Cairnryan
Stranraer
ENGLAND
HERN LAND
Lough Neagh
Belfast
nagh
Newry
Isle of Man
Douglas
Heysham
OF
Dundalk
Fleetwood
Irish Sea
Manchester
Liverpool
Mostyn
DUBLIN
Dun Laoghaire
Holyhead
Liffey
Carlow
WALES
Carlow
Wexford
Rosslare
terford
Fishguard
St George's Channel
Rosslare/Cherbourg
Pembroke
Swansea
CARDIFF
Bristol
Bristol Channel

Address to

Chas S. Parnell, Esq.

President of the Irish National Land League

Sir, We

tender you on behalf of the tenant farmers of Ireland a hearty Cead Mile Failte home again to the country you have so nobly served during your brief sojourn in the United States. Short as your stay has been in that mighty Western Republic it has nevertheless been signalised by the most splendid and opportune services to the present wants of our starving people, while being at the same time pregnant with encouraging hope for the future welfare of our fatherland. While thousands of families, pauperised through the operation of an infamous land system have been saved by your wondrous and indefatigable exertions from the fate which befel our famine-slaughtered kindred in '47 and '48, the heart of Ireland has followed in the wake of your triumphal progress among a generous and sympathetic people, and throbbed with expectant joy as they pledged you the moral support of America in our struggle against felonious landlordism.

As the representative of the Irish People and delegate of the National Land League, you and your colleague Mr. John Dillon, have had extended to you honours and manifestations of encouragement outpassing any yet conferred by the land of Washington Franklin and Carroll upon the champions of oppressed nationalities; and your country felt proudly raised once more to the dignity of a recognised nation when the House of Representatives bestowed upon you the proud privilege of advocating the cause of Ireland before the most representative assembly of the greatest Government in the world. From the St. Lawrence to the Potomac — from the Atlantic seaboard to the plains of Minnesota — the landlord-banished portion of our people have pledged anew their fidelity to Ireland and their vows for her deliverance, when by those enthusiastic greetings immense demonstrations and military parades they welcomed you as the ambassador of their resurgent Sireland while their munificent contributions and promised continued cooperation infuses a spirit of sanguine expectation into our impoverished people that the felt cause of their poverty and humiliation will soon fall beneath the united efforts of our entire race.

You are landing in Ireland at a time which may be deemed a momentous period in the history of that coercive and infamous Union which has been such a political scourge to our Country and when the spirit of Irish nationality is endangered by the virulent attacks of a truculent and unscrupulous Government. We sincerely hope that you have sped across the waters like another Perseus to save the Andromeda of nations from the political monster now threatening her with national destruction and that her deliverance from immediate danger achieved you will return to the assistance of your colleagues to complete the mission you were sent on by the body of which you are the honoured and trusted Head.

Signed

Patrick Egan	J. F. Grehan	Thomas Sexton
A. J. Kettle	R. J. Donnelly	Michael Davitt

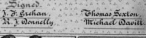

PARNELL ADDRESSING THE UNITED STATES HOUSE OF REPRESENTATIVES IN SESSION.
WASHINGTON, FEB 2nd 1880.

THE HISTORY OF DUBLIN

*T**he city of Dublin first took form in the early 9th century when Vikings founded one of their largest settlements outside Scandinavia on the site of the present city. Since then, it has suffered wars and conflict over many centuries. In the 20th century Dublin established its own identity and today it is a thriving, modern city, rich in history and proud of its past.***

Archaeological digs show evidence of civilization in the Dublin area as early as 7500 BC. The 4th millennium BC saw the influx of Neolithic farmers and herdsmen who built monumental tombs such as those found at Newgrange *(see pp120–21)*.

The Celts arrived around 700 BC and things changed little for 1,000 years. When St Patrick arrived in AD 432 bringing Christianity with him to Ireland, the Celts were quick to embrace the religion. During the golden age of Celtic Christianity the Dublin area was home to several churches and it is said that the present-day St Patrick's Cathedral (built in 1192) is where the saint baptized converts around AD 450. This era produced high levels of Christian scholarship, resulting in such treasures as the elaborately decorated Book of Kells *(see p40)*.

The city's modern Gaelic name of "Baile Atha Cliath" derives from a Celtic settlement on the north bank of the River Liffey. Known then as Ath Cliathe ("the ford over the hurdles") it was the only crossing over the river and lay at the junction of four major

Engraving showing St Patrick banishing snakes from Ireland

roads. It was the community at Ath Cliathe that bore the brunt of the island's first planned naval invasion by the Vikings.

THE VIKINGS

Norse Vikings established their first harbour in Dublin in AD 841 and left in AD 902, under pressure from local chieftains. They returned 15 years later and built a stronghold situated between the present location of Dublin Castle and Wood Quay. It was here that the rivers Liffey and Poddle converged in a body of dark, still water which the Vikings called *Dyfflin* or *Dubh Linn* (or "black pool").

In 919 at the Battle of Dublin the Vikings fended off the King of Tara and by the mid-1100s they started to intermarry with the Celts. The Vikings were then defeated at the Battle of Clontarf in 1014 by Brian Ború, the Irish High King. Under King Sitric the Silkbeard, Dublin became a Christian vassal state. He oversaw the construction of a wooden cathedral (later rebuilt as Christ Church). By this time Dublin's population was around 5,000.

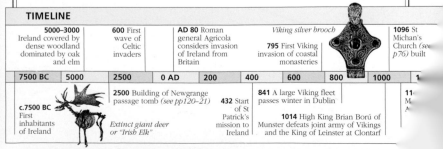

TIMELINE

5000–3000 Ireland covered by dense woodland dominated by oak and elm	**600** First wave of Celtic invaders	**AD 80** Roman general Agricola considers invasion of Ireland from Britain	*Viking silver brooch* **795** First Viking invasion of coastal monasteries	**1096** St Michan's Church *(see p76)* built

7500 BC	5000	2500	0 AD	200	400	600	800	1000	1

c.7500 BC First inhabitants of Ireland *Extinct giant deer or "Irish Elk"*	**2500** Building of Newgrange passage tomb *(see pp120–21)*	**432** Start of St Patrick's mission to Ireland	**841** A large Viking fleet passes winter in Dublin **1014** High King Brian Ború of Munster defeats joint army of Vikings and the King of Leinster at Clontarf

◁ **Address to Charles Stewart Parnell by the Land League**

ANGLO-NORMAN CONQUEST

Feuds in Ireland led to Dermot Mac-Murrough, the King of Leinster, asking Henry II of England to send an army to aid him. This resulted in the appearance of Richard de Clare, better known as Strongbow, in 1169. Within a year he had taken control of Dublin and married MacMurrough's daughter. He was also the instigator of the construction of Christ Church Cathedral *(see pp64–5)*.

The Marriage of Strongbow and Aoife, by Daniel Maclise (1854)

When MacMurrough died in 1171, Strongbow was in line to succeed him. Henry II sent an army to Ireland to check his ambitions, in part by recognizing Strongbow's suzerainty over the province of Leinster. Henry then spent four months in Dublin establishing control.

Under Anglo-Norman control, the structure and size of the city grew. Fortified walls and watchtowers were built, and in 1205 construction on Dublin Castle started. St Patrick's was made a cathedral in 1220 and underwent massive expansion while, in its shadows, the Liberties, the city's earliest suburbs, were growing in strength. The city became overcrowded and in 1348 was struck by the terrifying plague known as the Black Death.

TUDOR AND STUART RULE

Like the Vikings before them, the Anglo-Normans had entwined themselves in Irish society through marriage and religion. Some of them, such as the Fitzgeralds, the Butlers and the Burkes, effectively controlled dynasties. One of them, "Silken" Thomas Fitzgerald, son of the 9th Earl of Kildare, staged a revolt against London in 1534. This was defeated by King Henry VIII who, in 1541, passed the Act of Supremacy that made him King of Ireland and the head of the Church which, under the English Reformation, had broken from Rome. All land was the property of the English crown and, by dissolving the monasteries and sentencing to death all men of the Fitzgerald family, he indicated the start of a strongarm rule and the introduction of Protestantism to Ireland.

The reign of Elizabeth I witnessed the development of the island into a British colony, with plantations set up throughout Ireland. In 1592, on the site of a dissolved monastery near Dublin, she founded Trinity College as a seat of Protestant learning: a status it retained well into the 20th century.

Henry VIII with Bishop Sherbourne by Lambert Barnard (1519)

TIMELINE

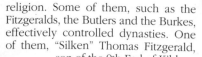

1166 Dermot MacMurrough, King of Leinster, flees overseas	**1297** First Irish Parliament meets in Dublin	**1366** Statutes of Kilkenny forbid marriage between Anglo-Normans and Irish
1172 Pope affirms King Henry II of England's lordship over Ireland		

1200	1250	1300	1350	1400	1450

1471 8th Earl of Kildare made Lord Deputy of Ireland

Strongbow's Normans at invitation of King of Dermot ...ough

A section of Strongbow's tomb

1348 The Black Death: one third of population dies within three years

1394 King Richard II lands with army to reassert control; returns five years later but with inconclusive results

1487 Kildare crowns Lambert Simnel, Edward VI in Dublin

London's grip over Ireland intensified in 1649, when Oliver Cromwell arrived in Dublin. His infamous campaigns left several thousand dead or deported and he forced the Irish from their fertile lands in the east to the barren western province of Connaught.

The Rotunda Hospital in 1795, Dublin's first maternity hospital

THE PENAL LAWS

In 1690, the Catholic ex-king of England, James II, was defeated by the Dutch Protestant William Prince of Orange (King William III) at the Battle of the Boyne. In the years following, religious persecution was formalized into a Penal Code. Catholics were prohibited from voting, trading, buying land, holding elected or state office, or entering professions.

THE PROTESTANT ASCENDANCY

While William III's Penal Laws were spelling hard times for the Catholic population in the rest of Ireland, Dublin's middle classes and aristocrats (many of them absentee landlords who came to Ireland during the entertaining season) enjoyed a very comfortable existence. Throughout the 18th century they commissioned ostentatious homes such as Leinster House and Powerscourt House. The owners of the grand town houses employed master craftsmen from around the world, such as the German-English architect Richard Castle and the Swiss-Italian stuccodores Paolo and Filippo Francini.

William of Orange at the Battle of the Boyne

Among the desirable addresses at the time were St Stephen's Green, Marlborough Street to the north of the Liffey and Ely Place on the southside. If they were ill, the Royal Hospital at Kilmainham attended their needs. Dublin also boasted the Rotunda Lying-In Hospital, the first maternity hospital in the British Isles. Much of the funding for this venture came from the adjacent and ornate Rotunda Gardens (no longer in existence), where members of high society frequently met and attended concerts. In Georgian times the privileged Protestants were able to patronize the arts: Handel premiered the *Messiah* in the city in 1742. Eleven years earlier, the still extant Royal Dublin Society was founded to promote the arts, science and agriculture. Many great academics and novelists also emerged from Trinity College, including the philosopher Edmund Burke, and Jonathan Swift, author of *Gulliver's Travels* and the Dean of St Patrick's Cathedral *(see p61)* from 1713 to 1745.

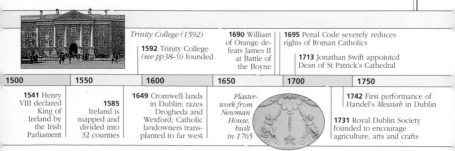

	Trinity College (1592)	**1690** William of Orange defeats James II at Battle of the Boyne	**1695** Penal Code severely reduces rights of Roman Catholics	
	1592 Trinity College *(see pp38–9)* founded		**1713** Jonathan Swift appointed Dean of St Patrick's Cathedral	
1500	**1550**	**1600**	**1650**	**1700**	**1750**
1541 Henry VIII declared King of Ireland by the Irish Parliament	**1585** Ireland is mapped and divided into 32 counties	**1649** Cromwell lands in Dublin; razes Drogheda and Wexford; Catholic landowners transplanted to far west	*Plasterwork from Newman House, built in 1765*	**1742** First performance of Handel's *Messiah* in Dublin **1731** Royal Dublin Society founded to encourage agriculture, arts and crafts

PUBLIC WORKS IN THE 18TH CENTURY

Many of the most impressive sights in Dublin today were built during the Protestant Ascendancy, in the Georgian era.

Among the most splendid structures of this period are Castletown House (1722–32), the Custom House (1791) and the Four Courts (1786–1802). The two latter buildings were both designed by James Gandon. Dublin was also one of the first cities in the world to enjoy planned development with the inauguration of the Wide Streets Commission in 1751. Further improvements came with the National Botanic Gardens in 1789.

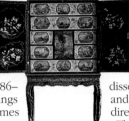

Lacquer cabinet, Castletown House

Commerce also helped shape the city. In the 1760s the Grand Canal was built and Ireland's most famous company began in 1759 when Arthur Guinness opened his brewery.

CATHOLIC EMANCIPATION AND RESISTANCE

Despite lengthy protests by pamphleteers and orators, the first real hint of relaxation of the penal laws came in 1782 when the Irish Parliament, led by Henry Grattan, passed a Declaration of Rights which, as well as pressing for independence for Ireland, also allowed Catholics to practise law. The unsuccessful 1798 revolt by the United Irishmen, led by Dublin Protestant Wolfe Tone, may have been instrumental in convincing the Westminster government to impose the 1800 Act of Union. This dissolved the Irish Parliament and saw the introduction of direct rule from England.

The first 19th-century revolt against British rule was led by Robert Emmet in 1803, who attempted to seize Dublin Castle. The most effective protest of the early part of the century was led by Daniel O'Connell, a Catholic lawyer, who later became known as "The Liberator" as a result of his efforts on behalf of the people who shared his religious beliefs. He supported mass peaceful protests and was elected an MP in 1828 but, as a Catholic, was unable to take his seat. In response to O'Connell's mass rallies and protests, the Emancipation Act of 1829 was passed. O'Connell was the first Catholic to be elected Mayor of Dublin in 1841 but, when he later called for a repeal of the Act of Union, he was jailed.

James Gandon's impressive Custom House, on the north bank of the Liffey

TIMELINE

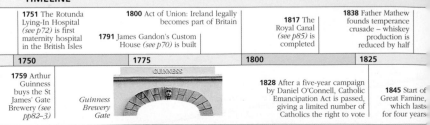

1751 The Rotunda Lying-In Hospital (*see p72*) is first maternity hospital in the British Isles

1791 James Gandon's Custom House (*see p70*) is built

1800 Act of Union: Ireland legally becomes part of Britain

1817 The Royal Canal (*see p85*) is completed

1838 Father Mathew founds temperance crusade – whiskey production is reduced by half

1750   1775   1800   1825

1759 Arthur Guinness buys the St James' Gate Brewery (*see pp82–3*)

Guinness Brewery Gate

1828 After a five-year campaign by Daniel O'Connell, Catholic Emancipation Act is passed, giving a limited number of Catholics the right to vote

1845 Start of Great Famine, which lasts for four years

THE GREAT FAMINE AND FURTHER REBELLIONS

The history of 19th-century Ireland is dominated by the Great Famine of 1845–8, which was caused by the total failure of the potato crop. Although Irish grain was still being exported to England, around one million people died from hunger or disease. By 1900, the pre-famine population of eight million had fallen by

O'Connell Street shortly after the Easter Rising

Ration card from Famine period

half. Many of the poor moved into Dublin and the middle-class Dubliners moved out to the suburbs. Rural hardship fuelled a campaign for tenants' rights that evolved into demands for independence from Britain. Great strides towards "Home Rule" were made in Parliament by the charismatic politician, Charles Stewart Parnell.

SUPPORT FOR HOME RULE GROWS

In 1902 Arthur Griffith founded the Sinn Féin newspaper; its name, meaning "We, Ourselves", expressed their central policy thrust and it soon gave rise to a political party of the same name. In 1913 the Irish Volunteers (the forerunners of the Irish Republican Army) were formed. Political freedom was increasingly important at this time of stark poverty and violent clashes between workers and employers. One of the leaders of the workers' side, James Connolly, would soon broaden his political agenda to Republicanism.

Daniel O'Connell, "The Liberator"

WORLD WAR I AND THE EASTER RISING

Although the Home Rule Bill made its final passage through the British parliament, its implementation was suspended due to the outbreak of war. A small contingent felt that the best time to launch an attack on British rule was when Britain was at its weakest. Hence, on Easter Monday 1916, Patrick Pearse and other members of a provisional government proclaimed the Declaration of Independence from the General Post Office (see p71) in O'Connell Street. The band of rebels occupied several buildings in the capital.

The Easter Rising was put down within a few days but only after 300 citizens were killed and much of the city centre razed to the ground. The British forces lost patience with the Irish cause and the rebel leaders were shot for treason at Kilmainham Gaol. This overreaction made those executed into martyrs and renewed resentment towards Britain.

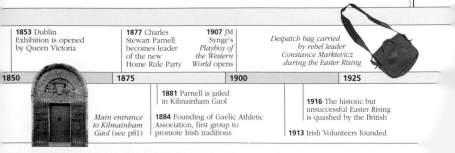

1853 Dublin Exhibition is opened by Queen Victoria	**1877** Charles Stewart Parnell becomes leader of the new Home Rule Party	**1907** JM Synge's *Playboy of the Western World* opens	*Despatch bag carried by rebel leader Constance Markievicz during the Easter Rising*

1850	1875	1900	1925

1881 Parnell is jailed in Kilmainham Gaol

1916 The historic but unsuccessful Easter Rising is quashed by the British

Main entrance to Kilmainham Gaol (see p81)

1884 Founding of Gaelic Athletic Association, first group to promote Irish traditions

1913 Irish Volunteers founded

View of O'Donovan Bridge which links the north and south sides of modern Dublin

INDEPENDENCE AND CIVIL WAR

The years after World War I were some of the bloodiest in Dublin's history. The resentment over the treatment of the Rising leaders, and a plan to bring in conscription in Ireland, helped the cause of the Sinn Féin party, which won three-quarters of Irish seats in the 1918 election. These new MPs refused to take up their seats and instead met at a newly formed Dáil Éireann (Parliament of Ireland) at the Mansion House *(see p41)*. The Dáil's Minister of Finance was Michael Collins, who was also head of the Irish Volunteers' campaign of urban guerrilla warfare. On the morning of 21 November 1920, Collins ordered the assassination of 14 undercover British officers in Dublin. That afternoon, British forces retaliated in what soon became known as Bloody Sunday, when they shot 12 spectators at a big Gaelic football game at Croke Park. Other skirmishes continued throughout the city, including the burning of the

Custom House *(see p70)* in May 1921. Soon after this, the British government instigated a truce and both sides signed the Anglo-Irish Treaty.

The treaty gave limited independence to what was to be called the Irish Free State, but six Ulster counties were to be excluded, and members of the Free State parliament (the Dáil) would have to swear allegiance to the British crown. A faction of the Dáil led by Eamon De Valera opposed the treaty, and in June 1922 Civil War broke out. Anti-treaty forces occupied the Four Courts building *(see p76)*, but this was bombed by the army under Collins. The Free State government proved ruthless in its imprisonment and later execution of anti-treaty rebels, but Collins himself finally became a victim when he was ambushed and shot. In May 1923 De Valera ordered an end to the fighting by anti-treaty rebels and left Sinn Féin.

Eamon De Valera, a major figure in modern Irish politics

TIMELINE

RECENT HISTORY

Within three years De Valera had formed a new party called Fianna Fáil (meaning "Warriors of Ireland"). By 1932, his party had acquired power. With only two short periods of time out of office, De Valera held the post of

Young Irish dancers

Taoiseach (prime minister) until 1959, when he became president for a further 14 years. His policies were largely insular and mirrored the Catholic Church on social issues. During World War II, De Valera kept Ireland neutral, so Dublin only experienced one Luftwaffe bombing.

European City of Culture doorway

After the war, Fianna Fáil were beaten in the election by Fine Gael. Though they were the descendants of the pro-treaty side, it was Fine Gael who oversaw the creation of the Republic of Ireland in 1949, which severed all ties with Britain by leaving the Commonwealth.

Dublin remained relatively immune to the political situation in Northern Ireland, as it does today, though in 1966 the IRA bombed the huge Nelson Pillar. Then, in 1972, the British Embassy in Dublin was petrol-bombed, in retaliation for the shooting of 13 civilians on a protest march in Derry, in Northern Ireland, on what became known thereafter as Ireland's second Bloody Sunday. In May 1974 a series of car bombs in Dublin and Monaghan killed 33 people. The Ulster Volunteer Force claimed responsibility.

DUBLIN INTO THE MILLENNIUM

In 1991 Dublin was named European City of Culture, which spurred the rejuvenation of Temple Bar *(see pp58–9)* into a world-class cultural quarter. The majority of new development was in the wealthier areas south of the river, though the divide between north and south has narrowed since the late 1990s.

In 2007, Unionists and Nationalists agreed to share power in a new Northern Ireland government, in a deal largely brokered by then Taoiseach Bertie Ahern and British Prime Minister Tony Blair. Ahern's successor Brian Cowen was at the helm during the 2009 economic downturn, which came to a head in November 2010, with Ireland forced to request financial help from the International Monetary Fund.

Grafton Street in modernized southwest Dublin

1972 Ireland joins European Community	1988 Dublin celebrates its millennium; most historians, however, trace its founding to an even earlier date	President Mary Robinson (1990–97)	1998 Peace talks between the British and Irish governments, and parties in Northern Ireland, result in the Good Friday Agreement	2010 Dublin is designated a UNESCO City of Literature
970	**1980**	**1990**	**2000**	**2010**	**2020**
1976 British ambassador assassinated in Dublin	1979 Pope John Paul II celebrates mass in front of more than one million people	1996 Investigative journalist Veronica Guerin murdered / 1990 Mary Robinson is the first woman elected as President of Ireland	2007 Unionists and Nationalists agree to share power in a new Northern Ireland government	

DUBLIN AT A GLANCE

Although it is a fairly small city, Dublin offers a wealth of different attractions which draw in millions of visitors each year. Those in the city centre or a short way outside Dublin are covered in the *Area by Area* section of this book. Sights further out of the city include the elegant stately homes of Castletown House and Powerscourt. In central Dublin, Temple Bar offers shopping, eating and drinking and the arts in a trendy, relaxed environment. Alternatively the glittering treasures of the National Museum or the liquid treasures of the Guinness Storehouse may lure you inside. A selection of Dublin's most popular sights is given below.

DUBLIN'S TOP TEN ATTRACTIONS

Guinness Storehouse
See pp82–3

Trinity College
See pp38–9

National Museum
See pp44–5

Castletown House
See pp106–7

National Gallery
See pp48–51

St Patrick's Cathedral
See p61

Powerscourt
See pp114–15

Temple Bar
See pp58–9

Custom House
See p70

Christ Church Cathedral
See pp64–5

◁ The bell tower in Trinity College

Celebrated Visitors and Residents

For many centuries Dublin has produced some of the greatest literary names in history. However, Dubliners are also famous for music, philosophy and politics. Edmund Burke, widely considered to be the father of British Conservatism, was born to the north of the Liffey. Writers such as Yeats, Beckett and Wilde lived in the city intermittently, having been born in Ireland. Jonathan Swift began the tradition of brilliant Irish writing at around the beginning of the 18th century. Great Irish writing continues to this day, with such prize-winning authors as Seamus Heaney, William Trevor, Anne Enright, John Banville and Roddy Doyle.

The Duke of Wellington
Wellington was born in Dublin, close to what is now Wellington Quay, in 1769. He became one of the most successful generals and politicians in British history.

G F Handel
The German-born composer decided to première his most famous oratorio, the Messiah, in the new Music Hall in Fishamble Street in 1741.

NORTH OF THE LIFFEY

SOUTHWEST DUBLIN

Jonathan Swift
Famous as the author of many literary works, including Gulliver's Travels, *Swift became Dean of St Patrick's Cathedral in 1713.*

D. SWIFT

Bram Stoker
The author of Dracula, *one of the most famous horror stories ever written, was born in Dublin in 1847 and lived on Harcourt Street just off St Stephen's Green.*

James Joyce
*Quite possibly Dublin's most
famous author. Two of his greatest
works,* Ulysses *and* Dubliners,
*are set in Dublin. Many of the
characters and places in*
Ulysses *are based on reality.*

William Butler Yeats
*Born in Sligo, in northwest Ireland,
Yeats was one of the founders of
the Abbey Theatre. The poet spent
much of his adult life in London
but returned to Ireland frequently.*

Samuel Beckett
*The playwright was
born south of
Dublin and studied
at Trinity College
(see pp38–9). One
of his most famous
and enigmatic
works is
Waiting
for Godot.*

SOUTHEAST
DUBLIN

Oscar Wilde
*This flamboyant author and playwright
was born in Dublin – his family home
can still be seen on the corner of Merrion
Square. He enjoyed great success with such
plays as* The Importance of Being Earnest.

0 metres   200

0 yards   200

Dublin's Best: Pubs

Everyone knows that Dublin is famous for its vast number of drinking establishments but, on arrival in the city, the choice can seem overwhelming. All the pubs are different – they range from vibrant, trendy bars to traditional pubs. Whatever your choice of environment and beverage, you can be guaranteed to find it in Dublin. These pages offer just a taster of the most popular pubs in the city and what they are famous for, but for a more complete listing, turn to pages 146–7.

Slattery's
Once a popular music pub just north of the Liffey, Slattery's has been totally modernized and is just as much of a success in its reincarnation as a trendy bar.

NORTH OF THE LIFFEY

The Stag's Head
This gorgeous Victorian pub has a long mahogany bar and has retained its original mirrors and stained glass. Located down an alley off Dame Street, this atmospheric pub is well worth seeking out.

SOUTHWEST DUBLIN

The Brazen Head
Reputedly the oldest pub in Dublin. The present building, still with its courtyard for coach and horses, dates back to 1750. The interior is full of dark wood panelling and old photographs of Dublin.

Hogan's
A café bar rather than a pub, Hogan's is a stylish establishment serving excellent drinks, and is popular with a young, trendy crowd. It is centrally situated on George's Street.

Oliver St John Gogarty

This famous old pub in the heart of Temple Bar is renowned for its live music throughout the day, and good food. It is named after the poet and friend of James Joyce. The atmosphere is relaxed and it is popular with visitors keen to sample a part of traditional Dublin.

O'Neill's

Just round the corner from Grafton Street, O'Neill's is one of the best places in the city for pub food. Its cosy atmosphere and location close to Trinity College make it a favourite with Dublin's student population.

LIFFEY

SOUTHEAST
DUBLIN

0 metres   200
0 yards   200

McDaid's

Playwright Brendan Behan downed many a pint in this pub, which dates from 1779. Though on the tourist trail, McDaid's retains a bohemian charm and bars upstairs and downsta provide space for a leisurely d

O'Donoghue's

A good mix of locals and tourists, y old, frequent this pub in the hear Dublin which has been a city f years. Famous as the pub wh folk group began in the 1⁹ today for its live traditi

DUBLIN THROUGH THE YEAR

The city is at its busiest in July and August, which are the most popular months for visiting Dublin. June and September can be pleasant but don't count on the weather, since Ireland's lush beauty is the product of a wet climate. Most Dublin sights are open all year round but, in the low season (generally November to March), some of them have limited opening hours or close

Revellers at the St Patrick's Day parade

completely. In summer, events are held in honour of anything from gardens to James Joyce, but a common thread is music, and few festivals are complete without it. Dublin is at its best when celebrating and is thus a treat at Christmas or New Year. Look out for the word *fleadh* (festival) in the city, but remember, too, that the Irish are a spontaneous people: festivities can spring from the air, or from a tune on a fiddle.

St Patrick's Day Festival parade through the streets of Dublin (March)

SPRING

After the relative quiet of the winter months, spring sees a flurry of festivals and events in Dublin. St Patrick's Day, on 17 March, is said to mark the beginning of the tourist season. This important national holiday in honour of Ireland's patron saint is celebrated with music and carnival-style abandon throughout the city. Accommodation is often in short supply around this time, so be sure to book well in advance.

MARCH

St Patrick's Day Festival *(around 17 Mar)*. Numerous street-theatre acts and performers fill the city during colourful celebrations that centre on a parade on St Patrick's Day itself.
St Patrick's Day Celtic Winners Show *(mid-Mar)*, Cloghran. Popular annual championship dog show.
Colours Boat Race *(late Mar)*. A rowing race along the Liffey between University College Dublin and Trinity College.

APRIL

Handel's Day *(13 Apr)*. This free celebration of music and history commemorates the première of Handel's *Messiah*, which took place on Fishamble Street on 13 April 1742.
Dublin: One City One Book *(Apr)*.

During this month-long event aimed at promoting the pleasures of reading, the whole city is invited to enjoy the same book.
Poetry Now Festival *(early Apr)*. Held in Dun Laoghaire, events include readings, masterclasses, workshops and children's activities.

MAY

May Day Parade *(first Mon in May)*. Celebrations and colourful parades through the city streets.

May Day Parade in central Dublin

Bloom in the Park *(late May or early Jun)*. Phoenix Park. Ireland's largest gardening event features gardening designs, floral displays and a food pavilion.
Laytown Beach Races *(late May or early Jun)*. Horse races on a beach north of Dublin.
Tour of Ireland Cycle Challenge *(second week)*. A five-day cycle race which starts in Dublin and ends in Lisburn.

of Handel's **ril)**

AVERAGE DAILY HOURS OF SUNSHINE

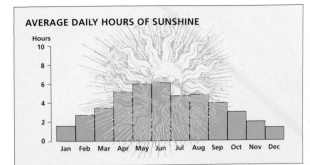

Hours

| 10 | 8 | 6 | 4 | 2 | 0 |

Jan Feb Mar Apr May Jun Jul Aug Sep Oct Nov Dec

Sunshine Chart
Hours of sunshine in rainy Dublin are few and far between for most of the year. In summer, however, the days are often long, hot and very sunny. As in the rest of the country, the weather is notoriously unpredictable, so skies can cloud over in minutes.

SUMMER

Summer represents the height of the festive calendar for the visitor and the Dubliner alike and is the city's busiest time of year. There is a succession of outdoor music, arts and community festivals of all kinds, culminating in the city's top social event, the annual Dublin Horse Show.

JUNE

Temple Bar Cultural Trust Summer Programme *(May–Aug, see p159)*. Free, family-friendly events which include open-air cinema, weekly markets and a chocolate festival.
Dublin Writer's Festival *(first week)*. An international literary festival celebrating Dublin's literary heritage and the very best of Irish and international writing.
Docklands Maritime Festival *(first week)*. A community festival that centres on

Blues performance at one of Dublin's many summer festivals

Pearse Street and City Quay, with shows and activities for all ages.
Summer in Dublin Festival *(Jun–Aug)*. Free music and family activities in the city's parks and public spaces.
County Wicklow Gardens Festival *(all month)*. Held at private and public gardens south of Dublin, including Powerscourt *(see pp114–15)*.
Bloomsday *(16 Jun)*. Walks, lectures and pub talks to celebrate James Joyce's *Ulysses*.

Scurlogstown Olympiad Celtic Festival *(mid-Jun)*, Trim *(see p122)*. Traditional Irish music, dance, fair and selection of a festival queen.
Music in Great Irish Houses *(second and third weeks)*. Classical music recitals in grand settings at various venues.
Darklight Film Festival *(end Jun)*. Festival for filmmakers, animators and artists which explores the convergence of art, film and technology and also features games and workshops.

The Dublin Horse Show (August)

JULY

Oxegen *(mid-Jul)*. Rock 'n' roll festival held over three days in Punchestown, outside Dublin.
Temple Bar Circus Festival *(mid-Jul)*. Temple Bar's streets and public spaces are transform... into a circus arena for f... days of performances...
Festival of World C... *or Aug)*. Dun Lao... *p90)*. A celebr... culturalism, ... music and...

AUG...

Powerscourt Gardens, part of the County Wicklow Gardens Festival

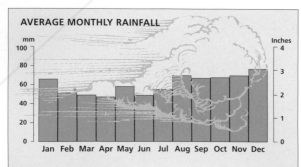

AVERAGE MONTHLY RAINFALL

Rainfall Chart

Ireland is one of the wettest countries in Europe, with rainfall distributed evenly throughout the year. Fortunately, Dublin is situated in the drier eastern half of the country, but visitors should still be prepared for rain at any time of year.

Revellers on Hallowe'en (October)

AUTUMN

Autumn kicks off with the Liffey Swim, a race along Dublin's river attempted only by the strong hearted. Later, the traditional sports of Gaelic football and hurling,

the latter a kind of aerial hockey, hold their popular national finals in the city. The theatre festival held in October is world class.

SEPTEMBER

The Liffey Swim *(first Sat)*. Swimmers brave the Liffey's murky waters from Watling Street Bridge to the Custom House *(see p70)*.
Culture Night *(third Fri)*. Arts and cultural organizations open their doors until late with special free events, tours, talks and performances.
Dublin Fringe Festival *(mid two weeks)*. Shows held at various venues in the city.
All-Ireland Hurling Final *(second Sun)*, Croke Park.

Carpets at the annual Irish Antique Dealers' Fair (September)

All-Ireland Football Final *(fourth Sun)*, Croke Park. Popular Gaelic football final.
Irish Antique Dealers' Fair *(last week)*, RDS Ballsbridge *(see p85)*. The country's most important antiques fair.

OCTOBER

Dublin Theatre Festival *(first two weeks)*. Features new works by Irish playwrights, plus many foreign productions.
Dublin City Marathon *(last Mon)*. Starting and finishing on O'Connell Street, the route takes in many Dublin landmarks, including Phoenix Park and Trinity College. Every year several thousand people participate.
Hallowe'en (Samhain) *(31 Oct)*. On the night when spirits rise, children wear fancy dress and celebrations include a parade and fireworks.

NOVEMBER

Dublin Toy and Train Fair *(mid-Nov)*, Clontarf Castle Hotel, Clontarf. Model cars, dolls, comics and teddy bears. Other fairs in February, May and September.

City Marathon (October)

AVERAGE MONTHLY TEMPERATURE

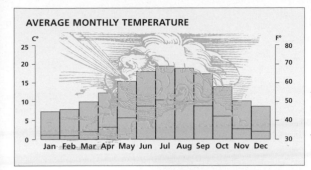

Temperature Chart
This chart gives the average minimum and maximum temperatures for the city. Extremes of temperature are rare: the winter is mild, with the mercury seldom falling below zero. In summer, however, the occasional day can be very warm.

WINTER

Although winter is a quiet time for festivals, there is a range of entertainment on offer, including sporting and theatrical events. Christmas is the busiest social period and there are plenty of informal celebrations. There is also a wide choice of National Hunt (steeplechase) race meetings, especially at Leopardstown, south of the city centre.

Glendalough *(see p110)* in the snow

Christmas scene at Mansion House

DECEMBER

Pantomime Season *(Dec–Jan)*. Traditional pantomime performed at theatres in Dublin and throughout Ireland.

St Stephen's Day *(26 Dec)*. On the day after Christmas, Catholic boys dress up as Wren boys (chimney sweeps with blackened faces) and sing hymns to raise money for charitable causes.

Leopardstown Races *(26–29 Dec)*. This four-day meeting is the biggest in the country.

New Year Festival *(30 Dec–1 Jan)*. Celebrations include the Solas Festival of Lights, carols at Christ Church Cathedral and a party at the Guinness Storehouse.

JANUARY

Salmon and Sea Trout Season *(1 Jan–Sep)*. Start of the season for this popular pastime.

Irish Champion Hurdle *(late Jan)*. Major horse race at Leopardstown *(see p105)*.

Temple Bar Tradfest *(Jan/Feb)*. Five-day festival of Irish music and culture.

Hurdlers at Leopardstown (January)

FEBRUARY

Six Nations Rugby Tournament *(on various weekends Feb–Apr)*. Ireland, England, Wales, Italy, Scotland and France compete; two/three matches in Dublin.

Dublin International Film Festival *(mid-Feb)*. Eleven days of movie premières, interviews and Q&A sessions.

PUBLIC HOLIDAYS

New Year's Day (1 Jan)
St Patrick's Day (17 Mar)
Good Friday
Easter Monday
May Day (1 May)
June Bank Holiday (first Mon in Jun)
August Bank Holiday (first Mon in Aug)
October Bank Holiday (last Mon in Oct)
Christmas Day (25 Dec)
St Stephen's Day (26 Dec)

DUBLIN AREA BY AREA

SOUTHEAST DUBLIN

This part of Dublin was virtually undeveloped until the founding of Trinity College in 1592. Even then, it was almost a hundred years before the land to the south was enclosed to create St Stephen's Green.

The mid-18th century saw the beginning of a construction boom in the area. During this time, public buildings such as the Old Library at Trinity College

Window in the Government buildings

and Leinster House were built. Many of the buildings in Merrion Square still have their original features.

Today, visitors are attracted to Southeast Dublin by the shops on Grafton Street and by the museums in the area, among them the fine National Gallery and the National Museum – Archaeology, with its displays of Irish Bronze Age gold treasures and Iron Age bog bodies.

SIGHTS AT A GLANCE

Museums, Libraries and Galleries

Genealogical Office Exhibition Space ❺
National Gallery pp48–51 ⓲
National Library ⓱
National Museum – Archaeology pp44–5 ⓮
Natural History Museum ⓯
Royal Hibernian Academy ⓴
Science Gallery ㉒

Historic Buildings

Bank of Ireland ❶
Government buildings ⓭
Iveagh House ⓫
Leinster House ⓰
Mansion House ❼
Newman House ❿
Number 29 ㉑
Royal College of Surgeons ❽
Trinity College pp38–9 ❷

Historic Streets

Ely Place ⓬
Grafton Street ❹
Merrion Square ⓳

Churches

St Ann's Church ❻
St Teresa's Church ❸

Parks and Gardens

St Stephen's Green ❾

KEY

- ▨ Street-by-Street map *See pp34–5*
- 🚆 Railway station
- Ⓓ DART station
- 🚋 Luas stop
- ℹ Tourist information

GETTING THERE

Buses 4, 4A, 5, 7, 8, 10, 13, 14A, 15A, 45 and 46A go along Nassau Street which is in walking distance of most of the sights in this area. If you are coming from further afield, both the Luas and the DART serve the area.

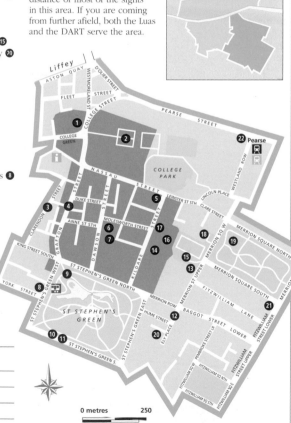

◁ The lush gardens of Merrion Square

Street-by-Street: Southeast Dublin

The area around College Green, dominated by the façades of the Bank of Ireland and Trinity College, is very much the heart of Dublin. The alleys and malls cutting across busy pedestrianized Grafton Street boast many of Dublin's better shops, hotels and restaurants. Just off Kildare Street are the Irish Parliament, the National Library and the National Museum – Archaeology. To escape the city bustle many head for sanctuary in St Stephen's Green, which is overlooked by fine Georgian buildings.

← Dublin Castle

Grafton Street
Brown Thomas department store is one of the main attractions on this pedestrianized street, alive with buskers and pavement artists ❹

Bank of Ireland
This grand Georgian building was originally built as the Irish Parliament ❶

Statue of Molly Malone (1988)

St Ann's Church
The striking façade of the 18th-century church was added in 1868. The interior features lovely stained-glass windows ❻

Mansion House
This has been the official residence of Dublin's Lord Mayor since 1715 ❼

Fusiliers' Arch (1907)

★ St Stephen's Green
The relaxing city park is surrounded by many grand buildings. In summer, lunchtime concerts attract tourists and workers alike ❾

COLLEGE GR

SUFFOLK ST

GRAFTON

GRAFTON STREET

DUKE ST

ANNE ST STH

DAWSON STREET

ST STEPHEN'S GREEN NORT

O'Connell Bridge

NORTH OF THE LIFFEY

SOUTHWEST DUBLIN

SOUTHEAST DUBLIN

LOCATOR MAP
See Street Finder map pp180–81

★ **Trinity College**
*Pomodoro's sculpture,
Sphere within Sphere
(1982), adds a modern
dimension to the
grand buildings
of the campus* ❷

National Library
*Saintly cherubs appear on the
frieze around the library's magnificent old reading room, once a
haunt of novelist James Joyce* ⑰

Leinster House
*This grand
house has been
the home of the
Irish Parliament
since 1922* ⑯

★ **National Museum –
Archaeology**
*The museum's
collection of antiqui-
ties includes a bronze
object known as the
Petrie Crown (2nd
century AD)* ⑭

NASSAU STREET

FREDERICK STREET

MOLESWORTH ST

KILDARE STREET

The Shelbourne Hotel
*Built in 1867, the Shelbourne
Hotel dominates the north
side of St Stephen's Green.*

STAR SIGHTS

★ Trinity College

★ National Museum

★ St Stephen's Green

0 metres   50

0 yards   50

KEY

— Suggested route

🚊 Luas stop

ℹ️ Tourist information

Original Chamber of the Irish House of Lords at the Bank of Ireland

Bank of Ireland ❶

2 College Green. **Map** D3.
Tel 677 6801. ◯ 10am–4pm Mon–
Fri (from 10:30am Wed, to 5pm Thu).
◯ public hols. **House of Lords** ▮
10:30am, 11:30am & 1:45pm Tue.

The prestigious offices of the
Bank of Ireland began life as
the first purpose-built parliament house in Europe. The
original central section was
started by Irish architect
Edward Lovett Pearce and
completed in 1739 after his
death. Sadly, Pearce's masterpiece, the great octagonal
chamber of the House of
Commons, was removed by
order of the British government in 1802. The House of
Lords, however, remains
intact. Attendants lead tours
that point out the coffered
ceiling and oak panelling.
There are also huge tapestries
of the *Battle of the Boyne*
and the *Siege of
Londonderry*, and a
1,233-piece crystal
chandelier that
dates from 1788.
  James Gandon
added the east
portico in 1785.
Further additions
were made
around 1797.
After the dissolu-
tion of the Irish
Parliament in
1800, the Bank
of Ireland
bought the
building.
The present
structure was
completed in

1808 with the transformation of
the former lobby of the House
of Commons into a cash office
and the addition of a curving
screen wall and the Foster
Place annexe. A statue by
John Foley of Henry Grattan
(see p16), the most formidable
leader of the old parliament,
stands on College Green.

Trinity College ❷

See pp38–9.

St Teresa's Church ❸

Clarendon St or Johnson Court.
Map D4. **Tel** 671 8466.
◯ 6:45am–6:30pm Mon–Fri,
6:45am–7:30pm Sat, 8:15am–7pm
Sun. ▮ 9:30am–5pm Mon–Sat.
www.clarendonstreet.com

The foundation stone of St
Teresa's was laid in 1793,
making it the first post-
Penal Law church to
be legally planned
and built in the
city after the
passing of the
Catholic Relief
Act the same
year *(see p16)*.
The land was
leased by a brew-
er named John
Sweetman and
was given
to the
Discalced
Carmelite
Fathers. The
church did
not in fact

Statue of the Virgin and child
in St Teresa's Church

open until May 1797.
The eastern transept
was added in 1863 and
the western transept
was completed in
1876, at which stage
it reached the form it
remains in today.
  Located in the middle
of Dublin, St Teresa's is
a relatively busy place
of worship. Its T-shaped
interior means that if you
enter through the main
door on Clarendon Street
and walk through the
church, you will arrive
in the tight alleyway of
Johnson Court, yards
from Grafton Street. There are
seven stained-glass windows
in the church by Phyllis Burke,
made in the 1990s, and a fine
sculpture of Christ by John
Hogan beneath the altar.

Street musicians outside Brown
Thomas on Grafton Street

Grafton Street ❹

Map D4.

The spine of Dublin's most
popular and stylish shopping
district runs south from Trinity
College to the glass-covered
St Stephen's Green Shopping
Centre. At the north end, at
the junction with Nassau
Street, is a bronze statue
by Jean Rynhart of *Molly
Malone* (1988), the celebrated
"cockles and mussels" street
trader from the traditional
Irish folk song.
  This busy pedestrianized
strip, characterized by numerous energetic buskers and
talented street theatre artists,
boasts many shops, including
many British chain stores.
Next, River Island, HMV and
Monsoon all contribute
toward making it Dublin's
fashion centre. Its most
exclusive store, however,
is Brown Thomas, one of

Monkeys playing billiards outside the Genealogical Office Exhibition Space

Dublin's most elegant department stores *(see p150)*, selling designer clothes, exclusive perfumes and fabulous shoes by designers such as Patrick Cox. Dublin's largest and most exclusive jewellers, Weir's, is also here.

The shops here attract Dublin's most beautiful people, and Grafton Street itself can seem like one long fashion catwalk. But it's not all about shopping, indeed No. 78 stands on the site of Samuel Whyte's school, whose illustrious roll included Robert Emmet *(see p16)*, leader of the 1803 Rebellion, and the Duke of Wellington. At this time, Grafton Street was actually paved with pinewood blocks to deaden the area from the harsh sound of horses' hooves and carriage wheels.

On many of the sidestreets off Grafton Street there are numerous pubs providing welcome refreshment for the exhausted shopper, among them the famous Davy Byrne's *(see p146)*, for years frequented by Dublin's literati.

Genealogical Office Exhibition Space ❺

2 Kildare St. **Map** E4. **Tel** 603 0200. **National Library Reading Room** ◻ 9:30am–9pm Mon–Wed, 9:30am–5pm Thu & Fri, 9:30am–1pm Sat. **Exhibition Space** ◻ 9:30am–8pm Mon–Wed, 10am–4:30pm Thu & Fri, 10am–12:30pm Sat. **www**.nli.ie

The Genealogical Office is part of the National Library and offers free advice to anyone wishing to trace their Irish ancestry. Professional genealogists and library staff offer expert assistance together with access to reference material and finding aids.

The exhibition space is worth a visit for its varied programme, featuring treasures from the National Library collection *(see p46)*. It is housed in a red-brick building in the Venetian style, which is unusual for Dublin. The exterior features some fanciful decorative aspects such as three monkeys playing billiards and bears playing violins just to the right of the entrance.

Window depicting Faith, Hope and Charity in St Ann's Church

St Ann's Church ❻

Dawson St. **Map** D2. **Tel** 676 7727. ◻ 10am–4pm Mon–Fri. ✝ 12:45pm Mon–Fri, 10:45am, 6:30pm Sun. **www**.stannschurch.ie

Founded in 1707, St Ann's striking Romanesque façade was added by the architects Deane and Woodward in 1868. The best view of the façade is from Grafton Street, looking down Anne Street South. Inside the church are many colourful stained-glass windows that date back to the mid-19th century. St Ann's has a long tradition of charity work: in 1723 Lord Newton left a bequest specifically to buy bread for the poor. The original shelf used for the bread still stands adjacent to the altar.

Famous past parishioners of St Ann's include the Irish patriot Wolfe Tone *(see p16)*, who was married here in 1785; Douglas Hyde, the first president of Ireland; and Bram Stoker (1847–1912), the author of *Dracula (see p22)*.

The milling crowds filling the pedestrianized Grafton Street

Trinity College ❷

Trinity College was founded in 1592 by Queen Elizabeth I on the site of an Augustinian monastery. It was originally a Protestant college, and it was not until the 1970s that Catholics started entering the university. Among the many famous students to attend the college were playwrights Oliver Goldsmith and Samuel Beckett, and political writer Edmund Burke. Trinity's lawns and cobbled quads provide a pleasant haven in the heart of the city. The major attractions are the Old Library and the *Book of Kells*, housed in the Treasury.

Trinity College coat of arms

★ Campanile
The 30-m (98-ft) bell tower was built in 1853 by Sir Charles Lanyon, architect of Queen's University, Belfast, in Northern Ireland.

Reclining Connected Forms (1969) by Henry Moore

Dining Hall (1761)

Chapel *(1798)*
This is the only chapel in the Republic to be shared by all denominations. The painted window above the altar dates from 1867.

Parliament Square

Statue of Edmund Burke (1868) by John Foley

Main entrance

SAMUEL BECKETT (1906–89)

Nobel prizewinner Samuel Beckett was born at Foxrock, south of Dublin. In 1923 he entered Trinity, where he was placed first in his modern literature class. He was also a keen member of the college cricket team. Forsaking Ireland, Beckett moved to France in the early 1930s. Many of his works such as *Waiting for Godot* (1951) were written first in French, and then later translated, by Beckett, into English.

Statue of Oliver Goldsmith (1864) by John Foley

Provost's House (c. 1760)

Examination Hall
Completed in 1791 to a design by Sir William Chambers, the hall features a gilded oak chandelier and ornate ceilings by Michael Stapleton.

Library Square
The red-brick building (known as the Rubrics) on the east of Library Square was built around 1700 and is the oldest surviving part of the college.

VISITORS' CHECKLIST

College Green. **Map** D3. **Tel** 896 1000. ⬛ DART to Pearse St. 🚌 14, 15, 46 and other routes. **Old Library and Book of Kells** ⬤ 9:30am–5pm Mon–Sat, 9.30am 4:30pm Sun (winter: noon–4:30pm); last adm: 30 min before closing. ⬤ 10 days at Christmas. 🖼 📷 ♿ ❚ 🚻 by appt. **Chapel** ⬤ by appt. **Douglas Hyde Gallery** ⬤ for exhibitions only. **www**.tcd.ie

Shop and entrance to Old Library

The Museum Building, completed in 1857, is noted for its Venetian exterior, and its magnificent multicoloured hall and double-domed roof.

New Square

Sphere within Sphere
(1982) was given to the college by its sculptor Arnaldo Pomodoro.

Berkeley Library Building by Paul Koralek (1967)

Fellows' Square

Entrance from Nassau Street

The Douglas Hyde Gallery was built in the 1970s to house temporary art exhibitions.

★ **Treasury**
This detail is from the Book of Durrow, *one of the other magnificent illuminated manuscripts housed in the Treasury along with the celebrated* Book of Kells *(see p40).*

★ **Old Library** *(1732)*
The spectacular Long Room measures 64 m (210 ft) from end to end. It houses 200,000 antiquarian texts, marble busts of scholars and the oldest surviving harp in Ireland.

STAR FEATURES

★ Old Library

★ Treasury

★ Campanile

The Book of Kells

The most richly decorated of Ireland's illuminated manuscripts, the *Book of Kells*, may have been the work of monks from Iona, who fled to Kells, near Newgrange *(see pp120–21)*, in AD 806 after a Viking raid. The book, which was moved to Trinity College *(see pp38–9)* in the 17th century, contains the four Gospels in Latin. The scribes who copied the texts embellished their calligraphy with intricate spirals as well as human figures and animals. Some of the dyes used were imported from as far as the Middle East.

Pair of moths

Stylized angel

The Greek letter "X"

The symbols *of the four evangelists are used as decoration throughout the book. The figure of the man symbolizes St Matthew.*

The letter that looks like a "P" is a Greek "R".

The letter "I"

Interlacing motifs

Cat watching rats

Rats eating bread could be a reference to sinners taking Holy Communion. The symbolism of the animals and people decorating the manuscript is often hard to interpret.

MONOGRAM PAGE

This, the most elaborate page of the book, contains the first three words of St Matthew's account of the birth of Christ. The first word "XRI" is an abbreviation of "Christi".

A full-page portrait *of St Matthew, shown standing barefoot in front of a throne, precedes the opening words of his Gospel.*

The text *is in a beautifully rounded Celtic script with brightly ornamented initial letters. Animal and human forms are often used to decorate the end of a line.*

Mansion House ❼

Dawson St. **Map** E4. 🔘 *to the public.* 🔳 **www**.mansionhouse.ie

Set back from Dawson Street, the Mansion House is an attractive Queen Anne-style building. It was built in 1710 for the aristocrat Joshua Dawson, after whom the street is named. The Dublin Corporation bought it in 1715 as the official residence of the city's Lord Mayor. A grey stucco façade was added in Victorian times.

The Dáil Éireann *(see p46)*, which adopted the Declaration of Independence, first met here on 21 January 1919. The Fire Restaurant in the old supper room is in period style and is open to the public.

Royal College of Surgeons ❽

123 St Stephen's Green. **Map** E4. **Tel** 402 2100.

The west side of St Stephen's Green is home to one of the most striking buildings in the square, namely the squat granite-faced Royal College of Surgeons. The college opened in 1810 and 15 years later its façade was extended from three to seven bays when a central pediment was added. On top of this are three statues which from left to right are Hygieia, goddess of health, Asclepius, god of medicine and son of Apollo,

Royal College of Surgeons, which overlooks St Stephen's Green

and Athena, the goddess of wisdom and patron of the arts. Today, the main entrance is through the modern extension on York Street. The academy has almost 1,000 students.

The building itself played an important part in Irish history. During the 1916 Easter Rising *(see p17)*, a section of the Irish Citizen Army under Michael Mallin and Countess Constance Markievicz were in control of the college. They were the last detachment of rebels to surrender and, although Mallin was executed, Markievicz escaped sentence because of her gender and public status. She was later to become the first woman to be elected as an MP at Westminster in London, though she refused to take her seat in parliament. The front columns of the building still feature the old bullet holes, an ever-present reminder of its colourful past.

St Stephen's Green ❾

Map D5. 🔘 *daylight hours.*

Originally one of three ancient commons in the old city, St Stephen's Green was enclosed in 1664. The 9-ha (22-acre) green was laid out in its present form in 1880, using a grant given by Lord Ardilaun, a member of the Guinness family. Landscaped with flowerbeds, trees, a fountain and a lake, the green is dotted with memorials to eminent Dubliners, including Ardilaun himself. There is a bust of James Joyce *(see p23)*, and a memorial by Henry Moore (1967) dedicated to W B Yeats *(see p23)*. At the Merrion Row corner stands a massive monument (1967) by Edward Delaney to 18th-century nationalist leader Wolfe Tone – it is known locally as "Tonehenge". The 1887 bandstand still has free daytime concerts in summer.

The busiest side of the Green is the north, known during the 19th century as the Beaux' Walk and still home to several gentlemen's clubs. The most prominent building is the venerable Shelbourne Hotel *(see p130)*. Dating back to 1867, its entrance is adorned by statues of Nubian princesses and attendant slaves. It is well worth popping in for a look at the chandeliered foyer and for afternoon tea in the Lord Mayor's Lounge.

Dubliners relaxing by the lake in St Stephen's Green

Stucco work in the Apollo room of No. 85 in Newman House

Newman House ⑩

85 & 86 St Stephen's Green. **Map** D5.
Tel 716 7422. ☐ Jun–Aug: noon–4pm Tue–Fri; Sep–May: by appt only for groups. ▨ **www**.ucd.ie

Numbers 85 and 86 on the south side of St Stephen's Green are collectively known as Newman House, named after John Henry Newman, later Cardinal Newman and the first rector of the Catholic University of Ireland.

Founded as an alternative to the Protestant Trinity College, it became part of University College Dublin in 1907 and is still owned by that institution.

During the 1990s it saw one of the most painstaking and diligent restorations ever undertaken in the city. It is the much smaller No. 85, designed by Richard Castle in 1738, that contains the most beautiful rooms with plaster-work by the Franchini brothers. Of particular interest are the Apollo Room, with a figure of the god above the mantle, and the upstairs Saloon. In the late 1800s the Jesuits covered the naked plaster bodies on the ceiling of the Saloon with rudimentary plaster casts to conceal what they thought to be shameful nudity. One of the figures is still covered today. A class-room, decorated as it would have been in the days when James Joyce was a student here, is open to the public,

as is the studio residence of the poet Gerard Manley Hopkins, who was a professor here in the late 19th century. Other famous past pupils include the writer Flann O'Brien and former president Eamon De Valera.

Iveagh House and Iveagh Gardens ⑪

80 & 81 St Stephen's Green. **Map** D5.
◑ to the public. **Gardens** ☐ daily.

Iveagh House, on the south side of St Stephen's Green, was originally two freestanding townhouses. No. 80 was designed in the 1730s by Richard Castle – his first commission in the city. The houses were combined in the 1860s when Sir Benjamin Guinness bought them. None of the original façade remains as Guinness linked the houses under a Portland stone façade and had the family arms engraved on the pediment. The Guinness family also carried out much interior reconstruction, including the addition of a large ballroom, with a domed ceiling and liberal amounts of marble and onyx, to the rear of the house. Iveagh House was given to the state by Rupert Guinness, the second Earl of Iveagh, in 1939. It is now used by the Department of Foreign Affairs, both as the office of the minister and as a venue for state receptions. The rear

Enjoying the secluded peace of Iveagh Gardens

of Iveagh House faces on to Iveagh Gardens, an almost secret park that offers a quiet alternative to St Stephen's Green. It owes its tranquillity partly to the fact that its three entrances are discreet: one is behind the National Concert Hall on Earlsfort Terrace, another is off Clonmel Street and a new one, with disabled access, is off Hatch Street.

Ely Place ⑫

Map E5.

A cul-de-sac with several well-preserved Georgian houses, Ely Place is at the end of Merrion Street Upper. Most of the houses along the street were built in the 1770s, and Ely Place soon became one of the most desirable addresses in the city at this time. Behind its red brick façade, 8 Ely Place, known as Ely House, has elegant plasterwork by the stuccodore Michael Stapleton and an ornate staircase covered with engravings of characters from the tales of the Labours of Hercules below the banister rail.

Modern buildings seal the end of the street. The Royal Hibernian Academy Gallagher Gallery (see p47) was built in 1973 and looks somewhat out of place on this rather grand stretch, but it offers one of the best gallery spaces in the city, exhibiting contemporary Irish and international art.

Detail of stucco from Ely House, featuring the mythical dog Cerberus

The elegant, Neo-Classical façade of the Government buildings

Government buildings **⑬**

Upper Merrion St. **Map** E4. **Tel** 662 4888. ⬭ Sat 10:30am–12:30pm, 1:30–3:30pm (call to check). Tickets available from National Gallery. ⬭ hourly from 10:30am–1:30pm. **www**.gov.ie/taoiseach

Alongside the Natural History Museum and the National Gallery on Upper Merrion Street, facing the attractive Georgian townhouses, stand the imposing Government buildings, built in a Neo-Georgian style.

The complex was opened in 1911 as the Royal College of Science (RCS) and it has the distinction of being the last major project planned by the British in Dublin. In 1922 the Irish government took over the north wing as offices and the RCS became part of University College Dublin. Academic pursuits continued here until 1989, when the government moved into the rest of the buildings and ordered a massive restoration of the façade. The city grime on the Portland stone was blasted away to restore it to its original near-white appearance.

The elegant domed buildings are set apart from the street by a cobbled courtyard and a large colonnade with columns that are strongly reminiscent of Gandon's Custom House (see p70). The tour takes in the office of the Taoiseach (pronounced Tee-Shuck) and the cabinet office. The interior is decorated with examples of works by contemporary Irish artists, most notably a huge stained-glass window, situated above the grand staircase, called *My Four Green Fields* by Dublin artist Evie Hone, which depicts the island's four provinces. This was designed for the 1939 World's Fair in New York. It was displayed in the Irish Pavilion there and afterwards returned to Dublin. For a number of years it lay packed away, until the 1960s, when it was put on display for a while in the Dublin Bus offices in O'Connell Street. It was finally moved to its present home in the Government buildings in 1991.

National Museum – Archaeology **⑭**

See pp44–5.

Natural History Museum **⑮**

Merrion St. **Map** E4. **Tel** 677 7444. ⬭ 10am–5pm Tue–Sat, 2–5pm Sun. ⬤ Good Fri, 25 Dec. ⬭ limited. **www**.museum.ie

This museum was opened to the public in 1857 with an inaugural lecture by Scottish explorer Dr David Livingstone, and it remains virtually unchanged from Victorian times. It is crammed with glass cabinets housing stuffed animals from around the world.

Inside the front door are three skeletons of the extinct giant deer known as the "Irish elk". The ground floor houses the Irish Room, which is devoted to local wildlife, including badgers, deer, seals, bats and a variety of insects.

The upper floor, accessed via a restored grand stone staircase, illustrates the range of mammals inhabiting our planet. Among the most fascinating exhibits are the primates (monkeys, apes and lemurs), a Bengal tiger and a pangolin. There is also the skeleton of a hamster, showing the cheek pouches where this animal stores food.

Hanging from the ceiling are the skeletons of a 20-m (66-ft) fin whale and a humpback whale, both found stranded on the Irish coast.

Lawn and front entrance of the Natural History Museum on Merrion Street Upper

National Museum – Archaeology ⓮

The National Museum of Ireland – Archaeology was built in the 1880s to the design of Sir Thomas Deane. Its splendid domed rotunda features marble pillars and a zodiac mosaic floor. The Treasury houses items such as the Broighter gold boat, while an exhibition on Ireland's Bronze Age gold contains some beautiful jewellery. The museum shows life in prehistoric Ireland and at the time of the Vikings.

Egyptian Mummy
This mummy of the lady Tentdinebu is thought to date back to c.945–716 BC. Covered in brilliant colours, it is part of the stunning Egyptian collection.

★ Ór – Ireland's Gold
This is one of the most extensive collections of Bronze Age gold in Western Europe. This gold lunula (c.1800 BC), found in Athlone, is one of many pieces of ancient jewellery in this exhibition.

KEY TO FLOORPLAN

- ☐ Kingship and Sacrifice
- ☐ Ór – Ireland's Gold
- ☐ The Treasury
- ☐ Prehistoric Ireland
- ☐ Medieval Ireland
- ☐ Viking Ireland
- ☐ Ancient Egypt
- ■ Rites of Passage at Tara
- ☐ Temporary exhibition space
- ☐ Non-exhibition space
- ☐ Ceramics and Glass from Ancient Cyprus
- ☐ Life and Death in the Roman World

★ Bog Bodies
This preserved hand (c.600 BC) is one of the pieces in a fascinating exhibition of Iron Age bodies discovered in 2003.

Main entrance

GALLERY GUIDE

The ground floor holds The Treasury, Ór – Ireland's Gold exhibition, Kingship and Sacrifice and the Prehistoric Ireland display. On the first floor is the Medieval Ireland exhibition, which illustrates many aspects of life in later medieval Ireland. Also on the first floor are artifacts from Ancient Egypt and from the Viking settlement of Dublin.

The domed rotunda, based on the design of the Altes Museum in Berlin, makes an impressive entrance hall.

The Treasury houses masterpieces of Irish crafts including the Ardagh Chalice.

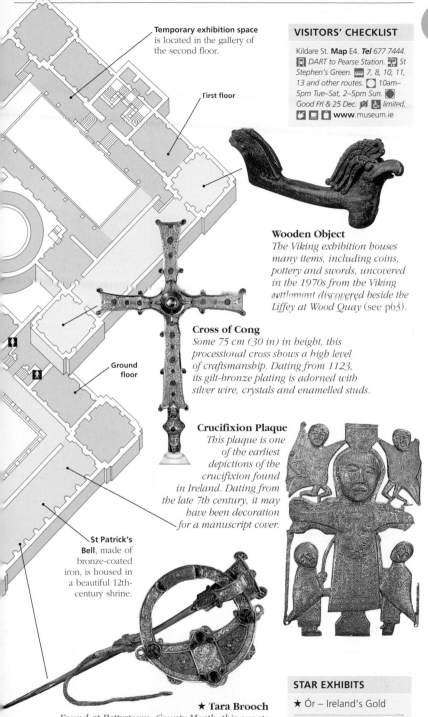

Temporary exhibition space is located in the gallery of the second floor.

First floor

Ground floor

Wooden Object
The Viking exhibition houses many items, including coins, pottery and swords, uncovered in the 1970s from the Viking settlement discovered beside the Liffey at Wood Quay (see p63).

Cross of Cong
Some 75 cm (30 in) in height, this processional cross shows a high level of craftsmanship. Dating from 1123, its gilt-bronze plating is adorned with silver wire, crystals and enamelled studs.

Crucifixion Plaque
This plaque is one of the earliest depictions of the crucifixion found in Ireland. Dating from the late 7th century, it may have been decoration for a manuscript cover.

St Patrick's Bell, made of bronze-coated iron, is housed in a beautiful 12th-century shrine.

★ Tara Brooch
Found at Bettystown, County Meath, this ornate brooch dates from the 8th century AD. It is decorated on the front and rear with a filigree of gold wire entwined around settings of amber and enamel.

STAR EXHIBITS

★ Ór – Ireland's Gold

★ Bog Bodies

★ Tara Brooch

Domed reading room on the first floor of the National Library

Leinster House ⑯

Kildare St. **Map** E4. **Tel** 618 3000.
⬤ groups by appointment only
(foreign tourists must book through
their own embassy). ⬤ phone for
details. **www**.oireachtas.ie

This stately mansion houses
the Dáil and the Seanad – the
two chambers of the Irish
Parliament. It was originally
built for the Duke of Leinster
in 1745. Designed by Richard
Castle, the Kildare Street
façade resembles that of a
large townhouse. The rear,
which looks out on to Merrion
Square, has the air of a country
estate. The Royal Dublin
Society bought the building in
1815. The government bought
the entire building in 1924.
   Visitors can arrange to tour
the main rooms, including the
Seanad chamber.

National Library ⑰

Kildare St. **Map** E4. **Tel** 603 0200.
⬤ 9:30am–9pm Mon–Wed,
9:30am–5pm Thu & Fri, 9:30am–
1pm Sat. ⬤ public hols. **www**.nli.ie

Designed by Sir Thomas
Deane, the National Library
was opened in 1890. It was
built to house the collection
of the Royal Dublin Society
(see p85). The Library
contains first editions of every
major Irish writer and a copy
of almost every book ever
published in Ireland. There

is a huge collection of old
maps, papers and a number
of significant manuscripts. The
first-floor reading room has
green-shaded lamps and well-
worn desks. To go in, ask an
attendant for a visitor's pass. An
exhibition space, bookshop
and coffee shop are open to
both readers and non-readers.

National Gallery ⑱

See pp48–51.

Merrion Square ⑲

Map F4.

Merrion Square, a large and
grand Georgian square,
covers about 5 ha (12 acres)
and was laid out by John
Ensor around 1762.
   On the west
side are the
impressive
façades of
the Natural

**Statue of Oscar Wilde by Danny
Osbourne in Merrion Square**

THE IRISH PARLIAMENT

The Irish Free State, the
forerunner of the Republic
of Ireland, was first
inaugurated in 1922 (see
p18), although an unofficial
Irish parliament, the Dáil,
had already been in existence since 1919. Today,
the Irish parliament is
made up of two houses:
the Dáil (House of Repre-
sentatives) and Seanad
Éireann (Senate). The
prime minister is the
Taoiseach and the deputy,
the Tánaiste. The Dáil's
166 representatives –
Teachta Dála, commonly
known as TDs – are
elected by proportional
representation every five
years. The 60-strong
Seanad is appointed by
various individuals and
authorities, including the
Taoiseach and the
University of Dublin.

**The first parliament of the Irish
Free State in 1922**

History Museum, the National
Gallery and the front garden
of Leinster House. However,
they do not compare with
the attractive Georgian townhouses on the other three
sides. Many have brightly
painted doors with original
features such as wrought-iron
balconies and ornate door-
knockers. The oldest and finest
houses are on the north side.
   Many are now offices, with
plaques detailing the rich and
famous who once lived in
them. These include Catholic
emancipation leader Daniel
O'Connell (see p16), who lived
at No. 58 and poet W B Yeats
(see p23), who lived at No. 82.
Oscar Wilde (see p23) spent

his childhood at No. 1. The attractive central park served as an emergency soup kitchen during the Great Famine of the 1840s (see p17). On the northwest side stands the restored Rutland Fountain, originally erected in 1791 for the sole use of Dublin's poor.

Just off the square, at No. 24 Merrion Street Upper, is the birthplace of the Duke of Wellington.

Royal Hibernian Academy ⑳

15 Ely Place. **Map** E5. **Tel** 661 2558. ◯ 11am–7pm Mon–Sat, 2–5pm Sun. ⬤ public hols and between exhibitions. ♿ **www**.royalhibernian academy.com

The academy is one of the largest exhibition spaces in the city. It puts on exhibitions of Irish and international artists showing both traditional and innovative forms of visual art. This modern brick-and-plate-glass building does, however, look out of place at the end of Ely Place, an attractive Georgian cul-de-sac.

Number 29 ㉑

29 Fitzwilliam St Lower. **Map** F5. **Tel** 702 6165. ◯ 10am–5pm Tue–Sat, noon–5pm Sun. ⬤ two weeks prior to Christmas. ♿ ♿ **www**.esb.ie/numbertwentynine

The recreated Georgian kitchen of Number 29, Fitzwilliam Street Lower

Number 29 is a corner townhouse, built in 1794 for a Mrs Olivia Beattie whose late husband was a wine and paper merchant. This museum gives visitors a behind-the-scenes look at how middle-class Georgians lived. Tours work their way through the building from the cellar upwards. Along the way are mahogany tables, chandeliers, Turkish carpets and landscape paintings, but of most interest are some of the quirkier items. Guides point out rudimentary hostess trolleys, water filters and even a Georgian baby walker, as well as an early exercise machine, used to tone up the muscles for horse riding. A tea caddy takes pride of place in one of the reception rooms: at today's prices a kilo of tea would have cost €800.

Science Gallery ㉒

Trinity College, Pearse Street. **Map** E3. **Tel** 896 4091. ◯ varies. ⬤ Mon. **www**.sciencegallery.com

The Science Gallery is a venture aiming to make science and technology accessible to all, especially young people. The focus on how it affects our lives now and in the future is explored through installations, festivals, performances and workshops promoting interaction and discussion. Past exhibitions at the state-of-the-art premises have featured light and sound installations and technological innovations in fashion, such as spray-on dresses and shirts that hug. The gallery was also once transformed into a neuroscience research lab.

The elegant gardens in Merrion Square, a quiet backwater in the centre of Dublin

National Gallery ®

This purpose-built gallery was opened to the public in 1864. It houses many excellent exhibits, largely due to generous bequests, such as the Milltown collection of works of art from Russborough House *(see p108)*. Playwright George Bernard Shaw was also a benefactor, leaving a third of his estate to the gallery. Although the emphasis is on Irish art, the major schools of European painting are well represented. During the current major refurbishment of the historic Dargan and Milltown wings, the location of exhibits is subject to change.

The Houseless Wanderer by John Foley

★ Pierrot
This Cubist-style work, by Spanish-born artist Juan Gri[s] is one of many varia[tions he painted on the theme of Pierrot and Harlequin. Thi[s] particular one dates from 1921.

★ For the Road
The Yeats Museum houses works by Jack B Yeats (1871–1957). This mysterious painting reflects the artist's obsession with the Sligo countryside.

Mezzanine level

GALLERY GUIDE
The main entrance to the gallery is through the lofty Millennium Wing on Clare Street. The gallery is undergoing major refurbishments until 2014/15, and this will result in changes to the presentation of the collection. Visitors are advised to call or email in advance to confirm whether and where specific exhibits will be displayed.

STAR PAINTINGS

★ The Taking of Christ

★ Pierrot

★ For the Road

★ The Taking of Christ

Rediscovered in the Dublin Jesuit House of Study in 1990, this 1602 composition by Caravaggio has enhanced the gallery's reputation.

VISITORS' CHECKLIST

Clare St & Merrion Square West. **Map** E4.
Tel 661 5133. 🚊 DART to Pearse. 🚌 5, 7, 10, 13/13A, 44C, 48A. 🕒 9:30am–5:30pm Mon–Wed, Fri & Sat, 9.30am–8:30pm Thu, noon–5:30pm Sun. 🔴 Good Fri, 24–26 Dec. 🎫 for special exhibitions. 🚫 ♿ 🖥 www.nationalgallery.ie

Level 2

Level 1

Millennium Wing

Judith with the Head of Holofernes

This monochrome image by Andrea Mantegna (c.1431–1506) depicts the decapitation of an Assyrian chief.

The Sick Call

Painted in a Pre-Raphaelite style by Matthew James Lawless, this 1863 canvas evokes the suffering of the Irish population in the years following the Famine.

Entrance level

Main entrance
(Clare Street)

KEY TO FLOORPLAN

☐ Irish and British Schools

☐ European Sculpture and Decorative Arts

☐ Print Gallery

☐ Italian School

☐ Spanish School

☐ Northern European and French Schools

☐ Yeats Museum

☐ Temporary exhibitions

☐ Closed for refurbishment until 2014/15

☐ Non-exhibition space

Exploring the National Gallery

In addition to rooms dedicated to major Irish and European schools, there are displays on art in the Dutch provinces, Caravaggio and his followers and Italian influences in the Northern countries. The Millennium Wing also has a floor dedicated to the Irish schools. Throughout the refurbishment programme, displays will change, and visitors are advised to contact the gallery in advance if they wish to see a specific work of art.

IRISH SCHOOL

This is the largest collection on display and the richest part of the gallery. Stretching back to the late 17th century, works range from landscapes such as *A View of Powerscourt Waterfall* by George Barret to paintings by Nathaniel Hone the Elder, including *The Conjuror*. Portraiture includes work by James Barry and Hugh Douglas Hamilton.

The Romantic movement made a strong impression on artists in the early 19th century; Francis Danby's *The Opening of the Sixth Seal*, an apocalyptic interpretation from the Book of Revelations, is the best example of this genre. Other examples are the Irish landscapes of James Arthur O'Connor.

In the late 19th century many Irish artists lived in Breton colonies, absorbing Impressionist influences. Roderic O'Conor's *Farm at Lezaven, Finistère* and William Leech's *Convent Garden, Brittany*, with its

Convent Garden, Brittany, by William Leech (1881–1968)

refreshing tones of green and white, are two of the best examples from this period.

Jack B Yeats is regarded as Ireland's first internationally known modern artist and the Yeats Museum is dedicated to him and his talented family. It includes works by Anne Yeats and his father John B Yeats, a famous portrait artist. Jack B Yeats' paintings portray life in the west of Ireland in the early 20th century. His later paintings, such as *Men of Destiny* and *Above the Fair*, are also national treasures.

BRITISH SCHOOL

Works dating from the 18th century – in particular, by the likes of William Hogarth, Joshua Reynolds and Thomas Gainsborough – are well represented here. Reynolds was one of the great portrait painters of his time. The British School collection also showcases portraits by other artists such as Philip Reinagle, Francis Wheatley and Henry Raeburn, that perfectly capture the family, military and aristocratic life of that period.

BAROQUE ART

This collection encompasses a series of 17th-century paintings, including many by lesser-known artists. It also holds enormous canvases by more famous names such as Lanfranco, Jordaens and Castiglione. *The Annunciation* and *Peter Finding the Tribute Money* by Peter Paul Rubens are among the most eye-catching paintings.

The collection received a generous boost in 2008, when Sir Denis Mahon donated eight canvases, including works by Guercino, Guido Reni and Domenichino.

FRENCH SCHOOL

The paintings devoted to the French School date mainly from the 17th and 18th centuries but also include the Barbizon, Impressionist, post-Impressionist and Cubist movements.

Among the earlier works are *The Annunciation*, a fine 15th-century panel by Jacques Yverni, and the *Lamentation over the Dead Christ* by Nicolas Poussin (1594–1665), one of the founders of European classicism.

The early 19th century saw the French colonization of North Africa. Many works were inspired by the colonization, including *Guards at the Door of a Tomb*, a painting by Jean-Léon Gérôme. Another

A View of Powerscourt Waterfall, by George Barret the Elder (c.1728–84)

A Group of Cavalry in the Snow by Jan Chelminski (1851–1925)

fine 19th-century work is the painting known as *A Group of Cavalry in the Snow* by Jan Chelminski.

The Impressionist paintings are among the most popular in the gallery and include Monet's *Argenteuil Basin with a Single Sailboat* (1874). There are also works by Camille Pissarro and Alfred Sisley.

Argenteuil Basin with a Single Sailboat, by Claude Monet (1874)

SPANISH SCHOOL

Works from the Spanish school are rich and varied. One of the early pieces of note is El Greco's *St Francis Receiving the Stigmata*, a particularly dramatic work, dating from around 1595. Other notable acquisitions from this period are by Zurbarán, Velázquez and Murillo. There are several works by the controversial court painter Francisco de Goya (1746–1828), including a portrait of the actress Doña Antonia Zárata. Pablo Picasso's *Still Life With A Mandolin* and *Pierrot* by Juan Gris represent 20th-century Spanish art.

ITALIAN SCHOOL

A successful purchasing strategy and various bequests have resulted in the gallery having a strong collection of Italian art.

Works of the Italian School are spread over seven rooms. Andrea Mantegna's *Judith with the Head of Holofernes* is done in *grisaille*, a technique that creates a stone-like effect. Famous pieces by Uccello, Titian, Moroni and Fontana hang in this section, but it is Caravaggio's *The Taking of Christ* (1602) which is the most important item. It was discovered by chance in a Dublin Jesuit house where it had hung in obscurity for many years. It was first hung in the National Gallery in 1993.

Virgin and Child, by Paolo Uccello (c.1435–40)

NORTHERN EUROPEAN SCHOOLS

The early Netherlandish School is comprised largely of paintings with a religious theme. One exception is Brueghel the Younger's lively *Peasant Wedding* (1620). In the Dutch collection there are many 17th-century works, including some by Rembrandt. Other highlights include *A Wooded Landscape* by Hobbema and *Lady Writing a Letter With Her Maid* by Vermeer. Rubens and van Dyck are two more famous names here, but there are also fine works by less well-known artists, such as van Uden's *Peasants Merrymaking*. Portraits by artists such as Faber and Pencz from the 15th and 16th centuries dominate the German collection, though Emil Nolde's colourful *Two Women in the Garden* dates from 1915.

PORTRAITURE

The portraiture collection includes full-length historical portraits such as one of Charles Coote, the first Earl of Bellamont, dressed in flamboyant pink ceremonial robes. There are also portraits of those who have made a contribution to Ireland from the 16th century to the present.

Peasant Wedding, by Pieter Brueghel the Younger (1564–1637)

SOUTHWEST DUBLIN

The area around Dublin Castle was first settled in prehistoric times, and it was from here that the city grew. Dublin gets its name from the dark pool (*Dubh Linn*) which formed at the confluence of the Liffey and the Poddle, a river that originally ran through the site of Dublin Castle. It is now channelled underground. Archaeological excavations behind Wood Quay, on the banks of the River Liffey, reveal that the Vikings had a settlement here as early as AD 841.

Following Strongbow's invasion of 1170, a medieval city began to emerge; the Anglo-Normans built strong defensive walls around the castle.

A small reconstructed section of these old city walls can be seen at St Audoen's Church. More conspicuous reminders of the Anglo-Normans appear in the medieval Christ Church Cathedral and St Patrick's Cathedral. When the city expanded during the Georgian era, the narrow cobbled streets of Temple Bar became a quarter inhabited by skilled craftsmen and merchants. Today this area is a haven for culture and entertainment, and is home to a variety of alternative shops and cafés. The Powerscourt Townhouse is an elegant 18th-century mansion that has been converted into one of the city's best shopping centres.

Vibrant artwork typical of shops and galleries in Temple Bar

SIGHTS AT A GLANCE

Museums and Libraries
Chester Beatty Library ❷
Dublinia ⓭
Marsh's Library ❽

Historic Buildings
City Hall ❸
Dublin Castle pp56–7 ❶
Olympia Theatre ❺
Powerscourt Townhouse ❻
Tailors' Hall ⓫

Historic Areas
Temple Bar pp58–9 ❹

Churches
Christ Church Cathedral pp64–5 ⓮
St Audoen's Church ⓬
St Patrick's Cathedral ❾
St Werburgh's Church ❿
Whitefriar Street Carmelite Church ❼

KEY

Street-by-Street map
See pp54–5

GETTING AROUND

Buses 11, 16A, 16B, 19A, 121, 122 and 123 go close to Temple Bar. Buses 49A, 49B, 54A, 65A, 65B, 77, 123 and 151 go past St Patrick's and Christ Church cathedrals.

Street-by-Street: Southwest Dublin

Despite its wealth of ancient buildings,
such as Dublin Castle and Christ Church
Cathedral, this part of Dublin lacks the sleek
appeal of the neighbouring streets around
Grafton Street. In the 1990s, however,
redevelopment rejuvenated the area,
especially around Temple Bar, where the
attractive cobbled streets are lined with shops,
futuristic arts centres, galleries, bars and cafés.

Sunlight Chambers
*Built in 1900, the
delightful terra-
cotta decoration
on the façade
advertises Lever's
soap manufact-
uring business.*

Wood Quay is where the
Vikings established their first
permanent settlement in Ireland
around 841.

**Dublin Viking
Adventure**

★ **Christ Church Cathedral**
*Huge family monuments,
including that of the
19th Earl of Kildare,
can be found in
Ireland's oldest cathe-
dral, which also has a
fascinating crypt* **14**

St Werburgh's Church
*An ornate interior hides behind
the somewhat drab exterior of
this 18th-century church* **10**

Dublinia
*Medieval Dublin is
the subject of this
interactive museum,
located in the
former Synod Hall
of the Church of
Ireland. It is linked
to Christ Church
by a bridge* **13**

City Hall
*Originally built as the
Royal Exchange in
1779, the city's munic-
ipal headquarters is
fronted by a huge
Corinthian portico* **3**

★ **Dublin Castle**
*The Drawing Room, with its
Waterford crystal chandelier,
is part of a suite of luxurious
rooms built in the 18th century
for the Viceroys of Ireland* **1**

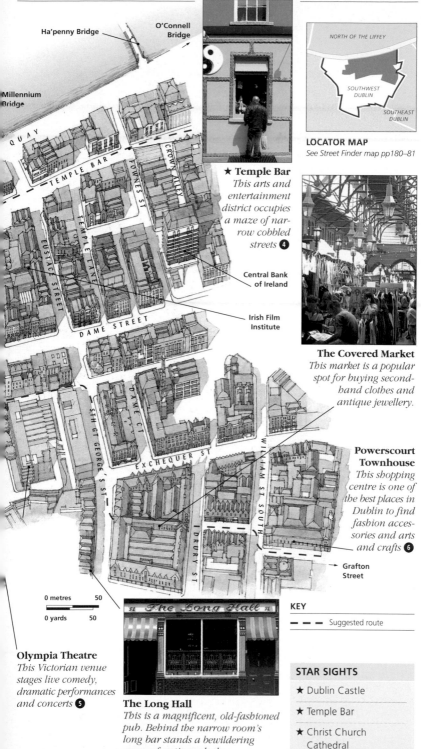

Ha'penny Bridge

O'Connell Bridge

Millennium Bridge

QUAY

TEMPLE BAR

FOWNES ST

CROW ALLEY

TEMPLE LANE

EUSTACE STREET

DAME STREET

STH GT GEORGE'S ST

DAME CT

EXCHEQUER ST

DRURY ST

WILLIAM ST SOUTH

LOCATOR MAP
See Street Finder map pp180–81

★ **Temple Bar**
This arts and entertainment district occupies a maze of narrow cobbled streets ❹

Central Bank of Ireland

Irish Film Institute

The Covered Market
This market is a popular spot for buying second-hand clothes and antique jewellery.

Powerscourt Townhouse
This shopping centre is one of the best places in Dublin to find fashion accessories and arts and crafts ❻

→ **Grafton Street**

0 metres 50
0 yards 50

KEY

– – – Suggested route

Olympia Theatre
This Victorian venue stages live comedy, dramatic performances and concerts ❺

The Long Hall
This is a magnificent, old-fashioned pub. Behind the narrow room's long bar stands a bewildering array of antique clocks.

STAR SIGHTS

★ Dublin Castle

★ Temple Bar

★ Christ Church Cathedral

Dublin Castle ❶

Dublin gets its name from the ancient black pool harbour, or *Dubh Linn*, that occupied the site of the present castle gardens. Part of the town's 10th-century defence bank is visible at the undercroft. The upper castle yard corresponds closely to the castle established by King John in 1204, which became the most important fortification in Ireland and was the seat of colonial rule and the centre of military, political and social affairs. On the castle's southern side, the magnificent state apartments include St Patrick's Hall and the drawing and throne rooms. They were built as the residential quarters of the viceregal court and now host important state functions.

St Patrick by Edward Smyth

Figure of Justice
Facing the Upper Yard above the main entrance from Cork Hill, this statue aroused much cynicism among Dubliners, who felt she was turning her back on the city.

★ **Throne Room**
The throne in this room was built in 1821 for King George IV's visit to Ireland.

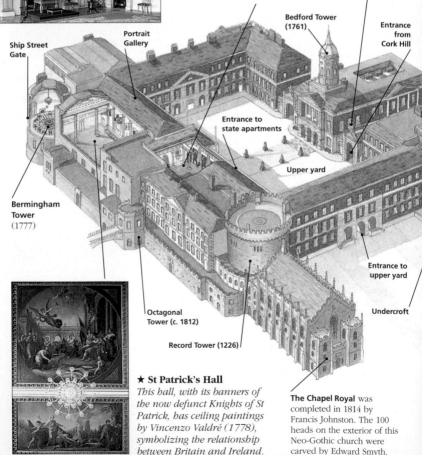

Ship Street Gate

Portrait Gallery

Bedford Tower (1761)

Entrance from Cork Hill

Entrance to state apartments

Upper yard

Bermingham Tower (1777)

Entrance to upper yard

Octagonal Tower (c. 1812)

Undercroft

Record Tower (1226)

★ **St Patrick's Hall**
This hall, with its banners of the now defunct Knights of St Patrick, has ceiling paintings by Vincenzo Valdré (1778), symbolizing the relationship between Britain and Ireland.

The Chapel Royal was completed in 1814 by Francis Johnston. The 100 heads on the exterior of this Neo-Gothic church were carved by Edward Smyth.

ROBERT EMMET

Robert Emmet (1778–1803), son of the state physician to the viceroy, led a failed attack on Dublin Castle in 1803. He was arrested and interrogated in the Record Tower. His final defiant and patriotic speech proved an inspiration to future generations of Irish freedom fighters. Publicly hung, drawn and quartered, the heroic Emmet became known as "the father of Irish Republicanism".

Treasury building

Lower yard

Dame Street and Palace Street Gate

STAR FEATURES

★ St Patrick's Hall

★ Throne Room

Manuscript (1874) from the Holy Koran written by calligrapher Ahmad Shaikh in Kashmir, Chester Beatty Library

Chester Beatty Library ❷

Clock Tower Building, Dubh Linn Gardens, Dublin Castle. **Map** C4. **Tel** 407 0750. ◯ May–Sep: 10am–5pm Mon–Fri; Oct–Apr: 10am–5pm Tue–Fri, 11am–5pm Sat, 1pm–5pm Sun all year. ◯ public hols. 🚻 📺 www.cbl.ie

This world-renowned collection of Oriental manuscripts and art was bequeathed to Ireland by the American mining magnate Sir Alfred Chester Beatty, who died in 1968. This generous act no doubt led to his selection as Ireland's first honorary citizen in 1957.

During his lifetime, Beatty accumulated almost 300 copies of the Koran, representing the works of master calligraphers from Iran, Turkey and the Arab world. Other exhibits include some 6,000-year-old Babylonian stone tablets, Greek papyri dating from the 2nd century AD and biblical material written in Coptic, the original language of Egypt.

In the Far Eastern collection is a display of Chinese jade books – each leaf is made from thinly cut jade. Burmese and Siamese art is represented in the fine collection of 18th- and 19th-century Parabaiks, books of illustrated folk tales. The Japanese collection also includes many books as well as paintings from the 16th to the 18th centuries.

Turkish and Persian miniatures, striking Buddhist paintings and Chinese dragon robes are among many other fascinating exhibits in this unusual museum.

City Hall ❸

Cork Hill, Dame St. **Map** C3. **Tel** 222 2204. ◯ 10am–5:15pm Mon–Sat, 2–5pm Sun & public hols. ◯ Good Fri, 24–26 Dec. 🎫 🚻 www.dublincity.ie

Designed by Thomas Cooley, this imposing building was built between 1769 and 1779 as the Royal Exchange. It was taken over by Dublin Corporation in 1852 as a meeting place for the city council, a role it keeps to this day.

Tours of the building, which has been restored to its original condition, are available. *Dublin City Hall – The Story of the Capital* is a permanent exhibition housed in the lower ground floor covering 1,000 years of history.

Façade of City Hall

Temple Bar ❹

The cobbled streets between Dame Street and the Liffey are named after Sir William Temple who acquired the land in the early 1600s. The term "bar" meant a riverside path. In the 1800s it was home to small businesses but over the years went into decline. In the early 1960s the land was bought up with plans to build a new bus station. Artists and retailers took short-term leases but stayed on when the redevelopment plans were scrapped. Temple Bar prospered and today it is an exciting place, with bars, restaurants, shops and galleries. Stylish and eco-friendly architectural development is contributing further to the area's appeal.

Palm tree seat

Modern, floor-lit entrance hall of the Irish Film Institute

Exploring Temple Bar
The most dramatic way to enter Temple Bar is through the **Merchants' Arch** opposite Ha'penny Bridge *(see p77)*. Underneath the arch is a short, dark alley lined with bazaar-like retail outlets. The alley opens out into the modern airy space of **Temple Bar Square**, a popular lunchtime hangout, where there is a small but eclectic **book market** at weekends. Along the east side is **Crown Alley**, with its brightly painted shops and cafés.

Galleries and gallery shops abound. In the northwest corner of the square is the **Temple Bar Gallery and Studios**, a renovated factory that combines exhibition and studio spaces. The **Graphic Studio Gallery** off Cope Street sells handmade prints.

The **Contemporary Music Centre**, on Fishamble Street, is Ireland's national archive and resource centre for new music, supporting the work of composers throughout the country. There is a performance space on the ground floor. **The Culture Box**, on Essex Street East, provides details of arts, culture and entertainment in the area.

Near Christ Church Cathedral in the Old City district, is **Cow's Lane**, a pedestrian street complete with designer shops and its own fashion and design market every Saturday (except in winter). **The Gutter Bookshop**, on Cow's Lane, is a well-stocked bookseller with a small but attractive children's corner.

In the evening, there are a huge number of restaurants, bars and pubs to choose from, many with live jazz, rock and traditional Irish music. **Button Factory** offers an exciting mix of mainly homegrown talent, from alternative to hip hop and electro. For international names, try the **Olympia**

Theatre, where the world's biggest bands have played. This Victorian theatre also stages comedy, musicals and, occasionally, drama.

Meeting House Square
Named after a Quaker place of worship which once stood here, this outdoor performance space is a wonderful asset to the city. It is one of the main venues for the Temple Bar Summer Programme *(see p159)*, which features lunchtime and evening concerts, and open-air theatre. Screenings of films and numerous family events also take place in the square. Every Saturday, the excellent Temple Bar Food Market is held here.

Project Arts Centre
39 East Essex Street.
Tel *881 9613/14.* ☐ *11am–7pm Mon–Sat; shows nightly.* ♿
www.project.ie
Project Arts Centre, which started in 1966, has an international reputation for its exciting year-round programme of avant-garde theatre, dance, music, film and visual art. The centre has launched the careers of actors Gabriel Byrne and Liam Neeson, and even the world-famous rock band U2 cut their teeth here. Two performance spaces showcase productions from some of Ireland's most successful festivals and companies, alongside the work of new and emerging artists. The gallery presents a series of free exhibitions throughout the year.

Enjoying a sunny day in Temple Bar

Gallery of Photography

Meeting House Square. **Tel** 671 4654.
⬜ 11am–6pm Mon–Sat, 1–6pm Sun.
🖥 www.galleryofphotography.ie
This bright, contemporary
space runs exhibitions of
high-quality Irish and international photography, some
of which feature talks by
the artist exhibiting. The
shop carries an extensive
selection of photos, postcards
and specialist titles.

National Photographic Archive

Meeting House Square. **Tel** 603
0374. ⬜ 10am–5pm Mon–Fri,
10am–2pm Sat. **www**.nli.ie
The National Library's
collection of around 300,000
photographs is housed here.
    The Archive has rolling exhi-
bitions, mainly featuring items
from the collections. Subject
matter ranges from social and
political history to early tourist
postcards and dramatic landscape shots, offering a window into a time when Ireland
really was a land of thatched
cottages and donkey carts.

Irish Film Institute

6 Eustace Street. **Tel** 679 5744.
⬜ daily. 🍴 🖥 www.irishfilm.ie
Opened in November 1992, in
the wake of international hits
such as *My Left Foot* (1989)
and *The Commitments* (1991),

Cheese stall at the weekly gourmet market in Meeting House Square

this was the first major cultural
project completed in Temple
Bar. A neon sign indicates the
main entrance, which runs
through a floor-lit corridor
before opening into an airy
atrium where visitors can
have a snack, meal or drink
in the bar and restaurant. The
IFI's three screens focus on
cult, arthouse and independent films as well as showing
archive screenings and
documentaries. There are also
seminars, workshops, seasons
on various themes, nations or
directors, and the Jameson
International Film Festival
each year. A small temporary
membership fee is payable
on top of the ticket price.

The Ark

11a Eustace Street. **Tel** 670 7788.
⬜ (box office) 10am–5pm Mon–Fri,
1 hr before performances and workshops Sat & Sun. 📷 ♿ www.ark.ie
Europe's first custom-built
children's cultural centre
opened in 1995 and is based
on the premise that children
have the same cultural
entitlements as adults. This
magical place for the young
boasts an indoor theatre, an
outdoor amphitheatre, gallery
spaces and a workshop.
    The year-round programme
of theatre, visual arts, music
and multi-disciplinary events
is designed to inspire and
excite, presenting work of a
world-class calibre.

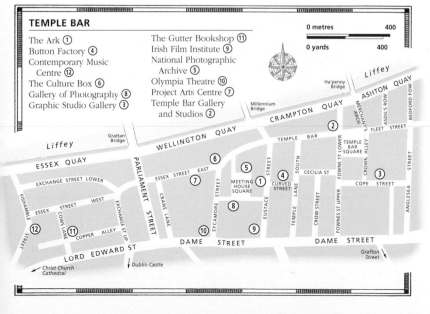

TEMPLE BAR

The Ark ①
Button Factory ④
Contemporary Music
    Centre ⑫
The Culture Box ⑥
Gallery of Photography ⑧
Graphic Studio Gallery ③

The Gutter Bookshop ⑪
Irish Film Institute ⑨
National Photographic
    Archive ⑤
Olympia Theatre ⑩
Project Arts Centre ⑦
Temple Bar Gallery
    and Studios ②

0 metres   400

0 yards   400

The light and airy interior of Powerscourt Townhouse shopping centre

Olympia Theatre ❺

73 Dame St. **Map** C3. **Tel** 679 3323. ⬚ 10:30am–8:30pm Mon–Sat (box office). See also **Theatre in Dublin** pp158–9.

Dublin's oldest theatre is a former Victorian music hall. The large auditorium is now used as both a theatre and a venue for live bands.

The theatre was originally built in 1879 by Dan Lowrey as the Star of Erin Music Hall and was eventually demolished and rebuilt as the Olympia Theatre in 1897. Its 19th-century Victorian canopy was accidentally destroyed in 2004, but it was painstakingly restored and unveiled in 2007.

Façade of Olympia Theatre

Powerscourt Townhouse ❻

South William St. **Map** D4. **Tel** 671 7000. ⬚ 10am–6pm Mon–Fri (8pm Thu), 9am–6pm Sat, noon–6pm Sun. See also **Shops and Markets** pp148–51. **www**.powerscourtcentre.com

Completed in 1774 by Robert Mack, this grand mansion was originally built as the city home of Viscount Powerscourt, who also had a country estate at Enniskerry, just south of Dublin. Granite from the Powerscourt estate was used in the construction of this mansion.

Today the building houses one of Dublin's best shopping centres. Inside it still features the original grand mahogany staircase, and finely detailed plasterwork by stuccodore Michael Stapleton.

In 1807, Powerscourt Townhouse was sold to the government, and the architect Francis Johnston was appointed to add three groups of buildings around the courtyard for use as a stamp office, and to erect the clock tower and bell on Clarendon Street.

The building became a drapery warehouse in the 1830s, and major restoration in the late 1970s turned it into a centre of galleries, antique shops, jewellery stalls and other shop units. The central courtyard café, topped by a glass dome, is a popular meeting place with many Dubliners. Another entrance is via the Johnson Court alley, just off Grafton Street.

Whitefriar Street Carmelite Church ❼

56 Aungier St. **Map** C4. **Tel** 475 8821. ⬚ 8am–6:30pm Mon & Wed–Fri, 8am–9pm Tue, 8am–7pm Sat, 8am–7:30pm Sun, 9.30am–1pm public hols. **www**.carmelites.ie

Designed by George Papworth, this Catholic church was built in 1827. It stands alongside the site of a medieval Carmelite foundation.

In contrast to the two Church of Ireland cathedrals, St Patrick's and Christ Church, which are usually full of tourists, this church is frequented by worshippers from all over Dublin. Every day they come to light candles to various saints, including St Valentine – the patron saint of lovers. His remains, previously buried in the cemetery of St Hippolytus in Rome, were offered to the church as a gift from Pope Gregory XVI in 1836. Today they rest beneath the commemorative statue to the saint, which stands in the northeast corner of the church beside the high altar.

Nearby is the figure of Our Lady of Dublin, a Flemish oak statue dating from the late 15th or early 16th century. It may have belonged to St Mary's Abbey (see p76) and is thought to be the only wooden statue of its kind to have escaped destruction when Ireland's monasteries were sacked during the time of the Reformation (see p14).

Statue of Our Lady of Dublin in Whitefriar Street Carmelite Church

The entrance to Marsh's Library, adjacent to St Patrick's Cathedral

Marsh's Library ⓼

St Patrick's Close. **Map** B4.
Tel 454 3511. ◯ 9:30am–1pm, 2–5pm Mon, Wed–Fri, 10am–1pm Sat. ◉ 24 Dec–2 Jan, public hols. 🖼🖥 **www**.marshlibrary.ie

Built in 1701 for Archbishop Narcissus Marsh, this is the oldest public library in Ireland. It was designed by Sir William Robinson, architect of the Royal Hospital Kilmainham (*see p84*).

To the rear of the library, at the bottom of the second gallery, wired cages can be found where readers were once locked in with rare books. The vast collection of over 25,000 books spans from the 16th to the 18th centuries.

St Patrick's Cathedral ⓽

St Patrick's Close. **Map** B4. **Tel** 475 4817. ◯ 9am–5pm Mon–Fri (to 6pm Sat), 10–11am, 12:30–2pm, 4:30–5:30pm Sun. Tours are not admitted during services. 🖼 ♿ **www**.stpatrickscathedral.ie

Ireland's largest church was founded beside a sacred well where St Patrick is said to have baptized converts around AD 450. The original building was just a wooden chapel and remained so until 1192, when Archbishop John Comyn rebuilt it in stone.

In the mid-17th century, Huguenot refugees from France arrived in Dublin, and were given the Lady Chapel by the Dean and Chapter as

their place of worship. The chapel was separated from the rest of the cathedral and used by the Huguenots until the late 18th century. Today St Patrick's is the Protestant Church of Ireland's national cathedral.

Much of the present building dates back to work completed between 1254 and 1270. The cathedral suffered over the centuries from desecration, fire and neglect but, thanks to Sir Benjamin Guinness, it underwent extensive restoration in the 1860s. The building is 91 m (300 ft) long; at the western end is a 43-m (141-ft) tower, restored by Archbishop Minot in 1370 and now known as Minot's Tower. The spire was added in the 18th century.

JONATHAN SWIFT (1667–1745)

Jonathan Swift was born in Dublin and educated at Trinity College (*see pp38–9*). He left for England in 1689, but returned in 1694 when his political career failed. He began a life in the church, becoming Dean of St Patrick's in 1713. In addition, he was a prolific political commentator – his best-known work, *Gulliver's Travels*, contains a bitter satire on Anglo-Irish relations. Swift's personal life, particularly his friendship with two younger women, Ester Johnson, better known as Stella, and Hester Vanhomrigh, attracted criticism. In later life, he suffered from Menière's disease (an illness of the ear), which led many to believe he was insane.

The interior is dotted with memorial busts, brasses and monuments. A leaflet available at the front desk helps identify and locate them. Famous citizens remembered in the church include the harpist Turlough O'Carolan (1670–1738), Douglas Hyde (1860–1949), the first President of Ireland and of course Jonathan Swift and his beloved Stella.

At the west end of the nave is an old door with a hole in it – a relic from a feud between the Lords Kildare and Ormonde in 1492. The latter took refuge in the Chapter House, but a truce was soon made and a hole was cut in the door by Lord Kildare so that the two could shake hands in friendship.

St Patrick's Cathedral with Minot's Tower and spire

Nave of St Werburgh's Church, showing gallery and organ case

St Werburgh's Church ⑩

Entrance through 7–8 Castle St. **Map** C4. **Tel** 478 3710. ⬤ 10am–4pm Mon–Fri, ring bell if doors locked.

Built on late 12th-century foundations, St Werburgh's was designed by Thomas Burgh in 1715, after an act of parliament which appointed commissioners to build a new church. Around 85 people made donations. By 1719 the church was complete but had an unfinished tower. Then in 1728 James Southwell bequeathed money for a clock and bells for the church on condition that the tower was completed within three years of his death. It was finally finished in 1732. After a fire in 1754 it was rebuilt with the financial help of George II. It served as the parish church of Dublin Castle, host-ing many state ceremonies, including the swearing-in of viceroys. However, this role was later taken over by the Church of the Most Holy Trinity within the castle walls.

Beyond the shabby pallor of its exterior walls lies some fine decorative work. There are massive memorials to members of the Guinness family, and a finely carved Gothic pulpit by Richard Stewart. Also worth seeing are the 1767 organ case and the beautiful stuccowork in the chancel.

Beneath the church lie 27 vaults including that of Lord Edward Fitzgerald, who died during the 1798 Rebellion *(see p16)*, and also Sir James Ware. The body of Fitzgerald's captor, Major Henry Sirr, is in the graveyard. John Field, the creator of the nocturne, was baptized here in 1782.

Tailors' Hall ⑪

Back Lane. **Map** B4. **Tel** 454 1786. ⬤ *to the public.* **www**.antaisce.org

Dublin's only surviving guild-hall preserves a delightful corner of old Dublin in an otherwise busy redevelop-ment zone. Built in 1706, it stands behind a limestone arch in a quiet cobbled yard. The building is the oldest guildhall in Ireland and was used by various trade groups including hosiers, saddlers and barber-surgeons as well as tailors. It was regarded as the most fashionable venue in Dublin for social occasions such as balls and concerts for many years until the New Music Hall in Fishamble Street opened and the social scene transferred to there. It also hosted many political meet-ings – the Protestant leader of the United Irishmen, Wolfe Tone, famously made a speech at the convention of the Catholic Committee on 2nd December 1792 before the 1798 rebellion *(see p16)*.

The building closed in the early 1960s due to neglect, but an appeal by Desmond Guinness saw the hall totally refurbished. Since 1985 it has been the home of An Taisce (the Irish National Trust).

Façade of Tailors' Hall, today the home of the Irish National Trust

St Audoen's Church ⑫

High St, Cornmarket. **Map** B3. **Tel** 677 0088. ⬤ May–Oct: 9:30am–5:30pm, last adm 4:45pm. ♿ ✚ **www**.heritageireland.ie

Sited in the heart of the walled Medieval City, and designated a National Monu-ment, St Audoen's Church is Dublin's earliest surviving medieval church. It is dedicated to Saint Ouen, the 7th century Bishop of

The 12th-century tower of St Audoen's Church, the oldest in Ireland

Rouen and Patron Saint of Normandy. The 15th-century nave remains intact and the three bells date from 1423. The Guild Chapel of St Anne houses an exhibition on the importance of this church in the life of the medieval city. To the rear, steps lead down to St Audoen's Arch, the last remaining gateway of the old city. Flanking the gate are restored sections of the 13th-century city walls.

Next door stands St Audoen's Roman Catholic Church, which was begun in 1841 and completed in 1847. It was built by Patrick Byrne, of Talbot Street, who studied at the Dublin Society School. The parish priest, Patrick Mooney, completed the plasterwork and also installed the organ. In 1884 the dome of the church collapsed and was replaced with a plaster circle. The portico was added to the building in 1899. The Great Bell, dedicated on All Saints Day in 1848 and known as The Liberator after Daniel O'Connell, rang to announce his release from prison and also tolled on the day of his funeral. The two Pacific clam shells by the front of the church hold holy water.

Medieval key in the Dublinia exhibition

Dublinia ⓭

St Michael's Hill. **Map** B3. **Tel** 679 4611. ◯ Apr–Sep: 10am–5pm daily; Oct–Mar: 10am–4:30pm daily. ◉ 17 Mar, 23–26 Dec. 🎫 minimum charge to enter Christ Church Cathedral via bridge. ♿ **www**.dublinia.ie

Managed by the non-profit-making Medieval Trust, the Dublinia exhibition covers the formative period of Dublin's history from the arrival of the Anglo-Normans in 1170 to the closure of the monasteries in the 1540s. The exhibition is housed in the Neo Gothic Synod Hall, which, up until 1983, was home to the ruling body of the Church of Ireland. The building and the bridge linking it to Christ Church Cathedral date from the 1870s. Before Dublinia

Former Synod Hall, now home to the Dublinia Exhibition

was established in 1993, the Synod Hall was briefly used as a nightclub.

The exhibition is entered via the basement where visitors walk through life-sized reconstructions of the Medieval City complete with realistic sounds and smells. These depict major events in Dublin's history, such as the Black Death and the rebellion of Silken Thomas (see p14). The ground floor houses a large-scale model of Dublin as it was around 1500, and reconstructions including the inside of a late medieval merchant's kitchen. There is also a display of artifacts from the Wood Quay excavation. This was the site of the first Viking settlement in Ireland. Excavations in the 1970s revealed remains of Norse and Norman villages, and artifacts including

pottery, swords, coins and leatherwork. Many of these finds are also on display at the National Museum (see pp44–5). However, the city chose not to develop the Wood Quay site, but instead built two large civic offices there. If you go to Wood Quay today all you will find is a plaque and an unusual picnic site by the Liffey in the shape of a Viking longboat. A fascinating exhibition depicts the world of archaeology. It is interactive, and enables visitors to become investigators of Dublin's Viking and Medieval past.

Also in the exhibition are information panels on the themes of trade, merchants and religion. On the first floor is the wood-panelled Great Hall, one of the finest examples of Victorian Gothic style in Dublin. The building's 60m-high (190-ft) St Michael's Tower offers one of the best vantage points for views of the city.

Mid 13th-century jug in Dublinia

Reconstruction of a Viking street in Dublinia

Christt Church Cathedral ⑭

Arms on Lord Mayor's pew

Christ Church Cathedral was established by the Hiberno-Norse king of Dublin, Sitric "Silkbeard", and the first bishop of Dublin, Dunan. It was rebuilt by the Anglo-Norman archbishop, John Cumin from 1186. It is the cathedral for the Church of Ireland (Anglican) diocese of Dublin and Glendalough. By the 19th century it was in a bad state of repair, but was completely remodelled by architect George Street in the 1870s. The vast 12th-century crypt was restored in 2000.

★ **Medieval Lectern**
This beautiful brass lectern was hand-made during the Middle Ages. It stands in the chapel of St Laud. The matching lectern on the south side is Victorian.

Medieval stone carvings are on display in the North Transept. Dating from about 1200, these exquisite Romanesque capitals include a troupe of musicians and two human faces enveloped by legendary griffons.

Nave
The 25-m (68-ft) high nave has some fine early Gothic arches. On the north side, the 13th-century wall leans out by as much as 50 cm (18 in) due to the foundations sinking in 1562.

Entrance

The bridge to the Synod Hall was added when the cathedral was being rebuilt in the 1870s.

★ **Strongbow Monument**
The large effigy in chain armour is probably not Strongbow (see p14). However, his remains are buried in the cathedral and the curious half-figure may be part of his original tomb.

STAR FEATURES

★ Strongbow Monument

★ Crypt

★ Medieval Lectern

Chapel of St Laud
The casket on the wall contains the heart of St Laurence O'Toole. The chapel features original medieval floor tiles.

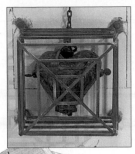

VISITORS' CHECKLIST

Christchurch Place. **Map** B3.
Tel 677 8099. 🚌 50, 66, 77 & many other routes. ⬭ 9:45am–5pm daily (Jun–Aug: 9am–6pm daily). ⬤ 26 & 27 Dec. 🛇
✝ 10am and 12:45pm Mon–Fri, 11am and 3:30pm Sun.
♿ limited. **www**.cccdub.ie

The Lady Chapel is used to celebrate the daily Eucharist.

★ Crypt
This decorated plate by Francis Garthorne is part of a collection presented to Christ Church Cathedral by King William III to mark his victory at the Battle of the Boyne in 1690.

Stairs to crypt

Crypt

The foundations of the original chapter house date back to the late 13th century.

Romanesque Doorway
Leading to the south transept, this ornately carved doorway is one of the finest examples of 12th-century Irish stonework.

TIMELINE

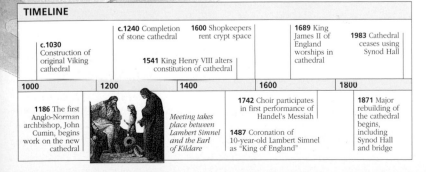

	c.1240 Completion of stone cathedral	**1600** Shopkeepers rent crypt space		**1689** King James II of England worships in cathedral	**1983** Cathedral ceases using Synod Hall
c.1030 Construction of original Viking cathedral		**1541** King Henry VIII alters constitution of cathedral			
1000	**1200**	**1400**	**1600**	**1800**	
1186 The first Anglo-Norman archbishop, John Cumin, begins work on the new cathedral	*Meeting takes place between Lambert Simnel and the Earl of Kildare*	**1487** Coronation of 10-year-old Lambert Simnel as "King of England"	**1742** Choir participates in first performance of Handel's Messiah	**1871** Major rebuilding of the cathedral begins, including Synod Hall and bridge	

NORTH OF THE LIFFEY

Dublin's north side was the last part of the city to be developed during the 18th century. The city authorities envisioned an elegant area of leafy avenues, but the reality of today's traffic has rather spoiled their original plans. Nonetheless, O'Connell Street is an impressive thoroughfare, lined with department stores, monuments and historic public buildings.

There are many notable buildings in the area, such as James Gandon's

Cart and barrels, Old Jameson Distillery

glorious Custom House and majestic Four Courts, together with the famous General Post Office, or GPO *(see p71)*. The Rotunda Hospital, Europe's first pupose-built maternity hospital, is another fine building. Dublin's two most celebrated theatres, the Abbey and the Gate, act as cultural magnets, as do the Dublin Writers' Museum and the James Joyce Cultural Centre, two museums that are dedicated to writers who spent most of their lives in the city.

SIGHTS AT A GLANCE

Historic Buildings
Custom House ❶
Four Courts ⓬
King's Inns ❽
Tyrone House ❹

Historic Streets and Bridges
Ha'penny Bridge ⓰
O'Connell Street ❸
Parnell Square ❼
Smithfield ❿

Theatres
Abbey Theatre ❷

Churches
St Mary's Church ⓯
St Mary's Pro-Cathedral ❺
St Michan's Church ⓭

Museums and Galleries
James Joyce Cultural Centre ❻
National Leprechaun Museum ❾
Old Jameson Distillery ⓫
St Mary's Abbey Exhibition ⓮

GETTING AROUND
Numerous buses, including the 3, 4, 11, 13, 16, 16A and 46A, go along O'Connell Street and round Parnell Square. To get to Smithfield, take a 67A, 68, 69, 79 or 90. The Tallaght to Connolly Station Luas line runs through the area.

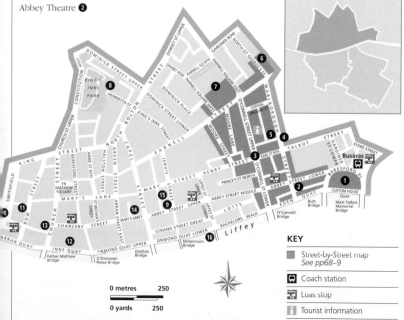

KEY

	Street-by-Street map *See pp68–9*
🚌	Coach station
🚊	Luas stop
ℹ	Tourist information

0 metres 250
0 yards 250

◁ **Portico of the Custom House, illuminated at night**

Street-by-Street: Around O'Connell Street

Throughout the Georgian era, O'Connell Street was the fashionable part of Dublin in which to live. However, the 1916 Easter Rising destroyed many of its fine buildings, including much of the General Post Office – only its original façade remains. Today, this main thoroughfare is lined with shops and businesses. Other nearby attractions include St Mary's Pro-Cathedral and James Gandon's Custom House, overlooking the Liffey.

Pavement mosaic, Moore Street

James Joyce Cultural Centre
This well-restored Georgian town house contains a small Joyce museum ❻

Parnell Monument (1911)

The Gate Theatre was founded in 1928 and is renowned for its productions of contemporary drama.

The Rotunda Hospital
Housing a chapel built in the 1750s to the design of German architect Richard Castle, this hospital features lovely stained-glass windows, fluted columns, panelling and intricate iron balustrades.

Moore Street Market
Be prepared for the cries of the stall holders offering an enormous variety of fresh fruit, vegetables and cut flowers.

The Monument of Light, an elegant stainless steel spire, rises to 120 m (394 ft).

The General Post Office, the grandest building on O'Connell Street, was the centre of the 1916 Rising.

James Larkin Statue (1981)

KEY

━ Suggested route

Luas stop

Tourist information

| 0 metres | 50 |
| 0 yards | 50 |

STAR SIGHTS

★ Custom House

★ O'Connell Street

St Mary's Pro-Cathedral
Built around 1825, this is Dublin's main place of worship for Catholics. The plaster relief above the altar in the sanctuary depicts The Ascension ❺

LOCATOR MAP
See Street Finder map pp180–81

The statue of James Joyce (1990)
This work by Marjorie Fitzgibbon commemorates one of Ireland's most famous novelists. Born in Dublin in 1882, Joyce catalogued the people and streets of Dublin in his celebrated books.

Abbey Theatre
Ireland's national theatre is known throughout the world for its productions by Irish playwrights, such as Sean O'Casey and JM Synge ❷

★ O'Connell Street
This monument to Daniel O'Connell by John Foley took 19 years to complete from the laying of its foundation stone in 1864 ❸

Butt Bridge

O'Connell
Bridge

Trinity
College

★ Custom House
This striking head, by Edward Smyth, symbolizes the River Liffey. It is one of 14 carved keystones that adorn the building ❶

Illuminated façade of the Custom House reflected in the Liffey

Custom House ❶

Custom House Quay. **Map** E2.
Tel 888 2538. ⬭ 10am–12:30pm
Mon–Fri (Nov–Mar: Wed–Fri),
2–5pm Sat, Sun. 🖼 ♿ weekdays.

This majestic building was designed as the Custom House by the English architect James Gandon. However, the 1800 Act of Union (see p16) transferred the custom and excise business to London, rendering the building practically obsolete. In 1921, Sinn Féin voters celebrated their election victory by setting light to what they saw as a symbol of British imperialism. The fire blazed for five days causing extensive damage. Reconstruction took place in 1926, but the building was not completely restored until 1991, when it re-opened as government offices.

The main façade is made up of pavilions at each end with a Doric portico in its centre. The arms of Ireland crown the two pavilions, and a series of 14 allegorical heads by Dublin sculptor Edward Smyth form the keystones of arches and entrances. These

heads depict Ireland's main rivers and the Atlantic Ocean. A statue of Commerce tops the central copper dome.

The best view of the building is from the south of the Liffey beyond Matt Talbot Bridge.

Logo of the Abbey Theatre

Abbey Theatre ❷

26 Lower Abbey St. **Map** E2. **Tel** 878
7222 Box office. ⬭ for performances,
some tours. See also **Entertainment**
pp154–9. **www**.abbeytheatre.ie

Founded in 1898 with WB Yeats and Lady Gregory as co-directors, the Abbey staged

its first play in 1904. The early years of this much lauded national theatre saw works by W B Yeats, J M Synge and Sean O'Casey. Many were controversial: nationalist sensitivities were severely tested in 1926 at the premiere of O'Casey's *The Plough and the Stars*, when the flag of the Irish Free State appeared in a scene featuring a pub frequented by prostitutes.

While presenting the work of eminent foreign authors from time to time, the prime objective of the Abbey, and the smaller Peacock Theatre downstairs, is to provide a performance space for Irish dramatic writing. Some of the most acclaimed performances have been Brian Friel's *Dancing At Lughnasa*, Patrick Kavanagh's *Tarry Flynn*, *The Colleen Bawn* by Dion Boucicault and Hugh Leonard's *Love in the Title*.

O'Connell Street ❸

Map D1–D2.

O'Connell Street is very different from the original plans of Irish aristocrat Luke Gardiner. When he bought the land in the 18th century, Gardiner envisioned a grand residential parade with an elegant mall running along its centre. Such plans were short-lived. The

O'Connell Bridge spanning the Liffey, viewed from the Butt Bridge

construction of Carlisle (now O'Connell) Bridge in 1790 transformed the street into the city's main north-south route. Also, several buildings were destroyed during the 1916 Easter Rising and the Irish Civil War. Since the 1960s many of the old buildings have been replaced by the plate glass and neon of fast food joints and amusement arcades.

A few venerable buildings remain, such as the General Post Office (1818), Gresham Hotel (1817), Clery's department store (1822) and the Royal Dublin Hotel, part of which occupies the street's only original townhouse.

A walk down the central mall is the most enjoyable way to see the street's mix of architectural styles. At the south end stands a huge monument to Daniel O'Connell (see p16), unveiled in 1882. The street, which throughout the 19th century had been called Sackville Street, was renamed for O'Connell in 1922. Higher up, almost facing the General Post Office, is an expressive statue of James Larkin (1867–1943),

Clock outside Clery's department store

leader of the Dublin general strike in 1913. The next statue is of Father Theobald Mathew (1790–1856), founder of the Pioneer Total Abstinence Movement. At the north end of the street is the obelisk-shaped monument to Charles Stewart Parnell (1846–91), who was leader of the Home Rule Party and known as the "uncrowned King of Ireland" (see p17). Completed in 2003, the Monument of Light was erected on the site where Nelson's column used to be. The monument is a stainless-steel conical spire that tapers from a 3-metre (9.8-ft) diameter base to a 10-cm (4-in) pointed tip of optical glass at a height of 120 metres (393 ft).

Tyrone House ❹

Marlborough St. **Map** D2.
⬤ to the public.

Considered to be the most important Dublin building by German-born Richard Castle (also known as Cassels) after

Leinster House, this Palladian-style structure was completed around 1740 as a townhouse for Sir Marcus Beresford, later Earl of Tyrone. Its interior features elaborate plasterwork by the Swiss Francini brothers, as well as a grand mahogany staircase. The premises were bought by the government in the 1830s and today house a section of the Department of Education; the minister has one of the most ornate state offices in what used to be a reception room.

Austere Neo-Classical interior of St Mary's Pro-Cathedral

St Mary's Pro-Cathedral ❺

Marlborough St. **Map** D2. **Tel** 874 5441. ⬤ 7:30am–6:45pm Mon–Sat, 9am–1:45pm, 5:30–7:30pm Sun. **www**.procathedral.ie

Dedicated in 1825 before Catholic emancipation (see p16), St Mary's backstreet site was the best the city's Anglo-Irish leaders would allow a Catholic cathedral.

The façade is based on the Temple of Theseus in Athens. Its six Doric columns support a pediment with statues of St Laurence O'Toole, 12th-century Archbishop of Dublin and patron saint of the city, St Mary and St Patrick. The most striking feature of the interior is the intricately carved high altar.

St Mary's is home to the famous Palestrina Choir. In 1904 the great Irish tenor, John McCormack, began his career with the choir, which sings at the 11am Sunday service.

THE GENERAL POST OFFICE (GPO)

Built in 1818, the GPO became a symbol of the 1916 Irish Rising after being seized by the Irish Citizen Army on Easter Monday. Patrick Pearse (see p17) read out the Proclamation of the Irish Republic from its steps. At first, many Irish people viewed the Rising unfavourably. However, as WB Yeats wrote, matters "changed utterly" when, during the following weeks, 14 of the leaders were shot at Kilmainham Gaol (see p81). Inside the GPO is a sculpture of the Irish mythical warrior Cúchulainn, dedicated to those who died.

Irish Life magazine cover showing the 1916 Easter Rising

An on-site museum displays a copy of the Proclamation and reveals the little-known story of the GPO staff who were on duty that Easter Monday.

James Joyce Cultural Centre **6**

35 North Great George's St. **Map** D1. **Tel** 878 8547. ⬛ 10am–5pm Tue–Sat, noon–5pm Sun (last adm 4:30pm). ⬛ Good Fri, 23–27 Dec. ⬛ ⬛ www.jamesjoyce.ie

Although born in Dublin, Joyce spent most of his adult life in Europe. He used Dublin as the setting for his major works, including *Ulysses*, *A Portrait of the Artist as a Young Man* and *Dubliners*.

This centre is located in a 1784 townhouse which was built for the Earl of Kenmare. Michael Stapleton, one of the greatest stuccodores of his time, contributed to the plasterwork with noteworthy friezes.

The main literary display is an absorbing set of biographies of around 50 characters from *Ulysses*, who were based on real Dublin people. Professor Dennis J Maginni, a peripheral character in *Ulysses*, ran a dancing school from this townhouse. Leopold and Molly Bloom, the central characters of *Ulysses*, lived a short walk away at No. 7 Eccles Street. The centre also organizes walking tours of Joyce's Dublin, so a visit is a must for all Joycean zealots.

At the top of the road, on Great Denmark Street, is the Jesuit-run Belvedere College attended by Joyce between 1893 and 1898. He recalls his unhappy schooldays there in *A Portrait of the Artist as a Young Man*. The college's interior contains some of Stapleton's best and most colourful plasterwork (1785).

Portrait of James Joyce (1882–1941) by Jacques Emile Blanche

Parnell Square **7**

Once as affluent as the now-restored squares to the south of the Liffey, Parnell Square is today sadly neglected. However, it still holds many points of interest, including the historic Gate Theatre and the peaceful Garden of Remembrance. There are hopes that this once-elegant part of the city will one day be renovated and restored to its original splendour.

Stained-glass window (c.1863) in the Rotunda Hospital's chapel

Gate Theatre

1 Cavendish Row. **Map** D1. **Box Office Tel** 874 4045. ⬛ 10am–7pm Mon–Sat, for performances at 8pm. See also **Entertainment in Dublin** pp140–45. www.gate-theatre.ie

Originally the grand supper room in the Rotunda, today the Gate Theatre is renowned for its staging of contemporary international drama in Dublin. It was founded in 1928 by Hilton Edwards and Mícheál Mac Liammóir. The latter is now best remembered for *The Importance of Being Oscar*, his long-running one-man show about the writer Oscar Wilde *(see p23)*. An early success was Denis Johnston's *The Old Lady Says No*, so-called because of the margin notes made on one of his scripts by Lady Gregory, founding director of the Abbey Theatre *(see p70)*. Although still noted for staging productions of new plays, the Gate's current output often includes classic Irish plays including Sean O'Casey's *Juno and the Paycock*.

Entrance to the Gate Theatre

Many famous names in the acting world got their first break at the Gate Theatre, including James Mason and a teenage Orson Welles.

Rotunda Hospital

Parnell Square West. **Map** D1. **Tel** 873 0700.

Standing in the middle of Parnell Square is Europe's first purpose-built maternity hospital. Founded in 1745 by Dr Bartholomew Mosse, the design of the hospital is similar to that of Leinster House *(see p46)*. The German-born architect Richard Castle designed both buildings. At the east end of the hospital is the Rotunda, after which the hospital is named. It was built in 1764 by John Ensor as Assembly Rooms to host fundraising functions and concerts. Franz Liszt gave a concert here in 1843.

On the first floor is a chapel featuring striking stained-glass windows and Rococo plasterwork and ceiling (1755) by the stuccodore Bartholomew

Cramillion. On the other side of the road from the hospital is Conway's Pub. Opened in 1745, it has been popular with expectant fathers for years.

Garden of Remembrance
Parnell Square. **Map** C1.
⬭ *dawn–dusk daily.*
At the northern end of Parnell Square is a small, peaceful park, dedicated to the men and women who have died in the pursuit of Irish freedom. The Garden of Remembrance marks the spot where several leaders of the Easter Rising were held overnight before being taken to Kilmainham Gaol *(see p81)*, and is also where the Irish Volunteers movement was formed in 1913.

Designed by Daithí Hanly, the garden was opened by President Eamon de Valera *(see p18)* in 1966, to mark the 50th anniversary of the Easter Rising. In the centre is a cruciform pool with a mosaic depicting broken swords, shields and spears, symbolizing peace. At one end of the garden is a large bronze sculpture by Oisín Kelly (1971) of the legendary *Children of Lir*, the children of King Lir who were changed into swans by their jealous stepmother.

Gallery of Writers at Dublin Writers' Museum

Children of Lir in the **Garden of Remembrance**

Dublin Writers' Museum
18 Parnell Square North. **Map** C1.
Tel 872 2077. ⬭ *10am–5pm Mon–Sat, 11am–5pm Sun & public hols (last adm 4:15pm).* ⬛ 25 & 26 Dec. ▨ www.writersmuseum.com
Opened in 1991, the museum occupies an 18th-century townhouse. There are displays relating to Irish literature over the last thousand years, although there is little about writers in the latter part of the 20th century. The exhibits include paintings, manuscripts, letters, rare editions and mementoes of Ireland's finest authors. There are many temporary exhibits and a lavishly decorated Gallery of Writers. The museum also hosts poetry readings and lectures.

There is also a pleasant café and a specialist bookstore, which provides a useful out-of-print search service.

Hugh Lane Municipal Gallery of Modern Art
Charlemont House, Parnell Square North. **Map** C1. *Tel* 222 5550.
⬭ *10am–6pm Tue–Thu, 10am–5pm Fri & Sat, 11am–5pm Sun.* ⬛ 24–26 Dec, public hols. ▨
www.hughlane.ie
Noted art collector Sir Hugh Lane donated his valuable collection of Impressionist paintings to Dublin Corporation in 1905. However, the failure to find a suitable location for them prompted Lane to consider transferring his gift to the National Gallery in London. The Corporation then proposed Charlemont House, the townhouse of Lord Charlemont, who built Marino Casino *(see p88)* and Lane relented. However, in 1915, before Lane's revised will could be witnessed, he died on board the torpedoed liner *Lusitania*. This led to a 50-year dispute which has been resolved by Dublin Corporation and the National Gallery swapping the collection every five years.

There are now 2000 works by national and international artists in the gallery. As well as the Lane bequest there is a sculpture hall with work by Rodin and others and a large collection of modern and contemporary Irish paintings. In 2001, the contents of Francis Bacon's studio at 7 Reece Mews, London, were donated by Bacon's sole heir, John Edwards, and reconstructed in the Gallery in their entirety.

***Sur la Plage* (c.1876) by Edgar Degas, Hugh Lane Municipal Gallery**

The impressive façade of the King's Inns, on Constitution Hill

King's Inns ❽

Henrietta St/Constitution Hill.
Map B1. ◐ *to the public, except the gardens.*

This classically proportioned public building was founded in 1795 as a place of both residence and study for barristers in Dublin. The King's Inns was the name taken by the Irish lawyers' society upon Henry VIII declaring himself King of Ireland.

To build it, James Gandon, famous as the architect of the Custom House *(see p70)*, chose to seal off the end of Henrietta Street, which was Dublin's first Georgian street and, at the time, one of the city's most fashionable addresses. In 1816, Francis Johnston added the graceful cupola, and the building was finally completed the following year.

Inside, there is a fine dining hall, and the Registry of Deeds (formerly the Prerogative Court). The west façade has two doorways flanked by elegant Classical caryatids (statues used in place of pillars) carved by sculptor Edward Smyth. The male figure, holding book and quill, is representative of the law.

Sadly, much of the area around Constitution Hill today is less attractive than it was in Georgian times. However, the King's Inns' gardens, which are open to the public, are still pleasant to stroll around.

National Leprechaun Museum ❾

Twilfit House, Jervis Street.
Map C2. **Tel** 873 3899. ◯
9:30am–6:30pm daily (last adm 5:45pm). 🎫 ♿ 🛍 www.leprechaunmuseum.ie

This charming interactive museum focuses on Irish myth and folklore, taking visitors inside Celtic culture to discover the truth about leprechauns, fairies, banshees and other mytholgical creatures. Visitors to the museum can take a trip to Fairy Hill, shrink to the size of a leprechaun and travel to the end of the rainbow while enjoying the lively storytelling of the expert guides. Children will enjoy the magical atmosphere of the museum, but there is plenty here to keep adults intrigued and amused too.

Statue at the entrance to King's Inns

Smithfield ❿

Map A2.

Laid out in the mid-17th century as a marketplace, Smithfield used to be one of Dublin's oldest trading and residential areas, playing host to people coming to the cattle- and horsefairs for which the area was famous. The traditional Horsefair still takes place here on the first Sunday of every month, even though the two-and-a-half-acre area underwent a €3.5-million regeneration in the 1990s and early 2000s. This created a modern public square surrounded by up-market apartment blocks and commercial units.

The transformation of Smithfield Plaza, commonly known as Smithfield Square, beside the famous fruit and fish markets, was part of Dublin Council's Historical Area Regeneration Programme, a project set up in 1995 in response to the severe decline suffered by the area between

Children riding saddle-free through the cobbled streets of Smithfield market

1940 and 1985. The remit of the programme was to make the inner city attractive again.

The cobbled pedestrian plaza is atmospherically lit by 12 gas lighting masts, each 26 m (85 ft) high, and provides the city with an impressive venue for outdoor civic events.

The transformation of Smithfield also includes some riverside public housing, a hotel, an art-house cinema and a small selection of bars and restaurants, as well as a number of artist-run galleries.

Horses tethered at the Sunday Horsefair

Old Jameson Distillery ⑪

Bow St. **Map** A2. *Tel* 807 2355.
⏲ 9am–6pm Mon–Sat, 10am–6pm Sun (last tour at 5:15pm). ⬤ Good Fri, 25 & 26 Dec. 🎫 📷 🚻 🛍
www.jamesonwhiskey.com

Proof of the significant investment made in the Smithfield area of Dublin's northside is evident in this large exhibition, set in a restored building that formed part of John Jameson's distillery. Whiskey was produced here from 1780 until 1971. While the place is run by Irish Distillers Limited, who are obviously keen to talk up their products (the four main names are Jameson, Paddy, Bushmills and John Power), it is an entertaining and educational experience. Visits start with a video, *Uisce Beatha* (the Water of Life; *uisce* meaning "water" and the origin of the word "whiskey"). Further whiskey-related

Sampling different whiskeys at the Old Jameson Distillery

facts are explained to visitors in the 40-minute tour. This moves around displays set out as a working distillery with different rooms devoted to the various stages of whiskey production, from grain storage through to bottling. The tour guides are keen to point out how the barley drying process differs from that used in the production of Scotch whisky: in Ireland the grain is dried through clean dry air, while in Scotland it is smoked over peat. They claim that this results in a smoother Irish tipple compared to its more smoky Scottish counterpart. At the end of the tour, visitors can test this claim in the bar, which features an extensive range of whiskeys, as well as a sample tray with tasting notes for self-tutoring.

IRISH WHISKEY

It is widely claimed that the Irish were the first to produce whiskey. This is quite possibly the case, since the monks spreading Christianity across Europe supposedly learnt the skills of distillation in the East where perfume was made. Some even believe that it was St Patrick who introduced the art. In the late 1800s and early 1900s Irish whiskey was superseded somewhat by the lighter blended Scotch. In addition, sales suffered in the United States as a result of the Prohibition. Today however, Irish whiskeys are enjoying a comeback and provide fierce competition for Scotch whiskies.

Old Bushmills *is a blended whiskey made from just one malt and a single grain. The end result is a pleasant blend of malty sweetness and aromatic dryness.*

Jameson 1780, *at 12 years old, has a classic smooth Jameson character. It is a hearty taste of Dublin's distilling heritage.*

Paddy *is the classic whiskey of Cork, Ireland's second city. It is firm-bodied, with the crisp finish typical of native Cork whiskeys.*

Power and Son's *Gold Label Irish, sometimes known as "Three Swallows", is a well-balanced and malty whiskey. Originally from Dublin, today it is very much a national brand.*

James Gandon's Four Courts overlooking the River Liffey

Four Courts ⑫

Inns Quay. **Map** B3. **Tel** 872 5555.
◯ 9:30am–12:30pm, 2–4:30pm
Mon–Fri (when courts in session).

Completed in 1796 by James Gandon, this majestic building was virtually gutted during the Irish Civil War *(see p17)* when government forces bombarded anti-Treaty rebels into submission. The adjacent Public Records Office, with documents dating back to the 12th century, was destroyed by fire. In 1932, the main buildings were restored using Gandon's original design. A copper-covered lantern dome rises above the six-columned Corinthian portico, which is crowned with the figures of Moses, Justice, Mercy, Wisdom and Authority. This central section is flanked by two wings holding the four original courts: Common Pleas, Chancery, Exchequer and King's Bench.

It is possible to walk in to the central waiting hall under the grand dome. An information panel to the right of the entrance details the building's history and functions.

St Michan's Church ⑬

Church St. **Map** B3. **Tel** 872 4154.
◯ mid-Mar–Oct: 10am–12:45pm, 2–4:45pm Mon–Fri, 10am–12:45pm Sat; Nov–mid-Mar: 12:30–3:30pm Mon–Fri, 10am–12:45pm Sat. 📷 ⚑ 🚻 ♿ limited.

Largely rebuilt in 1686 on the site of an 11th-century Hiberno-Viking church, the dull façade of St Michan's hides a more exciting interior. Deep in its vaults lie several bodies that have barely decomposed due to the dry atmosphere created by the church's magnesian limestone walls. Their wooden caskets have cracked

open, revealing the preserved bodies, complete with skin and hair. Among those thought to have been mummified in this way are the brothers John and Henry Sheares, leaders of the 1798 rebellion *(see p16)*, who were executed that year.

Other, less gory, attractions include the magnificent woodcarving of fruits and violins and other instruments above the choir. There is also an organ (1724) on which Handel is said to have played.

St Mary's Abbey Exhibition ⑭

Meetinghouse Lane. **Map** C2. **Tel** 833 1618. ◯ mid-Jun–mid-Sep: 10am–5pm Wed, Fri (last adm 4:30pm); by prior arrangement for groups. 📷 📷 off season; 086 606 2729. **www**.heritageireland.ie

Founded by Benedictine monks in 1139, but then transferred to the Cistercian order eight years later, this was one of the largest and most important monasteries in medieval Ireland. When it was built, the surrounding land was peaceful countryside; to-day, what is left of this historically

Detail of woodcarving (c.1724) at St Michan's Church

important abbey is hidden away in the sprawling back-streets that are found on the north side of the river Liffey.

As well as having control over extensive estates, including whole villages, mills and fisheries, the abbey acted as state treasury and meeting place for the Council of Ireland. It was during a council meeting in St Mary's that "Silken Thomas" Fitzgerald *(see p14)* renounced his allegiance to Henry VIII and marched out to raise the short-lived rebellion of 1534. The monastery was dissolved a few years later in 1539 and, during the 17th century, the site served as a quarry. Stone from St Mary's was pillaged and used in the construction of Essex Bridge (which was later replaced by Grattan Bridge in 1874), just to the south of the abbey.

Sadly, all that remains of the abbey today is the vaulted chamber of the old Chapter House. This houses a display on the history of the abbey and a model of how it would have looked 800 years ago.

The old vaulted Chapter House in St Mary's Abbey

St Mary's Church ⑮

Mary St (at Wolfe Tone St). **Map** C2. *Tel* 828 0102. **www**.thechurch.ie

In among the produce stalls and family-run stores in the warren of streets to the west of O'Connell Street stands what was once one of the most important society churches in 18th- and 19th-century Dublin. Dating back to 1627, its design is usually credited to Sir William Robinson, the Surveyor General who also built the beautiful Royal Hospital Kilmainham *(see p84)*, and it is reckoned to be the first church in the city with a

Impressive organ in St Mary's Church

gallery. Famous past parishioners here include Arthur Guinness, who got married here in 1793, and Wolfe Tone, the leader of the United Irishmen, who was born within a stone's throw of the church and baptized here in the 1760s. The cross street and the small park to the rear of the church are named in his honour today. The playwright Sean O'Casey was also baptized at St Mary's in 1880. Church services finally ceased in the mid-1980s. The building now houses several bars, a café, restaurant and nightclub and is called The Church. All the listed features were restored by specialist craftsmen and a church-like feel has been preserved in the decor. Look out for the organ and impressive stained-glass windows.

Detail of carving in St Mary's Church

Ha'penny Bridge ⑯

Map D3.

Linking Temple Bar and Liffey Street on the north bank of the river, this attractive high-arched footbridge is made of cast iron and is used by thousands of people every day to cross Dublin's river. It was built by John Windsor, an ironworker from Shropshire, England. One of Dublin's most popular and most photographed sights, it was originally named the Wellington Bridge, after the Duke of Wellington. Its official name today is in fact the Liffey Bridge, but it is also known simply as the Metal Bridge. Originally opened in 1816, the bridge got its better-known nickname from the halfpenny toll that was first levied on it. The toll was scrapped in 1919 but the nickname stuck and is still used with some fondness by Dubliners and visitors alike. In 2001, a restoration job that included the installation of original period lanterns made it even more attractive. This is particularly true at night, when the bridge is lit up as people cross over it to go through Merchant's Arch and into the bustling nightlife of the Temple Bar area *(see pp58–9)* with all its pubs, clubs and restaurants.

The Ha'penny Bridge looking from Temple Bar to Liffey Street

FURTHER AFIELD

There are many interesting sights just outside Dublin. In the western suburbs is the Museum of Modern Art, housed in the splendid setting of the Royal Hospital Kilmainham. Phoenix Park, Europe's largest city park, offers the opportunity for a stroll in a leafy setting. Further north are the National Botanic Gardens, home to over 20,000 plant species from around the world. Nearby, Marino Casino is a fine example of Palladian architecture. The magnificent coastline is easily admired by taking the DART railway. The highlight of the riviera-like southern stretch is around Dalkey village, especially lovely Killiney Bay. One of the many Martello towers built as defences now houses a museum to James Joyce. To the northeast, slightly further from the centre, is Malahide Castle, once home of the Talbot family.

Michael Collins' gravestone

SIGHTS AT A GLANCE

Museums and Galleries
Fry Model Railway Museum **14**
Guinness Storehouse **4**
Irish Museum of Modern Art –
    Royal Hospital Kilmainham **5**
James Joyce Tower **17**
Kilmainham Gaol **3**

National Museum – Decorative
    Arts & History **6**
Shaw's Birthplace **7**
Waterways Visitors' Centre **9**

Parks and Gardens
Dublin Zoo **2**
Glasnevin Cemetery **12**
National Botanic Gardens **11**
Phoenix Park **1**

Historic Buildings
Malahide Castle **13**
Marino Casino **10**

Towns and Villages
Ballsbridge **8**
Dalkey **18**
Dun Laoghaire **16**
Howth **15**
Killiney **19**

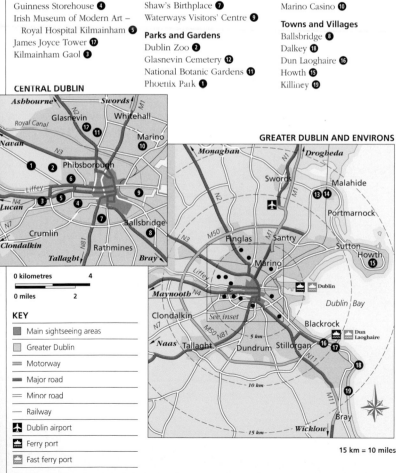

CENTRAL DUBLIN

0 kilometres   4
0 miles   2

KEY
■ Main sightseeing areas
□ Greater Dublin
= Motorway
▬ Major road
= Minor road
— Railway
✈ Dublin airport
⛴ Ferry port
⛴ Fast ferry port

GREATER DUBLIN AND ENVIRONS

15 km = 10 miles

Phoenix Park ❶

Park Gate, Conyngham Rd, Dublin 8.
🚍 *25, 26, 37, 38, 39, 46A, 70; plus shuttle bus service from Heuston (Park Gate St) through the park.* ⬤ *park: 24 hours daily; side gates: 7am–11pm.*
Visitor Centre *Tel 677 0095.* ⬤
Mar–Oct: 10am–6pm daily (last adm 5:15pm); Nov–Feb: 9:30am–5:30pm daily (last adm 4:45pm). 🔢 ♿ 🅿
Bike Hire *Tel 086 265 6258.*
www.phoenixparkbikehire.com
President's House 🎫 *10:30am– 4:30pm Sat (Oct–mid-Apr: to 3:30pm).*
www.heritageireland.ie

To the west of the city centre, ringed by an 11-km (7-mile) wall, is the largest enclosed city park in Europe. Phoenix Park is over 700 ha (1,700 acres) in size. The name "Phoenix" is said to be a corruption of the Gaelic *Fionn Uisce*, meaning "clear water". The **Phoenix**

The Phoenix Column topped by a statue of the mythical bird

Column is crowned by a statue of the mythical bird.

Phoenix Park originated in 1662, when the Duke of Ormonde turned the land into a deer park. Deer still roam in the park today. In 1745 it was landscaped and opened to the public by Lord Chesterfield.

Near Park Gate is the lakeside **People's Garden** – the only part of the park which has been cultivated. A little further on is the famous **Dublin Zoo**.

In addition to the Phoenix Column, the park has two other

striking monuments. The **Wellington Testimonial**, a 63-m (204-ft) obelisk, was begun in 1817 and completed in 1861. It allegedly took so long to be built because of the Duke of Wellington's fall from public favour. Its bronze bas-reliefs were made from captured French cannons. The 27-m (90-ft) steel **Papal Cross** marks the spot where Pope John Paul II celebrated Mass in front of more than one million people in 1979.

Most Saturdays, the visitors' centre issues tickets to the public for a free guided tour of **Áras an Uachtaráin**, the Irish President's official residence, which was built within the park in 1751. It was home to various British viceroys before becoming the residence of the president in 1937. **Deerfield**, also dating to the 18th century, is the residence of the US Ambassador and was once the home of Lord Cavendish, the British Chief Secretary for Ireland who was murdered in 1882 by an Irish nationalist. **Ashtown Castle**, a restored

Jogging in Phoenix Park

PHOENIX PARK

Áras An Uachtaráin ⑤
Ashtown Castle ①
Deerfield ②
Dublin Zoo ⑥
Papal Cross ③
People's Garden ⑧
Phoenix Column ④
Wellington Testimonial ⑦

KEY

🚍 Bus stop

🅿 Parking

ℹ Tourist information

▦▦▦ Park wall

0 metres   500
0 yards   500

Orang-utan mother and baby at Dublin Zoo

17th-century tower house, is adjacent to the Phoenix Park Visitor Centre.

Five times the size of Hyde Park in London and over double the size of New York's Central Park, Phoenix Park can fit playing fields for Gaelic football, hurling and polo, plus running, cycling and horseriding trails.

Visitors watching giraffe at Dublin Zoo

Dublin Zoo ❷

Phoenix Park, Dublin 8. *Tel 474 8900.* 🚌 *25, 25A, 26, 46A, 66, 66A, 66B, 67, 67A, 68, 69.*
🔾 *Mar–Sep: 9:30am–6pm daily; Oct–Jan: 9:30am–4pm daily; Feb: 9:30am–5pm daily.* 🏷 🔾 🍴 🏠
www.dublinzoo.ie

Opened in 1830 with one wild boar and an admission price of 6d (2.5 pence), Dublin Zoo was one of the world's first zoos. In its long history, there have been many changes, and today's facility would be unrecognizable to its first visitors.

The impressive African Plains sector, incorporating a 13-ha (32-acre) savannah with a large lake and mature woodland, is home to giraffes, rhinos, lions, zebras, hippos, cheetahs and ostriches.

Other sectors include the World of Primates, World of Cats, and Fringes of the Arctic, with highlights such as the orang-utan, Sumatran tiger, snow leopard and grey wolf.

Dublin Zoo has always prided itself on its breeding programme and cooperates with zoos worldwide in the conservation of endangered species. Lion breeding began in 1857, and 670 lions have been born here, including the lion that roars at the start of MGM movies.

Education is another aspect of the zoo's work: visitors will find skulls, skins, eggs and other objects at the Discovery Centre. Kids also enjoy the City Farm and the Nakuru Safari Train that runs daily in summer and at weekends in winter from the African Plains.

Kilmainham Gaol ❸

Inchicore Rd, Kilmainham, Dublin 8. *Tel 453 5984.* 🚌 *51B, 78A, 79, 79A.*
🔾 *Apr–Sep: 9:30am–6pm daily; Oct–Mar: 9:30am–5pm Mon–Sat, 10am–6pm Sun (last adm 1hr before closing).* 🔾 *25 & 26 Dec.* 🏷 🎥 🏠 🖥 www.heritageireland.ie

A long tree-lined avenue runs from the Royal Hospital Kilmainham to the grim, grey bulk of Kilmainham Gaol. The building dates from 1796, but was restored in the 1960s. From the 1790s to the mid-19th century, Kilmainham was used as a transportation depot for prisoners bound for Australia.

During its 130 years as a prison, Kilmainham housed many of those involved in the fight for Irish independence, including Robert Emmet *(see p16)* and Charles Stewart Parnell *(p17)*. The last prisoner held during the Civil War was Eamon de Valera *(p18)*, the future President of Ireland, who was released on 16 July 1924, just prior to the gaol's closure.

The tour of the Gaol starts in the chapel, where Joseph Plunkett married Grace Gifford just a few hours before he faced the firing squad for his part in the 1916 Rising *(see p17)*. The tour ends in the prison yard where Plunkett's badly wounded colleague James Connolly, unable to stand up, was strapped into a chair before being shot. It also passes the dank cells of those involved in the 1798, 1803, 1848 and 1867 uprisings, as well as a hard-labour yard. Of the 16 executions that took place in the few days following the Easter Rising, 14 were carried out here. There is a video presentation, and in the exhibition space are pieces depicting various events which took place in the gaol until it finally closed in 1924. There are also personal mementoes of some of the former inmates.

Doorway and gates of the historic Kilmainham Gaol

Tasting a pint of Guinness at a local pub

Guinness Storehouse ❹

St James's Gate, Dublin 8. **Tel** 408 4800. 🚌 51B, 78A, 123. ◯ 9:30am–5pm daily (to 7pm Jul–Aug). ● Good Fri, 24–26 Dec. 📷 (10% discount if booked online). 🚻 🏠 🍴 🖥 **www**.guinness-storehouse.com

The Guinness Storehouse is based in St James's Gate Brewery, the original house of Guinness, now completely remodelled. This 1904 listed building covers nearly four acres of floor space over seven storeys built around a huge pint glass atrium. A copy of the original lease signed by Arthur Guinness is enshrined on the floor. The tour starts with the Ingredients section, where visitors can touch, smell and feel the ingredients through interactive displays. Next, visitors enter an authentic Georgian anteroom to "meet" Arthur Guinness and see him at work. The Brewing Process is a noisy, steamy and "hoppy" area giving the impression of brewing all around with full explanation of the process. The historical development of Guinness cooperage is accompanied by video footage of the craft. Models and displays tell the story of Guinness's transportation, the appeal of Guinness worldwide, and their popular advertising campaigns. The archive includes an online search facility for visitors to see if their ancestors worked at the brewery. The tour ends with a tasting of draught Guinness, either in the Brewery Bar or the rooftop Gravity Bar with 360-degree views across Dublin.

The Brewing of Guinness

Label from a Guinness bottle

Guinness is a black beer, known as "stout", renowned for its distinctive malty flavour and smooth, creamy head. From its humble beginnings over 200 years ago, the Guinness brewery site at St James's Gate now covers 26 ha (65 acres) and has its own water and electricity supply. It is the largest brewery in Europe and exports beers to more than 120 countries. Other brands owned by Guinness include Harp Lager and Smithwick's Ale.

HOW GUINNESS IS MADE

The four main ingredients used to brew Guinness are barley, hops, yeast and water which, contrary to popular belief, comes from the Wicklow Mountains rather than the River Liffey.

Barley

Flaked barley

Malted barley

Roasted barley

Water

Grist mill

Grist

Masher

Kieve

1 Irish barley is prepared in three ways – malted, flaked and roasted (to give the distinctive tint). These are all ground together in a grist mill to form a grist.

2 The grist is mixed together with hot water and mashed into a porridge-like consistency. The mixture is strained into a kieve, or mash tun, and left to stand. Here starches are turned into sugars, producing a dark, sweet wort, or an infusion of malt.

Residual husks are removed

Sweet wort

GUINNESS FOR STRENGTH

Guinness advertising *has become almost as famous as the product itself. Since 1929, when the first advertisement announced that "Guinness is Good for You", poster and television advertising campaigns have employed many amusing images of both animals and people.*

ARTHUR GUINNESS

In December 1759, 34-year-old Arthur Guinness signed a 9,000-year lease at an annual rent of £45 to take over St James's Gate Brewery, which had lain vacant for almost ten years. At the time the brewing industry in Dublin was at a low ebb – the standard of ale was much criticized and in rural Ireland beer was virtually unknown, as whiskey, gin and poteen were the more favoured drinks. Furthermore, Irish beer was under threat from imports. Guinness started brewing ale, but was also aware of a black ale called porter, produced in London. This new beer was so called because of its popularity with porters at Billingsgate and Covent Garden markets. Guinness decided to stop making ales and develop his own recipe for porter (the word "stout" was not used until the 1920s). So successful was the switch that he made his first export shipment in 1769.

Arthur Guinness

Engraving (c. 1794) of a satisfied customer

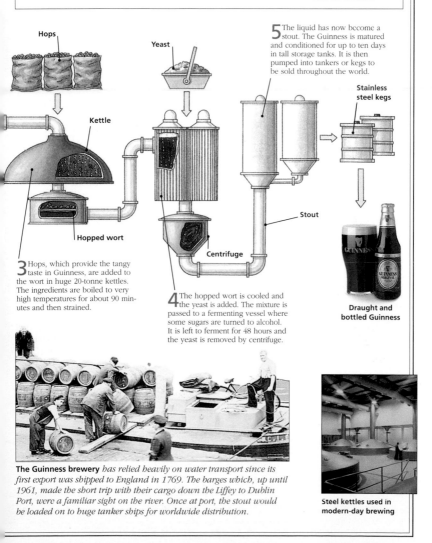

Hops

Yeast

5 The liquid has now become a stout. The Guinness is matured and conditioned for up to ten days in tall storage tanks. It is then pumped into tankers or kegs to be sold throughout the world.

Kettle

Stainless steel kegs

Hopped wort

Stout

Centrifuge

3 Hops, which provide the tangy taste in Guinness, are added to the wort in huge 20-tonne kettles. The ingredients are boiled to very high temperatures for about 90 minutes and then strained.

4 The hopped wort is cooled and the yeast is added. The mixture is passed to a fermenting vessel where some sugars are turned to alcohol. It is left to ferment for 48 hours and the yeast is removed by centrifuge.

Draught and bottled Guinness

The Guinness brewery *has relied heavily on water transport since its first export was shipped to England in 1769. The barges which, up until 1961, made the short trip with their cargo down the Liffey to Dublin Port, were a familiar sight on the river. Once at port, the stout would be loaded on to huge tanker ships for worldwide distribution.*

Steel kettles used in modern-day brewing

The elegant façade of the Royal Hospital Kilmainham

Irish Museum of Modern Art – Royal Hospital Kilmainham ❺

Kilmainham, Dublin 8. **Tel** 612 9900. 🚉 Heuston Station. 🚌 26, 51, 51B, 78A, 79, 90, 123. **Irish Museum of Modern Art** ◻ 10am–5:30pm Tue–Sun (from 10:30am Wed, from noon Sun & public hols); last adm 5:15pm. 🟢 Good Fri, 24–26, 29 Dec. 🎫 ▯ 🚻 ♿ limited. **www**.modernart.ie

Ireland's finest surviving 17th-century building was laid out in 1680, and styled on Les Invalides in Paris. It was built by Sir William Robinson, who also built Marsh's Library (see p61), as a home for 300 wounded soldiers, rather than as a hospital as its name suggests. It retained this role until 1927 and was the first such institution in the British Isles, erected even before the Chelsea Hospital in London. When it was completed, people were so impressed by its elegant Classical symmetry that it was suggested it would be better used as the main campus of Trinity College. The building's design is functional, but the Baroque chapel has fine wood carvings and intricate heraldic stained glass. The plaster ceiling is a replica of the original, which fell down in 1902.

In 1991, the hospital's former residential quarters were imaginatively converted to house the **Irish Museum of Modern Art**. The collection includes a cross-section of Irish and international modern and contemporary art. Works are displayed on a rotating basis and include group and solo shows, retrospectives and special visiting exhibitions.

National Museum – Decorative Arts & History ❻

See pp86–7.

Shaw's Birthplace ❼

33 Synge St, Dublin 8. **Tel** 475 0854. 🚌 16, 16A, 19, 19A, 122. ◻ May–Sep: 10am–1pm, 2–5pm Mon–Fri, 2–5pm Sat, Sun & public hols (groups by arrangement). 🟢 Wed. 🎫 ▯ **www**.visitdublin.com

Playwright and Nobel prize-winner George Bernard Shaw was born in this Victorian house on 26 July 1856. In 1876 he followed his mother to London. She had left four years

The recreated Victorian kitchen in Shaw's Birthplace

earlier with her daughters, fed up with her husband's drinking habits. In London, Shaw met his wife-to-be Charlotte Payne-Townsend. He never returned to Dublin, remaining in England until his death.

Inside the house, visitors can see the young Shaw's bedroom and the kitchen where the author drank "much tea out of brown delft left to 'draw' on the hob until it was pure tannin". Also on view are the nursery, the maid's room and the drawing room.

Although there is little in the museum on Shaw's productive years, the house does give an interesting insight into the lives of a typical middle-class Victorian family.

GEORGE BERNARD SHAW

Born in Dublin in 1856, Shaw moved to England at the age of 20 where he began his literary career somewhat unsuccessfully as a critic and novelist. It was not until his first play was produced in 1892 that his career finally took off. One of the most prolific writers of his time, Shaw's many works include *Heartbreak House, Man and Superman*, and, perhaps most famously, *Pygmalion*, which was later adapted into the successful musical *My Fair Lady*. He often attacked conventional thinking and was a supporter of many causes, including vegetarianism and feminism. He lived an abstemious life and died in 1950 at the age of 94.

Ballsbridge ⑧

Co Dublin. 🚌 *4, 4A, 7, 8, 18, 45.*

Laid out mostly between 1830 and 1860, the suburb of Ballsbridge is a very exclusive part of Dublin, attracting many wealthy residents. Many of the streets are named after military heroes. Running off Pembroke Road the elegant tree-lined streets such as Raglan Road and Wellington Road are lined with prestigious red-brick houses. The area is also home to several foreign embassies – look for the striking cylindrical US Embassy building at the junction of Northumberland and Eglin roads – as well as a number of upmarket hotels and guesthouses.

Close to Baggot Street Bridge is a statue of the poet Patrick Kavanagh, depicted reclining on a bench. This attractive stretch of the Grand Canal at Lower Baggot Street was one of the poet's favourite parts of Dublin.

The southeast sector of Ballsbridge, just across the River Dodder, is dominated by the Royal Dublin Society Showgrounds (often simply abbreviated to RDS). Founded in 1731 to promote science, the arts and agriculture, the Royal Dublin Society was an instrumental mover behind the creation of most of Ireland's national museums and

Late 18th-century engraving of a passenger ferry passing Harcourt Lock on the Grand Canal, taken from a painting by James Barralet

DUBLIN'S CANALS

The affluent Georgian era witnessed the building of the Grand and Royal canals linking Dublin with the River Shannon and the west coast. These two canals became the main arteries of trade and public transport in Ireland from the 1760s until the coming of the railways, which took much of the passenger business, almost a century later. However, the canals continued to carry freight until after World War II, finally closing to commercial traffic in 1960. Today the canals are well maintained and used mainly for pleasure-boating, cruising and fishing.

galleries. The two major events at the sprawling yet graceful showgrounds are the Spring Show in May and the Horse Show in August (*see p27*). Throughout the rest of the year the showground plays host to various conventions, exhibitions and concerts.

In May 2010, the Aviva stadium opened on the site of the former Lansdowne Road stadium, a landmark that was demolished in 2007. The state-of-the-art grounds are home to the Irish national rugby and soccer teams.

Stretch of the Grand Canal near the Waterways Visitors' Centre

Waterways Visitors' Centre ⑨

Grand Canal Quay, Dublin 2. *Tel 677 7510 or 087 122 6258.* 🚆 *DART to Grand Canal Dock.* 🚌 *2, 3.* ⏱ *10am–6pm Wed–Sun (last adm 5:30pm).* 🅿️ ♿ 🅿️ *on request.* **www**.waterwaysireland.org

A 15-minute walk from Trinity College, this visitors' centre, known as the "Box on the Docks", overlooks the Grand Canal Basin. Its audiovisual displays and models illustrate the history of Ireland's inland waterways. One of the most interesting focuses on their construction: in the 1700s, canals were called "navigations", and the men who built them were "navigators", a term that was shortened to "navvies". There are also exhibits on the wildlife found in the canals and surrounding marshlands.

The Royal Dublin Showground at Ballsbridge

National Museum – Decorative Arts & History ⑥

Silver coffee pot

Commissioned by William III in 1700, this was the largest barracks in his domain, with living accommodation for over 5,000 soldiers. Originally known as Dublin Barracks, it was renamed Collins Barracks after Michael Collins *(see p18)* following Irish independence. This decorative arts and history site of the National Museum *(see pp44–5)* displays the fine exhibits, from furniture to silver, by making full use of up-to-date technology including a multimedia catalogue and clever lighting. Currently occupying only two blocks, the museum is planned to extend eventually to fill all four wings.

Scientific Instruments
The fascinating display of surveying and navigation instruments includes this astrolabe (c.1580–90), which was made in Prague by Erasmus Habermel.

Skinners Alley Chair
Dating back to c.1730, this impressive gilt chair is part of the museum's collection of Irish period furniture. It was made for the Protestant aldermen of the Corporation of Skinners Alley, who were removed from the Dublin Assembly by James II. The society was eventually incorporated into the Orange Order.

South block

Entrance

Ground floor

East block

STAR EXHIBITS

★ William Smith O'Brien Gold Cup

★ Irish Silver

★ The Fonthill Vase

★ Irish Silver
This silver-gilt bowl by Thomas Bolton dates from 1703. Also known as a monteith, it was used for cooling wine glasses.

★ The Fonthill Vase

This beautiful 14th-century Chinese vase takes its name from Fonthill Abbey, near Salisbury in England, one of its many homes before it came to this museum.

VISITORS' CHECKLIST

Benburb Street, Dublin 7. **Tel** 677 7444. 🚌 25, 25A, 66, 67, 90. 🚃 Museum. ⏲ 10am–5pm Tue–Sat, 2–5pm Sun. ⦿ Good Fri, 25 Dec. 🎫 ♿ ▯ ⌀ www.museum.ie

★ William Smith O'Brien Gold Cup

After an uprising in 1848, O'Brien was sent to Australia and imprisoned. On his release he was presented with this 22-carat gold cup by his supporters in Australia.

Soldiers and Chiefs

This space includes The History of the Irish Soldier (1550–2001) and the Stokes Tapestry (below).

GALLERY GUIDE

Furniture, silver and scientific instrument collections are in the south block. In the west block exhibits include musical instruments, glass, clothing and jewellery. The Curators' Choice section displays 25 objects, individually chosen by the curators of the museum for their cultural significance.

Third floor

Second floor

West block

Main entrance

North block

First floor

Military History Wing

KEY TO FLOORPLAN

▢ Irish Country Furniture	▢ Exhibition Development
▢ A Dubliner's Collection of Asian Art	▢ Irish Silver
▢ The Way We Wore	▢ Curators' Choice
▢ Eileen Gray	▢ Origin of National Collections
▢ Period Furniture	▢ Temporary exhibitions
▢ Scientific Instruments	▣ Soldiers and Chiefs
▢ Out of Storage	▢ What's in Store?
	▢ Non-exhibition space

Marino Casino ⑩

Cherrymount Crescent, off Malahide Rd. **Tel** 833 1618. ⊞ DART to Clontarf. ⊞ 20A, 20B, 27A, 27B, 42, 42C, 123 IMP. ◯ May–Oct: 9am–5pm daily. For group bookings outside these times, call 086 606 2729. ⬚ ⬚ obligatory (last tour: 45 mins before closing). **www**.heritageireland.ie

This delightful little villa, designed by Sir William Chambers in the 1760s for Lord Charlemont, now sits next to a busy road. Originally built as a summer house for the Marino Estate, the villa survives today although the main house was pulled down in 1921. The Casino is one of the finest examples of Neo-Classical architecture in Ireland. Some innovative features were used in its construction, including chimneys disguised as urns and hollow columns that accommodate drains. Outside, four fine carved stone lions stand guard at each of the corners. The building's squat, compact exterior conceals 16 rooms arranged on three floors around a central staircase. The ground floor comprises a spacious hall and a saloon, with beautiful silk hangings. On the first floor is the state bedroom.

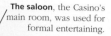

State bedroom

The saloon, the Casino's main room, was used for formal entertaining.

Entrance

The basement contains the servants' hall, the kitchen, pantry and wine cellar.

The hall ends in a semi-circular apse leading to the saloon.

Spectacular giant water lilies in the Lily House, National Botanic Gardens

National Botanic Gardens ⑪

Botanic Ave, Glasnevin, Dublin 9. **Tel** 857 0909. ⊞ 13, 19, 19A, 83, 134. ◯ Apr–Oct: 9am–6pm daily; Nov–Mar: 9am–4:30pm daily. ⬚ 25 Dec. ⬚ ⬚ ⬚ free at noon & 2:30pm Sun. **www**.botanicgardens.ie

Opened in 1795, these gardens are home to Ireland's foremost centre of botany and horticulture. They still possess an old-world feel, thanks to the beautiful cast-iron Palm House and other curvilinear glasshouses. These were built between 1843 and 1869 by Richard Turner, who was also responsible for the Palm House at Kew Gardens, London, and the glasshouses in Belfast's Botanic Gardens. The 20-ha (48-acre) park contains over 16,000 different plant species. A particularly attractive feature is the colourful display of Victorian carpet bedding. Other highlights include a renowned rose garden and rich collections of cacti and orchids. Pampas grass and the giant lily were first grown in Europe here.

One path, known as Yew Walk, has trees that date back to the early 18th century and there is also a giant redwood that towers to 30 m (100 ft).

Glasnevin Cemetery ⑫

Finglas Rd, Glasnevin. **Tel** 830 1133. ⊞ 40, 40A, 40B from Parnell St, 40C. ◯ 8am–4:30pm daily. **Glasnevin Museum Tel** 882 6590. ◯ 10am–5pm Mon–Fri, 11am–6pm Sat, Sun & public hols. ⬚ ⬚ ⬚ ⬚ **www**.glasnevinmuseum.ie

Impressive gravestones in Glasnevin Cemetery

Originally known as Prospect Cemetery, this is Ireland's largest graveyard – about 1.2 million people are buried here. Established in 1832 by Daniel O'Connell, it was viewed as a great achievement on his part, since Catholics were previously unable to conduct graveside ceremonies because of the Penal Laws. O'Connell's endeavours have earned him the most conspicuous monument – a 51-m (167-ft) tall roundtower in the early Irish Christian style standing over his crypt.

While the headstones exhibit a tremendous variety of designs – with high crosses and insignia such as harps, shamrocks and Irish wolfhounds – none, apart from O'Connell's, has been allowed to be too resplendent.

The most interesting sector is the oldest part by Prospect Square, on the far right-hand side. Two watchtowers built into the walls were erected as lookouts for the bodysnatchers hired by 19th-century surgeons. Before the Anatomy Act allowed corpses to be donated to science, this was the only way medical students could learn. Tours are available to visit the graves of people of interest, such as Charles Stewart Parnell and Eamon De Valera. A small Republican plot holds the remains of Countess Constance Markievicz and Maud Gonne MacBride, while the body of poet Gerard Manley Hopkins lies in the Jesuit Plot.

Glasnevin also reveals some interesting landscaping; the paths that run between the plots follow the same routes as the original woodland trails. In addition to mature sycamores and oaks, trees here include a Californian giant sequoia and a cedar of Lebanon.

The fascinating Glasnevin Museum, just inside the main cemetery gates, houses the Milestone Gallery, where visitors can find information on the lives of the many historical figures buried here.

Candelabra at Malahide Castle

The oak-beamed Great Hall at Malahide Castle

Malahide Castle ⓭

Malahide, Co Dublin. 🚌 🚆 42
Tel 846 2184. ◯ Apr–Sep: 10am–5pm Mon–Sat, 10am–5pm Sun, public hols; Oct–Mar: 10am–5pm Mon–Sat, 11am–5pm Sun, public hols. 🅿️ 🖥️ 📷 last tours 4:30pm.
www.malahidecastle.com

Near the seaside dormitory town of Malahide stands a huge castle set in 100 ha (250 acres) of grounds. The castle's core dates from the 14th century but later additions, such as its rounded towers, have given it a classic fairy-tale appearance. Originally a fortress, the building served as a stately home for the Talbot family until 1973. They were staunch supporters of James II: the story goes that, on the day of the Battle of the Boyne in 1690, 14 members of the family breakfasted here; none came back for supper.

Guided tours take in the impressive oak-beamed Great Hall, the Oak Room with its carved panelling, and the castle's collection of 18th-century Irish furniture. Part of the Portrait Collection, on loan from the National Gallery (see pp48–51), can be seen here. It includes portraits of the Talbot family, and other figures such as Wolfe Tone (see p16).

Fry Model Railway Museum ⓮

Malahide Castle grounds, Malahide, Co Dublin. **Tel** 846 3779. 🚌 42 from Beresford Place, near Busáras. 🚆 and DART to Malahide. ◯ Apr–Sep: 10am–1pm, 2–5pm Tue–Sat, 1–5pm Sun (last adm 4:30pm). ◯ Oct–Mar. 🅿️ ♿
www.malahidecastle.com

Set in the grounds of Malahide Castle, this collection of handmade models of Irish trains and trams was started by Cyril Fry, a railway engineer and draughtsman, in the 1920s. It is one of the largest such displays in the world. Running on a 32-mm wide (0-gauge) track, each detailed piece is made to scale and journeys through a landscape featuring the major Dublin landmarks, including the River Liffey complete with model barges. As well as historic trains, there are also models of the DART line, trains, buses and ferries.

A smaller room exhibits static displays of memorabilia and larger-scale models.

Howth ⑮

Co Dublin. 🚆 *DART.* **Howth Castle grounds** ◯ *8am–sunset daily.*

Yachts anchored in Dun Laoghaire harbour

The commercial fishing town of Howth marks the northern limit of Dublin Bay. Before Dun Laoghaire, or Kingstown as it was known then, took over, Howth was the main harbour for Dublin.

Howth Head, a huge rocky mass, has lovely views of the bay. A footpath runs around the tip of Howth Head, which is known locally as the "Nose". Nearby is Baily Lighthouse (1814). Sadly, much of this area – some of Ireland's prime real estate – has suffered from building development.

To the west of the town is Howth Castle, which dates back to Norman times. Its grounds are particularly beautiful in May and June when the rhododendrons and azaleas are in full bloom. The National Transport Museum in the grounds is worth a visit.

Ireland's Eye, an islet and bird sanctuary where puffins nest, can be reached by a short boat trip from Howth.

Dun Laoghaire ⑯

Co Dublin. 🚆 *DART.* **National Maritime Museum** *Tel* 280 0969. **Comhaltas Ceoltóirí Éireann** *Tel* 280 0295. ◯ *music Tue, Wed, Fri & Sat nights, céilis Fri.* 🖼 🅿 **Lambert Puppet Theatre** *Tel* 280 0974. ◯ *for performances 3:30pm Sat & Sun.* 🖼

Dublin's southern ferry port and yachting centre, with its bright villas, parks and palm trees, makes a surprising introduction to Ireland, usually known for its grey dampness. For a time Dun Laoghaire (pronounced Dunleary) was called Kingstown, after a visit by King George IV of England in 1821. Its original name was restored under the Free State in 1921, though the building of a rail line to Dublin in 1834 resulted in the demolition of the original *dún* or fort after which it is named.

Many visitors arriving on the ferry head straight for Dublin or the countryside. However, the town offers some great walks around the harbour. The east pier has sea-safari cruises, an ice-cream parlour and music on Sundays. The pretty **People's Park** at the end of George's Street has a coffee shop and hosts a flower show on the second weekend in August and a farmer's market every Sunday. The outlying villages of Sandycove and Dalkey can be reached via "The Metals", a footpath that runs alongside the railway line.

In the Mariners' Church is the **National Maritime Museum**, now under renovation. Exhibits include a longboat used by French officers during Wolfe Tone's unsuccessful invasion at Bantry in 1796.

Just up the road (or DART line) in Monkstown's Belgrave Square, is the **Comhaltas Ceoltóirí Éireann**, Ireland's main centre for traditional music and dancing, with regular music sessions and *ceilis* (dances). The **Lambert Puppet Theatre** on Clifton Lane offers classic pantomime fun for kids by the creators of the children's TV show *Wanderly Wagon.*

Martello Tower at Howth Head just north of Dublin

James Joyce Tower ⑰

Sandycove, Co Dublin. **Tel** 280 9265. 🚇 DART to Sandycove. ☐ Apr–Sep: 10am–5pm Mon–Sat, 2–6pm Sun, public hols. ● 1–2pm weekdays. 📷

Standing on a rocky promontory above the village of Sandycove is this Martello tower. It is one of 15 defensive towers which were erected between Dublin and Bray in 1804 to withstand a threatened invasion by Napoleon. They were named after a tower on Cape Mortella in Corsica. One hundred years later James Joyce (see p23) stayed in this tower for a week as the guest of Oliver St John Gogarty, poet and model for the Ulysses character Buck Mulligan. Gogarty rented the tower for a mere £8 per year. Today, inside the squat 12-m (40-ft) tower's granite walls is a small museum with some of Joyce's correspondence, personal belongings, such as his guitar, cigar case and walking stick, and his death mask. There are also photographs and several first editions of his works, including a deluxe edition (1935) of Ulysses illustrated by Henri Matisse. The roof, originally a gun platform but later used as a sunbathing deck by Gogarty, affords

Guitar at the museum, James Joyce Tower

marvellous views across Dublin Bay. Directly below the tower is the Forty Foot Pool, which was traditionally an all-male nude bathing spot, but is now open to both sexes.

Dalkey ⑱

Co Dublin. 🚇 DART.

Dalkey was once known as the "Town of Seven Castles", but only two of these fortified mansions, dating from the 15th and 16th centuries, now remain. They are both on the main street of this attractive village whose tight, winding roads and charming villas give it a Mediterranean feel.

A little way offshore is tiny Dalkey Island, a rocky bird sanctuary with a Martello tower and a medieval Benedictine church, both now in a poor state of repair. In summer the island can be reached by a boat ride from the town's Coliemore Harbour. The island was, at one time, held by Danish pirates. In the 18th century, a Dublin club used to gather on the island to crown a mock "King of Dalkey" and his officers of state. Originally done simply for fun, the ceremony was stopped in 1797 by Lord Clare when it became a political issue. It began again in the late 1970s.

Shopfronts lining the main street of Dalkey village

Killiney ⑲

Co Dublin. 🚇 DART to Dalkey or Killiney.

South of Dalkey, the coastal road climbs uphill before tumbling down into the winding leafy lanes around Killiney village. The route offers one of the most scenic vistas on this stretch of the east coast, with views that arc often compared to those across the Bay of Naples in Italy. Howth Head is clearly visible to the north, with Bray Head (see p116) and the foothills of the Wicklow Mountains (see p113) to the south. There is another exhilarating view from the top of windswept Killiney Hill Park, off Victoria Road. It is well worth tackling the steep trail up from the village to see it. Down below is the popular pebbly beach, Killiney Strand.

View southwards from Killiney Hill over Killiney Bay towards the Wicklow Mountains

THREE GUIDED WALKS

The scale of the city and the lack of many hills make Dublin an ideal place for walking. Many of the tourist attractions and the loveliest Georgian squares are within short distances of each other. The weather can be changeable, but that is a good excuse to drop into a local pub for a drink until the rain clears up.

Draught and bottled Guinness

The following walks give you a sense of three very different faces of the city. You can discover remnants of the old Viking town around Christ Church Cathedral; follow in the footsteps of Dublin's best-known literary figures; or take a trip to the nearby medieval village of Dalkey. There, you can enjoy great views of Dublin Bay and the beautiful Wicklow Mountains, only a short distance away. In addition to these walks, each of the three areas in the *Area-by-Area* section of the book offers a short walk on its *Street-by-Street* map.

CHOOSING A WALK

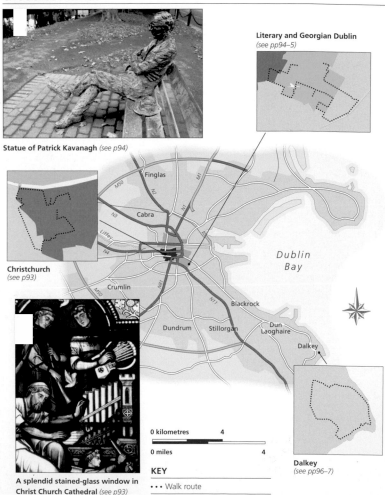

Statue of Patrick Kavanagh (see p94)

Literary and Georgian Dublin
(see pp94–5)

Christchurch
(see p93)

Dublin Bay

Finglas

Cabra

Crumlin

Blackrock

Dundrum   Stillorgan

Dun Laoghaire

Dalkey

A splendid stained-glass window in Christ Church Cathedral (see p93)

Dalkey
(see pp96–7)

0 kilometres   4

0 miles   4

KEY

••• Walk route

A 45-Minute Walk Around Christchurch

Although every part of Dublin boasts a rich heritage, it is in Christchurch, at the heart of the original Viking town, that the layers of history lie thickest on the ground. Much evidence of the past has sadly been lost through development; however, a few precious hints remain, including sections of the city wall and street names that suggest past uses, stories and personalities.

The bridge to the Synod Hall, part of Christ Church Cathedral ⑦

Begin at **City Hall** ① *(see p55)* and head up Parliament Street towards the Liffey. You will pass an old sign for **Thomas Reade's Cutlers** ②, a 17th-century sword shop. Turn left into **Essex Gate** ③, one of the old entrances into the town.

Looking through the ground-level bar grille of the corner building on Exchange Street, you will see the base of **Isolde's Tower** ④, part of the 13th-century Anglo-Norman wall. Go down Essex Street West, then turn into Cow's Lane for coffee at **Queen of Tarts** ⑤. Go back to Essex Street West and continue to Fishamble Street ⑥, named after the fish market that was located here in medieval times.

Cross over to John's Lane East, behind the spectacularly imposing **Christ Church Cathedral** ⑦ *(see pp64–5)*, Ireland's oldest cathedral. Viewing windows allow you to admire a section of the Hiberno-Norse town wall, located in the basement of the **Civic Offices** ⑧.

Head up Winetavern Street, on to Merchant's Quay and pause at **Father Matthew Bridge** ⑨, site of the original ford over the Liffey where the city was founded. Stop for a drink at the **Brazen Head** ⑩ *(see p146)*, the city's oldest pub. Turn left onto Cook Street and cross the grounds of **St Audoen's Church** ⑪ *(see pp62–3)* via its famous arch, the last remaining gateway of the old city. Turn right and follow Thomas Street West until the crossroads with St Augustine Street. This former Gaelic crossing point pre-dates the Vikings. Go down **Francis Street** ⑫, lined with a number of attractive antiques shops. Turn left towards **St Patrick's Cathedral** ⑬ *(see p61)*, Ireland's largest church. Cross the grounds to Golden Lane and turn left onto Ship Street Great, behind ancient **Dublin Castle** ⑭ *(see pp56–7)*. Follow Ship Street Little to **St Werburgh's Church** ⑮ *(see p62)*, and back on to Christchurch Place where you can catch a bus to various points across the city.

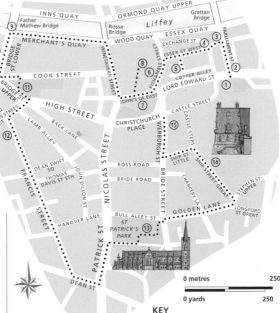

KEY

• • • Walk route

0 metres 250
0 yards 250

The sign for Thomas Reade's Cutlers, a 17th-century sword shop ②

TIPS FOR WALKERS

Starting point: *City Hall.*
Length: *2.5 km (1.5 miles).*
Getting there: *Buses 49X, 50, 50X, 51B, 77X, 78A, 123 and 206 to Christchurch Place. Stopping-off points: Queen of Tarts for a coffee; the Brazen Head for a pint or Guinness stew; and Leo Burdock's (see p141) for the best fish 'n' chips in Dublin.*

A 90-Minute Walk Through Literary And Georgian Dublin

Dublin has an enviable literary heritage and, as a result, there are endless routes one could take to follow in the footsteps of world-famous poets, dramatists and novelists. The walk detailed below passes through some of the city's loveliest Georgian squares and parks and along an attractive section of the Grand Canal, finishing up where many Irish writers got their inspiration – their local pubs.

Trinity to the Grand Canal

Begin at **Trinity College** ① *(see pp38–40)*, alma mater to Jonathan Swift *(see p61)*, author of the world-famous *Gulliver's Travels*; JM Synge, a renowned Irish dramatist; and Nobel Prize-winning playwright Samuel Beckett *(see p23)*, best known for *Waiting for Godot*. Walk east from the Lincoln Place entrance, passing Westland Row, where the prolific literary genius Oscar Wilde *(see p23)* was born. At the corner of Lincoln Place is **Sweeny's Chemist** ②, where Leopold Bloom, the protagonist of James Joyce's masterpiece *Ulysses (see p23)*, would buy lemon soap. Head to Merrion Square. As a child, Wilde lived at **No. 1** ③, and it was on this corner that Joyce was stood up on a first date by his future wife, Nora Barnacle. Continue to the reclining **Wilde Statue** ④ and then to the plaques on the square's south

side, commemorating the celebrated poet WB Yeats, who lived at **No. 82** ⑤; influential Irish writer AE

Russell worked at **No. 84** ⑥; and Joseph Le Fanu, a Gothic writer who impressed both Bram Stoker *(see p22)* and Joyce, lived at **No. 70** ⑦. On the corner of Mount Street Upper is **Number 29** ⑧ *(see p47)*, a re-creation of a Georgian house. Continue to **St Stephen's Church** ⑨. Pass Herbert Street, on your right, where the successful Irish dramatist Brendan Behan lived in the 1950s. The Grand Canal is ahead. Turn right, following the path by the water.

KEY

••• Walk route

Grand Canal to the RHA

On Herbert Place is a plaque to novelist Elizabeth Bowen, born at **No. 15** ⑩ in 1899. As a boy, Flann O'Brien (aka Brian O'Nolan), author of *The Third Policeman*, lived at **No. 25** ⑪. Continue along the canal to the **Statue of Patrick Kavanagh** ⑫. This immensely popular poet often referred to the canal and nearby streets in his works. Turn up Cumberland Road to **Fitzwilliam Square** ⑬. In the 1930s, WB Yeats lived at No. 42. Exit the square, returning to Fitzwilliam Street, and continue to Baggot Street Lower. At No. 3 is the

Pretty Georgian terrace houses lining Fitzwilliam Square ⑬

United Arts Club ⑭, founded in 1907 by WB Yeats and AE Russell among others to promote writing, visual art and music. Continue down Baggot Street to **Toner's Pub** ⑮, the only Dublin bar Yeats ever had a drink in. At the next crossroads, you come to **Ely Place** ⑯ *(see p42)*. Oscar Wilde proposed to Constance Lloyd at No. 1, while surgeon and writer Oliver St John Gogarty lived at what is now the Royal Hibernian Academy *(see p47)*.

Plaque for Bram Stoker

St Stephen's Green to the Carmelite Church

Continue on Merrion Row to St Stephen's Green, past the 17th-century **Huguenot Cemetery** ⑰ (closed to visitors) and the **Shelbourne Hotel** ⑱ *(see p130)*.

Among the writers who lived on or around **St Stephen's Green** ⑲ *(see p41)* are the 19th-century poet James Clarence Mangan; 19th-century Gothic writer Charles Maturin; and James Stephens, poet and writer of fairy tales. Gothic master Bram Stoker was born at No. 30 Kildare Street, just off the green to the right. Cross the green to emerge at **Newman House** ⑳ *(see p42)* to the south. Poet Gerard Manley Hopkins lived and taught here. You can see his room and the classroom of James Joyce, who studied here when it was part of University College Dublin. Continue round the green, taking a left at York Street. Walk to the **Whitefriar Street Carmelite Church** ㉑ *(see p60)*.

The façade of the grand Shelbourne Hotel on St Stephen's Green ⑱

Ghosts, pubs and old books

Also on Aungier Street is the birthplace of poet Thomas Moore at No. 12, now a pub. Joseph Le Fanu based some ghost stories around here, too.

Take a right on to Stephen Street Lower for Chatham Street, and visit **McDaid's** ㉒, Brendan Behan's local pub; he and Patrick Kavanagh were never allowed in at the same time to avoid fisticuffs. Turn left into Grafton Street and right to Duke Street. More refreshment awaits in three famous pubs: **Davy Byrne's** ㉓, the setting for a famous scene in *Ulysses*, and **The Duke** ㉔ and **The Bailey** ㉕, both frequented by Brendan Behan, Patrick Kavanagh, Flann O'Brien, James Joyce among others. Finally, go into **Cathach Books** ㉖ to browse through rare editions of old favourites. Catch a bus from Nassau Street.

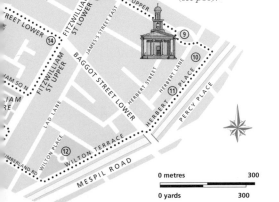

The tranquil surroundings of the Grand Canal

TIPS FOR WALKERS

Starting point: *Lincoln Gate, Trinity College.*
Length: *2.5 km (1.5 miles).*
Getting there: *DART to Pearse Street; a huge number of buses serve the area around Trinity. Stopping along Nassau Street are 4, 4A, 5, 7, 7A/B/C/D, 8, 11, 11A/B, 14, 14A, 45, 46A/B/C/D/E, 63, 74, 92, 116, 117, 118, 145.*
Stopping-off points: *There are several pleasant eateries near Baggot Street Bridge, or you can have lunch on La Peniche barge restaurant (see p140), near the Kavanagh statue, on the Grand Canal. Ely Winebar (see p139) is on Ely Place, and there are many pubs along the route for drinks.*

A 90-Minute Walk Around Dalkey

The picturesque village of Dalkey (see p91) has a fascinating history and stunning coastal views. In medieval times, it was Dublin's main deep-water port, and it thrived on maritime trade until the 1600s, when Dublin itself became a safe port for shipping. Dalkey then declined into a sleepy fishing village. Its fortunes turned once again in the 19th century, with the decision to build a protective pier at nearby Dún Laoghaire. Granite for the pier was quarried in Dalkey, bringing the town into the limelight once more. This walk goes along winding streets and past homely cottages snuggling up to grand mansions, now home to the rich and famous.

Roseate tern from a colony breeding off Dalkey Island

Castle Street to Coliemore Harbour and Dillon's Park

Start at the **Tramyard** ① on Castle Street, a short stroll from the Dart station. This is where trams from Dublin used to be parked for the night and the horses stabled. The last tram ran from Dublin to Dalkey in 1949.

The former site of most of Dalkey's seven medieval castles, **Castle Street** ② now boasts the only two surviving fortified mansions. Walk to the crossroads, turn left down Convent Road and take the first right into Coliemore Road. From here, you will catch tantalizing glimpses of the sea and Dalkey Island in-between colourful gardens, quirky cottages and grand mansions. Pass the fairy-tale **Cliff Castle** ③, a famous hotel in the 1920s and now the Moroccan embassy. Further along is **Inniscorrig** ④, a mansion once owned by Dominic Corrigan, a physician who brought running water to Dalkey. If the gate is open, you will see his face carved above the doorway.

At **Coliemore Harbour** ⑤, home to lobster fishermen, you will get a better view of Dalkey Island. Named after its shape (its Gaelic name, *Deilg Inis*, means "Thorn Island"), the island has been inhabited since 4,500 BC; these days only goats live there. On the island are the ruins of a 9th-century church and a Martello tower, one of 26 built between Dublin and Bray as defence posts against a Napoleonic invasion that never came. Note the outlying rocks, Lamb Island and Maiden Rock, which was named after some local girls who drowned while collecting shellfish. These are now a

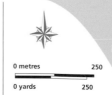

0 metres   250

0 yards   250

TIPS FOR WALKERS

Starting point: *Castle Street.*
Length: *2.5 km (1.5 miles).*
Getting there: *30 minutes by DART south from the city centre; buses number 8 (very infrequent) and 59 from Dún Laoghaire.*
Stopping-off points: *There are high-quality restaurants and cafés all along Castle Street. On Coliemore Road is Nosh (see p144).*

Pretty Coliemore Harbour ④**, with a clear view of Dalkey Island**

breeding ground for a rare species of roseate tern.

Continue to **Dillon's Park** ⑥. A Mrs Dillon operated tea rooms here in Victorian times. Take a rest, and enjoy the clear view of Dalkey Island.

Famous residents

Walk a little further and take the steps on the right up to **Sorrento Park** ⑦. Follow the path past a rock face with a mosaic of John Dowland, an Elizabethan poet said to have been born in Dalkey, who was a friend of William

Goats roaming on Dalkey Island

Shakespeare. As the path splits, veer left to reach **Sorrento Point** ⑧. Pause here to enjoy stunning views of Dalkey Island, Killiney Bay and Hill, and the Wicklow Mountains. This panoramic vista is often compared to the views across the Bay of Naples in Italy.

Exit the park and turn right to reach **Vico Road** ⑨, home

KEY

- • • Walk route
- 🚉 Dart station

to the ultra-wealthy. Further up the road, opposite a house called Strawberry Hill, the high wall on your right will break for zigzagging steps. Known as the **Cat's Ladder** ⑩, this is the hardest climb of the walk, but there are low walls for rest stops en route. At the top, turn right into Torca Road. A short way up on the left is **Torca Cottage** ⑪, the childhood home of renowned author/ playwright George Bernard Shaw. The road eventually turns into Ardbrugh Road. On your left is **Dalkey Quarry** ⑫, which supplied the granite used for the piers of nearby Dún Laoghaire Harbour. Just

The exterior of the 14th-century Goat Castle

before the road forks, a grassy slope down a steep hill appears on your right, separated from the road by bollards. This was the route of the funicular railway that serviced the quarry, and is marked by flagstones. Head down this hill and turn right onto Dalkey Avenue, then stop at the corner of Old Quarry and Summerfield House. Within the grounds of Summerfield House was **Clifton School** ⑬, which features in James Joyce's masterpiece *Ulysses*. At the end of Dalkey Avenue turn right, back into Castle Street.

Castles and Queens

On your right is **Archbold's Castle** ⑭, one of the street's two extant medieval mansions. Beside it is the **Church of the Assumption** ⑮. Cardinal Newman, first rector of the Catholic University of Ireland, spent time here while he lived in Dalkey.

Almost opposite is **Dalkey Castle & Heritage Centre** ⑯, in the 14th-century Goats Castle. The centre provides entertaining, in-depth historical and literary walking tours of the area, plus a tour of the castle led by characters in full period dress. Entrance includes access to the 10th-century St Begnet's Church and a Rathdown Slab, one of 28 unique to the area, believed to be a 10th-century Viking burial marker.

End your walk with a drink at **The Queens** ⑰ *(see p144),* a landmark pub that's been here since 1745. Turn right at the end of Castle Street to return to the DART station.

Herb garden, Ardgillan Castle ▷

BEYOND DUBLIN

BEYOND DUBLIN

A short way out of central Dublin, the beautiful Irish countryside offers a wealth of pretty villages, dramatic mountains and elegant stately homes to visit. South of Dublin, the coastline down to Dun Laoghaire and beyond, with its dramatic backdrop of the Wicklow Mountains, is stunning. To the north can be found traces of some of the earliest residents in the area – the Celts.

North of Dublin, the fertile Boyne Valley in County Meath was settled during the Stone Age. The remains of ancient sites from this early civilization fill the area and include New-grange, the finest Neolithic tomb in Ireland. In Celtic times, the focus shifted south to the Hill of Tara, the seat of the High Kings of Ireland and the Celts' spiritual and political capital. Tara's heyday was in the 3rd century AD, but it retained its importance until the Norman invasion in the 1100s.

Coracle from the Millmount Museum in Drogheda

Norman castles, such as the immense fortress at Trim in County Meath, attest to the shifting frontiers around the region of English influence known as the Pale *(see p108)*. By the end of the 16th century, this area incorporated nearly all the counties in the Midlands. The Boyne Valley returned to prominence in 1690, when the Battle of the Boyne ended in a land-mark Protestant victory over the Catholics *(see p15)*.

The area to the south of Dublin had the strongest English influence in all of Ireland. From the 18th century onwards, wealthy Anglo-Irish families were drawn to what they saw as a stable zone, and felt confident enough to build fine mansions like the Palladian masterpieces of Russborough, Newbridge and Castletown.

For a refreshing breath of fresh air, stroll along the cliffs at Bray Head, or follow one of the invigorating walking routes in the Wicklow Mountains.

Traditional kitchen in Newbridge House

◁ View towards the sea beyond Ardgillan Castle

Exploring Beyond Dublin

The countryside around Dublin is stunning and
offers everything from stately homes to ancient
burial sites and dramatic mountains to seaside
villages. The Wicklow Mountains have excellent
walking territory and are also home to some of
the best sights, such as the elegant gardens of
Powerscourt House and the monastic complex
at Glendalough. The coastal stretch to the south
of Dublin towards Bray is particularly scenic.

The lush gardens at Ardgillan Demesne,
situated on the coast north of Dublin

SIGHTS AT A GLANCE

Castlepollard   N52

Athboy   N

Lough
Deeravaragh   R395   Delvin

Royal Canal   N4   Ballivor   TRIM

R392   ㉘ MULLINGAR

W E S T M E A T H   Kinnegad
Lough Ennell   N52   M6   M4
Galway   M6   Rochfortbridge   Enfield
KILBEGGAN ㉙ ⊞   R400
Grand Canal
BOG OF ALLEN
NATURE CENTRE ③
Tullamore   O F F A L Y   ROBERTSTO

N80   R420   KILDAR

Portarlington
Mountmellick   MONASTEREVIN ④   ⑤ 🏠 KILDAR

Portlaoise   M7   N78
R417
Stradbally   Ballitor
Portlaoise   N80   Athy
L A O I S   Barrow
Ballylynan

Carlow
⑦
BROWNE'S HILL
DOLMEN

CARLO

The extensive gardens at Avondale House

0 kilometres   20
0 miles   10

Elegant stuccoed hall and staircase in Castletown House

KEY

▬	Motorway
▬	Major road
▬	Secondary road
▬	Minor road
▬	Scenic route
▬	Main railway
▬	Minor railway
▬	International border
▬	County border

SEE ALSO

• **Where to Stay** pp128–33

• **Where to Eat** pp138–45

GETTING AROUND

Several motorways and main roads fan out from Dublin. The M1 goes north to Dundalk, the N11 south, following the scenic coastline. Regular train services operate around the country from Heuston and Connolly stations. Coach services also run all around the country from Dublin. The DART railway line runs north and south from the city along the coast and has several stops in central Dublin.

Castletown House ❶

See pp106–7.

Robertstown ❷

Co Kildare. 🏠 *240.* 🖥 **www.** robertstownholidayvillage.com

Ten locks west along the Grand Canal from Dublin, Robertstown is a characteristic 19th-century canalside village, with warehouses and cottages flanking the waterfront. Freight barges plied the route until about 1960, but pleasure boats have since replaced them. Barge cruises leave from the quay and the old Grand Canal Company's Hotel, built in 1801 for canal passengers, is now used for banquets.

Near Sallins, about 8 km (5 miles) east, the canal is carried over the River Liffey along the **Leinster Aqueduct**, an impressive structure built in 1783.

Bog of Allen Nature Centre ❸

Lullymore, Co Kildare. **Tel** 045 860133. 🚌 to Newbridge & Kildare. 🚌 to Allenwood. ⏰ all year: 10am–4pm Mon–Fri. 📷 ♿ limited. **www.**ipcc.ie

Anyone interested in the natural history of Irish bogs should visit the Nature Centre, an exhibition housed in an old farm at Lullymore, 9 km (6 miles) northeast of Rathangan. It lies at the heart of the Bog of Allen, a vast expanse of raised bog that extends across the counties of Offaly, Laois and Kildare.

Japanese Gardens at Tully near Kildare

The exhibition explains the history and ecology of the bog, and features displays of flora and fauna as well as archaeological finds from the surrounding area. Guided walks are also organized to introduce visitors to the bog's delicate ecosystem and the careful conservation work that is being done.

Stacking peat for use as fuel

Monasterevin ❹

Co Kildare. 🏠 *2,200.* 🚌

This Georgian market town lies west of Kildare, where the Grand Canal crosses the River Barrow. Waterborne trade brought prosperity to Monasterevin in the 18th century, but the locks now see little traffic. However, you can still admire the aqueduct, which is a superb example of canal engineering.

Moore Abbey, next to the church, was built in the 18th century on the site of a Cistercian monastery which was founded by St Evin, but the grand Gothic mansion owes a great deal to Victorian remodelling. Originally the ancestral seat of the earls of Drogheda, in the 1920s Moore Abbey became the home of the internationally celebrated Irish tenor, John McCormack. It is now a Sisters of Charity convent.

Kildare ❺

Co Kildare. 🏠 *4,200.* 🚌 🚆 ℹ️ Market House, May–Sep: 045 521 240. 🛒 Thu.

The charming and tidy town of Kildare is dominated by **St Brigid's Cathedral**, which commemorates the saint who founded a religious community on this site in AD 480. Unusually, monks and nuns lived

The Grand Canal Company's Hotel in Robertstown

here under the same roof, but this was not the only orthodox practice associated with the community. Curious pagan rituals, including the burning of a perpetual fire, continued until the 16th century. The fire pit is visible in the grounds today. So too is a round tower, which was probably built in the 12th century and has a Romanesque doorway. The cathedral was rebuilt in the Victorian era, but the restorers largely adhered to the original 13th-century design.

🏰 St Brigid's Cathedral
Market Square. ⬜ *May–Sep: daily.* 🖼 *donation.* ♿

Environs
Kildare lies at the heart of racing country: the Curragh racecourse is nearby, stables are scattered all around and bloodstock sales take place at Kill, northeast of town.

The **National Stud** is a semi state-run bloodstock farm at Tully, just south of Kildare. It was founded in 1900 by an eccentric Anglo-Irish colonel, William Hall-Walker. He sold his foals on the basis of their astrological charts, and put skylights in the stables to allow the horses to be "touched" by sunlight or moonbeams. Hall-Walker received the title Lord Wavertree in reward for bequeathing the farm to the British Crown in 1915.

Visitors can explore the 400-ha (1,000-acre) grounds and watch the horses being exercised. Mares and stallions are generally kept in separate paddocks. The breeding stallions are expected to cover more than 100

HORSE RACING IN IRELAND

Ireland has a strong racing culture and, thanks to its non-elitist image, the sport is enjoyed by all. Much of the thoroughbred industry centres around the Curragh, a grassy plain in County Kildare stretching unfenced for more than 2,000 ha (5,000 acres). This area is home to many of the country's studs and training yards, and every morning horses are put through their paces on the gallops. Most of the major flat races, including the Irish Derby, take place at the Curragh racecourse just east of Kildare. Other popular fixtures are held at nearby Punchestown – most famously the steeplechase festival in April – and at Leopardstown, which also hosts major National Hunt races *(see p29).*

Finishing straight at the Curragh racecourse

mares per season. There is a foaling unit where the mare and foal can rest for a few days after the birth.

The farm has its own forge and saddlery, and also a Horse Museum. Housed in old stable block, this illustrates the importance of horses in Irish life. Exhibits include the frail skeleton of Arkle, the champion steeplechaser who raced to fame in the 1960s.

Sharing the same estate as the National Stud are the **Japanese Gardens**, created by Lord Wavertree at the height of the Edwardian penchant for Orientalism. The gardens were laid out in 1906–10 by a Japanese landscape gardener called Tassa Eida, with the help of his son Minoru and 40 assistants. The impressive

array of trees and shrubs includes maples, mulberries, bonsai, magnolias, cherry trees and sacred bamboos.

The gardens take the form of an allegorical journey from the cradle to the grave, beginning with life emerging from the Gate of Oblivion (a cave) and leading to the Gateway of Eternity, a Zen rock garden.

St Fiachra's Garden was a millennium project completed in 1999. It was designed by Professor Martin Hallinan and commemorates St Fiachra, the Patron Saint of Gardeners.

🌿 National Stud, Japanese & St Fiachra Gardens
Tully. **Tel** *045 521 617.* ⬜ *mid-Feb–23 Dec: 9:30am–5pm daily.* 🖼 ♿ 📷 *Stud only.* 📺 📷 *www.irish-national-stud.ie*

St Brigid's Cathedral and roofless round tower in Kildare town

Castletown House ❶

Built in 1722–32 for William Conolly, the Speaker of the Irish Parliament, the façade of Castletown was the work of Florentine architect Alessandro Galilei and gave Ireland its first taste of Palladianism. The magnificent interiors date from the second half of the 18th century. They were commissioned by Lady Louisa Lennox, wife of William Conolly's great-nephew, Tom,

Conolly crest on an armchair

who lived here from 1759. Castletown remained in the family until 1965, when it was taken over by the Irish Georgian Society. The state now owns the house and it is open to the public.

★ Long Gallery
The heavy ceiling sections and friezes date from the 1720s and the walls were decorated in the Pompeian manner in the 1770s.

Green drawing room

Red drawing room
The red damask covering the walls of this room is probably French and dates from the 19th century. This exquisite mahogany bureau was made for Lady Louisa in the 1760s.

West wing with kitchen

Boudoir wall paintings
The boudoir's decorative panels, moved here from the Long Gallery, were inspired by the Raphael Loggia in the Vatican.

The Dining Room with the compartmentalized ceiling was designed by Isaac Ware.

VISITORS' CHECKLIST

Celbridge, Co Kildare.
Tel 628 8252.
🚌 67, 67A from Dublin.
⭘ mid-Mar–end Oct: 10am–
6pm Tue–Sun, public hols. 🖼️
♿ 🚻 💻 📷 obligatory. First
tour 10:30am, last adm 4:45pm.
Summer concerts.
www.castletown.ie

★ **Print room**
*In this, the only intact 18th-century print room in Ireland,
Lady Louisa indulged her taste for Italian engravings. It was
fashionable at the time for ladies to paste prints directly on
to the wall and frame them with elaborate festoons.*

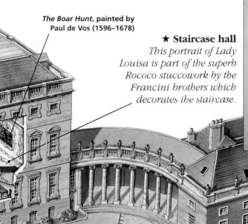

The Boar Hunt, painted by
Paul de Vos (1596–1678)

★ **Staircase hall**
*This portrait of Lady
Louisa is part of the superb
Rococo stuccowork by the
Francini brothers which
decorates the staircase.*

The east wing originally
housed the stables.

The entrance hall is an
austere Neo-Classical room.
Its most decorative feature is
the delicate carving on the
pilasters of the upper gallery.

Entrance

STAR FEATURES

★ Long Gallery

★ Print room

★ Staircase hall

CONOLLY'S FOLLY

This folly, which lies just
beyond the grounds of
Castletown House, provides
the focus of the view from
the Long Gallery. Speaker
Conolly's widow, Katherine,
commissioned it in 1740
as a memorial to her late
husband, and to provide
employment after a harsh
winter. The unusual structure
of superimposed arches
crowned by an obelisk was
designed by Richard Castle,
architect of Russborough
House *(see p108).*

Saloon in Russborough House with original fireplace and stuccowork

Russborough House ⑥

Blessington, Co Wicklow. **Tel** 045
865239. 🚌 65 from Dublin (check
times). ☐ May–Sep: 10am–6pm
daily; Apr & Oct: 10am–6pm Sun &
public hols only. 🎫 📷 obligatory.
💻 📷 www.russborough.ie

This Palladian mansion,
built in the 1740s for Joseph
Leeson, later Earl of Milltown,
is one of Ireland's finest
houses. Its architect, a
German called Richard Castle,
also designed Powerscourt
House (see pp114–15) and is
credited with introducing the
Palladian style to Ireland.
Unlike many grand estates in
the Pale, Russborough has
survived magnificently,
both inside and out.
The house claims
the longest
frontage in
Ireland, with a
façade adorned
by heraldic lions
and curved
colonnades. The
interior is even more
impressive. Many
rooms feature superb
stucco decoration, which was
done largely by the Italian
Francini brothers, who also
worked on Castletown House

**Vernet seascape in
the drawing room**

(see pp106–7). The best
examples are found in the
music room, saloon and
library, which are embellished
with exuberant foliage and
cherubs. Around the main
staircase, a riot of Rococo
plasterwork depicts a hunt,
with hounds clasping garlands
of flowers. The stucco mould-
ings in the drawing room
were designed especially to
enclose marine scenes by the
French artist Joseph Vernet
(1714–89). The paintings were
sold in 1926, but were tracked
down more than 40 years later
and returned to the house.

Russborough House has
many other treasures to be
seen, including finely worked
fireplaces made of Italian
marble, imposing mahogany
doorways and priceless
collections of silver, porcelain
and Gobelins tapestries.

Such riches aside, one of the
main reasons to visit
Russborough is
to see the **Beit
Art Collection**,
famous for its
Flemish, Dutch
and Spanish Old
Master paintings.
Sir Alfred Beit,
who bought the
house in 1952,
inherited the pictures
from his uncle,
also named Alfred Beit. The
family's wealth had come
from gold mines and diamond
dealing in Kimberley, South

An 18th-century family enjoying the privileged lifestyle
that was typical within the Pale

THE HISTORY OF THE PALE

The term "Pale" refers to an area around
Dublin which marked the limits of
English influence from Norman to Tudor
times. The frontier fluctuated but, at its
largest, the Pale stretched from Dundalk
in County Louth to Waterford town.
Gaelic chieftains outside the area could
keep their lands provided they agreed
to raise their heirs within the Pale.

The Palesmen supported their rulers'
interests and considered themselves the
upholders of English values. This widened
the gap between the Gaelic majority and
the Anglo-Irish, foretelling England's
doomed involvement in the country. Long
after its fortifications were dismantled,
the idea of the Pale lived on as a state
of mind. The expression "beyond the
pale" survives as a definition of those
outside the bounds of civilized society.

Africa. The Beit family donated Russborough to the Beit Foundation, opening the house to the public while living in one of the wings of the house. The West Wing has been converted to create self-catering accommodation under the stewardship of the Landmark Trust.

Only a selection of paintings is on view at any one time, while others are on permanent loan to the National Gallery in Dublin *(see pp48–51)*. Other paintings from the National Gallery are also on view in the house from time to time.

Russborough enjoys a fine position near the village of **Blessington**, which has a good view of the Wicklow Mountains. The house lies in the midst of wooded parkland rather than elaborate gardens. As Alfred Beit said of Irish Palladianism, "Fine architecture standing in a green sward was considered enough". Adjoining the house is a maze.

Environs

The **Poulaphouca Reservoir**, formed by the damming of the River Liffey, extends south from Blessington. The placid lake is popular with water-sports enthusiasts, while others come simply to enjoy the view of the nearby Wicklow Mountains.

Avondale House, with its colourful gardens in the foreground

Browne's Hill Dolmen ❼

Co Carlow. to Carlow. *daily.*

In a field 3 km (2 miles) east of Carlow, along the R726, stands a huge dolmen boasting the biggest capstone in Ireland. It stands in the area of Browne's Hill, where there is a stone house dating from 1763. Weighing a reputed 100 tonnes, this massive stone is embedded in the earth at one end and supported at the other by three much smaller stones. Dating back to 2000 BC, the Dolmen is thought to mark the tomb of a local chieftain. A path from the road skirts the field before reaching it.

Browne's Hill Dolmen, famous for its enormous capstone

Avondale House ❽

Co Wicklow. ***Tel*** *0404 46111.* *to Rathdrum.* **House and grounds** *mid-Mar–Oct: 11am–6pm daily (last adm to house: 5pm).* *Mar–Apr, Sep–Oct: Mon, Good Fri.*

Lying just south of Rathdrum, Avondale House was the birthplace of the 19th-century politician and patriot, Charles Stewart Parnell *(see p17)*. Built in 1779, it passed into the hands of the Parnell family in 1795 and Charles Stewart was born here on 27 June 1846. The Georgian mansion now houses a museum dedicated to Parnell and the fight for Home Rule. The birthplace of Irish Forestry, Avondale is managed by the Irish Forestry Board but the public is free to explore the 200 ha (512 acres) of grounds, complete with picnic and children's play areas. Known as **Avondale Forest Park**, the former estate includes an impressive arboretum which was first planted in the 18th century and has had many additions made to it since 1900.

Parnell's chair in Avondale House

There are some lovely walks through the woods, including the magnificent Great Ride, which is one of the best, with pleasant views along the River Avonmore. There is also much wildlife in the area, including hares, rabbits and otters.

Glendalough ⑨

Co Wicklow. 🚌 *St Kevin's bus from
Dublin.* **Ruins** ⬭ *daily.* 📷 *in summer.*
Visitors' centre *Tel 0404 45325/
45352.* ⬭ *Oct–mid-Mar: 9:30am–
5pm (last adm 4:15pm) daily; mid–
Mar–Sep: 9:30am–6pm (last adm
5:15pm).* ⬤ *24–27 Dec.* 🈳🚹📷
on request. **www**.*heritageireland.ie*

The steep, wooded slopes of
Glendalough, the "valley of the
two lakes", harbour an atmospheric monastic site. Established by St Kevin in the 6th
century, the settlement was
sacked time and again by the
Vikings but nevertheless
flourished for over 600 years.
Decline set in only after English
forces partially razed the site in
1398, though it functioned as a
monastic centre until the Disso-
lution of the Monasteries in
1539 *(see p14).* Pilgrims kept
on coming to Glendalough
even after that, particularly on
St Kevin's feast day, 3 June.

The age of the buildings is
uncertain, but most date from
the 8th to 12th centuries. Many

View along the Upper Lake at Glendalough

were restored in the 1870s. The
main group of ruins lies east
of the Lower Lake, but other
buildings associated with St
Kevin are found by the Upper
Lake. Here, where the scenery
is much wilder, it is possible
to enjoy more the tranquillity
of Glendalough
and to escape the
crowds which
inevitably descend
on the site. Try to
arrive as early as
possible in the day,
particularly during
the peak tourist
season. Enter the
monastery through the double
stone arch of the **Gatehouse**,
the only surviving example in
Ireland of a gateway into a
monastic enclosure.

A short walk leads to a
graveyard with a **Round tower**
in one corner. Reaching 30 m
(100 ft) in height, this is one
of the finest of its kind in the
country. Its cap was rebuilt in
the 1870s using stones found
inside the tower. The roofless
Cathedral nearby dates mainly

St Kevin's Kitchen

from the 12th century and is
the valley's largest ruin. At
the centre of the churchyard
stands the tiny **Priests' House**,
whose name derives from the
fact that it was a burial
place for local clergy. The
worn carving of a robed
figure above the door is
thought possibly to be
St Kevin, flanked by two
disciples. East of here,
St Kevin's Cross dates
from the 8th century
and is one of the best
preserved of Glen-
dalough's various High
Crosses. Made of gran-
ite, the cross may once have
marked the boundary of the
monastic cemetery. Below,
nestled in the lush valley, a tiny
oratory with a steeply pitched
stone roof is a charming sight.
Erected in the 11th century or
even earlier, it is popularly
known as **St Kevin's Kitchen**;
this is perhaps because its
belfry, which is thought to be
a later addition, resembles a
chimney. One of the earliest
churches at Glendalough,

**Remains of the Gatehouse, the
original entrance to Glendalough**

PLAN OF GLENDALOUGH

The visitors' centre explains the history of the
monastery and is the best place to start a tour.
You can see both groups of ruins, which
lie less than 1.5 km (1 mile) apart, in
about two hours, but to make the
most of the site allow
a full day.

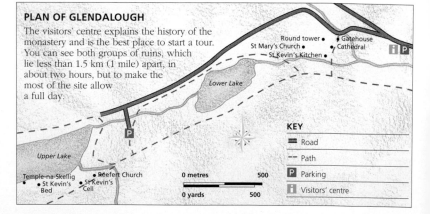

Round tower ●   ● Gatehouse
St Mary's Church ●   ● Cathedral   ℹ️ P
St Kevin's Kitchen ●

Lower Lake

Upper Lake

Temple-na-Skellig
● St Kevin's   ● Reefert Church
Bed   ● St Kevin's
Cell

0 metres   500
0 yards   500

KEY

▬ Road

┅ Path

P Parking

ℹ️ Visitors' centre

ST KEVIN AT GLENDALOUGH

St Kevin was born in 498, a descendant of the royal house of Leinster. He rejected his life of privilege, however, choosing to live instead as a hermit in a cave at Glendalough. He later founded a monastery here, and went on to establish a notable centre of learning devoted to the care of the sick and the copying and illumination of manuscripts. St Kevin attracted many disciples to Glendalough during his lifetime, but the monastery became more celebrated as a place of pilgrimage after his death in around 618.

Colourful legends about the saint make up for the dearth of facts about him. That he lived to the age of 120 is just one of the many stories told about him. Another tale claims that one day, when St Kevin was at prayer, a blackbird laid an egg in one of his outstretched hands. According to legend the saint remained in the same position until the bird was hatched.

possibly to have been used as a tomb in the Bronze Age, but it is more famous as St Kevin's favourite retreat. It was from this point that the saint allegedly rejected the advances of a naked woman by picking her up and throwing her into the lake.

Mount Usher Gardens ⑩

Ashford, Co Wicklow. *Tel 0404 40116.* 🚌 to Ashford. 🕐 1 Mar– 31 Oct: 10:30am–6pm daily (last adm 5:20pm). 🎫 ⬛ ⬛ (27 Apr– 31 Oct). ♿ limited. 🎫 call to book. www.mount-usher-gardens.com

Set on the banks of the River Vartry, just east of Ashford, are the Mount Usher Gardens. They were designed in 1868 by a Dubliner, Edward Walpole, who imbued them with their strong sense of romanticism.

The 8 ha (20 acres) are laid out in a wild, informal style and contain around 4,000 different species of plants including rare shrubs and trees, from Chinese conifers and bamboos to Mexican pines and pampas grass. The Maple Walk is particularly glorious in the autumn, and in spring the rhododendron collection is brilliant with reds and pinks.

The river provides the main focus of the Mount Usher Gardens and, amid the exotic and lush vegetation, the visitor can usually catch a glimpse of herons standing on the many weirs and little bridges that cross the river.

Round tower at Glendalough

St Mary's, lies across a field to the west. Some traces of hood moulding (intended to throw off water) are visible outside the east window. The path along the south bank of the river leads visitors to the Upper Lake. This is the site of more monastic ruins and is also the chief starting point for walks through the valley and to a number of abandoned lead and zinc mines.

Situated in a grove not far from the Poulanass waterfall are the ruins of the **Reefert Church**, a simple building. Its unusual name is a corruption of *Righ Fearta*, meaning "burial place of the kings"; the church may mark the site of an

ancient cemetery. Nearby, on a rocky spur overlooking the Upper Lake, stands **St Kevin's Cell**, the foundation of a beehive-shaped structure which is thought to have once been the home of the hermit.

There are two sites on the south side of the lake which cannot be reached on foot but are visible from the shore on the other side. **Temple-na-Skellig**, or the "church on the rock", was supposedly built on the site of the first church that was founded by St Kevin at Glendalough. To the east of it, carved into the cliff, is **St Kevin's Bed**. This small cave, in fact little more than a rocky ledge, is thought

Mount Usher Gardens, on the banks of the River Vartry

A Tour of the Military Road ⑪

Rare red squirrel

The British built the Military Road through the heart of the Wicklow Mountains during a campaign to flush out Irish rebels after an uprising in 1798 *(see p16)*. Now known as the R115, this winding road takes you through the emptiest and most rugged landscapes of County Wicklow. Beautiful countryside, in which deer and other wildlife flourish, is characteristic of the whole of this tour.

Glencree ①
The former British barracks in Glencree are among several found along the Military Road.

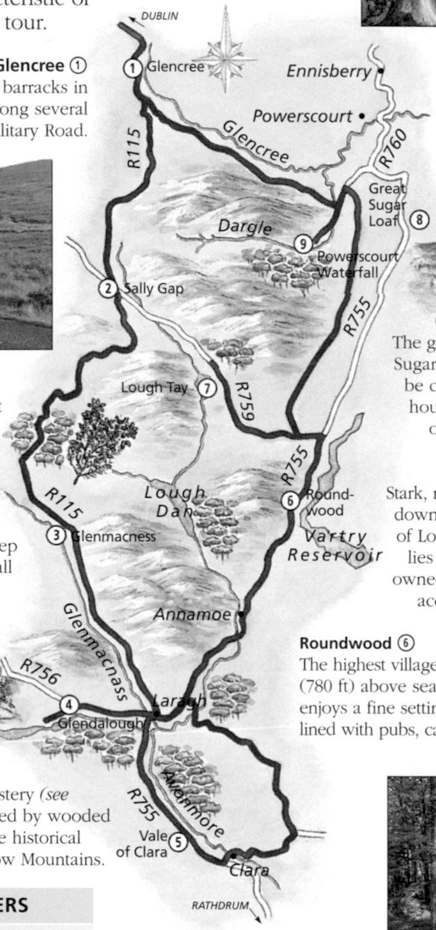

Powerscourt Waterfall ⑨
The River Dargle cascades 130 m (425 ft) over a granite escarpment to form Ireland's highest waterfall.

Great Sugar Loaf ⑧
The granite cone of Great Sugar Loaf Mountain can be climbed in under an hour from the car park on its southern side.

Sally Gap ②
This remote pass is surrounded by a vast expanse of blanket bog dotted with pools and streams.

Glenmacnass ③
After Sally Gap, the road drops into a deep glen where a waterfall spills dramatically over rocks.

Lough Tay ⑦
Stark, rocky slopes plunge down to the dark waters of Lough Tay. Though it lies within a Guinness-owned estate, the lake is accessible to walkers.

Roundwood ⑥
The highest village in Ireland at 238 m (780 ft) above sea level, Roundwood enjoys a fine setting. Its main street is lined with pubs, cafés and craft shops.

Glendalough ④
This ancient monastery *(see pp110–11)*, enclosed by wooded slopes, is the prime historical sight in the Wicklow Mountains.

Map labels: DUBLIN · Glencree ① · Ennisberry · Powerscourt · Glencree · R115 · R760 · Dargle · Great Sugar Loaf ⑧ · Powerscourt Waterfall ⑨ · Sally Gap ② · R755 · Lough Tay ⑦ · R759 · R115 · Lough Dan · Glenmacnass ③ · R755 · Round-wood ⑥ · Vartry Reservoir · Annamoe · Glenmacnass · R756 · Glendalough ④ · Laragh · R755 · Avonmore · Vale of Clara ⑤ · Clara · RATHDRUM

TIPS FOR DRIVERS

Length: 96 km (60 miles).
Stopping-off points: There are several pubs and cafés in Enniskerry (including Poppies, an old-fashioned tearoom), and also in Roundwood, but this area is better suited for picnics. There are numerous marked picnic spots south of Enniskerry.

0 kilometres   5

0 miles   3

KEY

━━━ Tour route

═══ Other roads

☼ Viewpoint

Vale of Clara ⑤
This picturesque wooded valley follows the River Avonmore. It contains the tiny village of Clara, which consists of two houses, a church and a school.

Wicklow Mountains ⑫

Co Wicklow. 🚃 *to Rathdrum &
Wicklow.* 🚌 *to Enniskerry, Wicklow,
Glendalough, Rathdrum & Avoca.*
🛈 *Rialto House, Fitzwilliam Square,
Wicklow, 0404 69117.*
www.eastcoastmidlands.ie

The inaccessibility of the
rugged Wicklow Mountains
meant that they once provided
a safe hideout for opponents
of English rule. Rebels who
took part in the 1798 uprising
sought refuge here. The building of the **Military Road**,
started in 1800, made the area
slightly more accessible, but
the mountains are still thinly
populated. There is little traffic
to disturb enjoyment of the
exhilarating scenery of rock-
strewn glens, lush forest and
bogland where heather gives
a purple sheen to the land.
Turf-cutting is still a thriving
cottage industry, and you can
often see peat stacked up by
the road. Numerous walking
trails weave through these
landscapes. Among them is the
Wicklow Way, which extends
132 km (82 miles) from Marlay
Park in Dublin to Clonegal in
County Carlow. It is marked
but not always easy to follow,
so do not set out without a
good map. Although no peak
exceeds 915 m (3,000 ft), the
Wicklow Mountains can be
dangerous in bad weather.

A good starting point for
exploring the northern area
is the picture-postcard estate
village of **Enniskerry**, close to

View across the Long Ponds to Killruddery House

Powerscourt *(see pp114–15)*.
To the south, you can reach
Glendalough *(see pp110–11)*
and the **Vale of Avoca**. The
beauty of this gentle valley
was captured in the poetry of
Thomas Moore (1779–1852):
"There is not in the wide world
a valley so sweet as that vale
in whose bosom the bright
waters meet" – a reference to
the confluence of the Avonbeg
and Avonmore rivers, the so-
called **Meeting of the Waters**
beyond Avondale House *(see
p109)*. Nestled among wooded
hills at the heart of the valley is
the hamlet of Avoca, where the
Avoca Handweavers produce
colourful tweeds in the oldest
hand-weaving mill in Ireland,
in operation since 1723.

Further north, towards the
coast near Ashford, the River
Vartry rushes through the deep
chasm of the **Devil's Glen**.
On entering the valley, the
river falls 30 m (100 ft) into a
pool known as the Devil's

Punchbowl. There are good
walks around here, with fine
views of the coast.

🏠 **Avoca Handweavers**
Avoca. **Tel** *0402 35105.* 🕐 *May–
Oct: 9am–6pm daily, Nov–Apr:
9:30am–5:30pm daily.* ⬤ *25 &
26 Dec.* **Weaving shed** 🕐 *8am–
4:30pm Mon–Fri, 10am–5pm Sat
& Sun.* 🍴 🏠 🚻 www.avoca.ie

Killruddery House and Gardens ⑬

Bray, Co Wicklow. **Tel** *0404 46024.*
Gardens 🕐 *Apr: 9:30am–5pm
Sat & Sun; May–Sep. 9:30am 5pm
daily.* **House** 🕐 *May, Jun, Sep:
1–5pm daily.* 📷 🚻 *limited.*
www.killruddery.com

Killruddery House lies just
to the south of Bray, in the
shadow of Little Sugar Loaf
Mountain. Built in 1651, it has
been the seat of the Earls of
Meath ever since, although it
was remodelled in the 1800s.

The house contains some
good carving and stuccowork.
The real charm stems from its
formal gardens. Laid out in the
1680s by a French gardener
who also worked at Versailles,
they feature romantic parterres
and an array of hedges, trees
and shrubs. The sylvan theatre,
a small enclosure surrounded
by a bay hedge, is the only
known example in Ireland.

The garden centres on the
Long Ponds, a pair of canals
which extend 165 m (550 ft)
and were once used to stock
fish. Beyond, an enclosed pool
leads to a Victorian arrangement of paths flanked by
statues and hedges of yew,
beech, lime and hornbeam.

Colourful moorland around Sally Gap in the Wicklow Mountains

Powerscourt 🄰

The gardens at Powerscourt are probably the finest in Ireland, both for their design and their dramatic setting at the foot of Great Sugar Loaf Mountain. The house and grounds were commissioned in the 1730s by Richard Wingfield, the first Viscount Powerscourt. The gardens fell into decline but, in 1840, the original scheme was revived. New ornamental gardens were completed in 1858–75 by the seventh Viscount, who added gates, urns and statues collected during his travels on the Continent. Gutted by an accidental fire in 1974, the ground floor and the ballroom on the first floor have been renovated.

Laocöon statue on upper terrace

Bamberg Gate
Made in Vienna in the 1770s, this gilded wrought-iron gate was brought to Powerscourt by the seventh Viscount from Bamberg Cathedral in Bavaria.

The walled gardens include a formal arrangement of clipped laurel trees but are also used for growing plants for Powerscourt's gardens.

Entrance

Statue of Laocöon

The pets' cemetery contains the graves of Wingfield family dogs, cats and even horses and cattle.

Dolphin pond
This pool, designed as a fish pond in the 18th century, is enclosed by exotic conifers in a lovely secluded garden.

POWERSCOURT HOUSE

In 1974 a fire at the Palladian mansion at Powerscourt left the building a burnt-out shell. The Slazenger family, who now own the estate, have restored part of the house; the ground floor now incorporates a terrace café, speciality shops and house exhibition describing the history of the estate. Originally built in 1731 on the site of a Norman castle, the house was designed by Richard Castle, also the architect of Russborough House *(see p108)*.

Powerscourt ablaze in 1974

★ The Perron
This superb Italianate stairway, added in 1874, leads down to the Triton Lake, which is guarded by two statues of the winged horse Pegasus and the emblem of the Wingfield family.

Pebble mosaic
Many tonnes of pebbles were gathered from nearby Bray beach to build the Perron and to make this mosaic on the terrace.

The Pepper Pot Tower was built in 1911.

The Italian garden is laid out on terraces which were first cut into the steep hillside in the 1730s.

★ Triton Lake
Made for the first garden, the lake takes its name from its central fountain, which is modelled on a 17th-century work by Bernini in Rome.

★ Japanese gardens
These enchanting Edwardian gardens, created out of bogland, contain Chinese conifers and bamboo trees.

STAR FEATURES

★ The Perron

★ Japanese gardens

★ Triton Lake

Bray ⑮

Co Wicklow. 👥 33,000.
🚉 DART. 🚌 ℹ️ Old Court House,
Main St, 286 7128/286 6796.
www.braytourism.ie

Once a refined Victorian resort, Bray is nowadays a brash holiday town, with amusement arcades and fish-and-chip shops lining the seafront. Its beach attracts huge crowds in summer, including many young families. Anyone in search of peace and quiet can escape to nearby Bray Head, where there is scope for bracing cliffside walks. Bray also makes a good base from which to explore the Wicklow Mountains (see p113), the delightful coastal villages of Killiney and Dalkey (see p91) and Powerscourt House and Gardens (see pp114–15).

Tourists on the popular seafront esplanade at Bray

Newbridge Demesne ⑯

Donabate, Co Dublin. **Tel** 843 6534.
🚉 to Donabate. 🚌 33B from
Swords. **House and Courtyard**
⭕ Apr–Sep: 10am–5pm Tue–Sat,
noon–6pm Sun & public hols;
Oct–Mar: 11am–4pm Tue–Sun.
⬤ 25 & 26 Dec. 📷 📹 house only
(obligatory). ♿ courtyard only.
Park ⭕ daily. **www**.newbridge
houseandfarm.com

Newbridge is located on the edge of the seaside village of Donabate, 19 km (12 miles) north of Dublin. The house itself is a delight for enthusiasts of Georgian architecture and decor. The house was designed by George Semple in 1737 for Archbishop Charles Cobbe,

Connemara Pony stabled at Newbridge House

and it remained the family home until 1986, when it was bought by the local council. The Cobbe family retains the use of the upstairs quarters.

The highlight of the house tour is the red drawing room, one of the best-preserved Georgian rooms in the country. Its rich red decor is complemented by fine plasterwork by Richard Williams and by some impressive portrait and landscape paintings. Its contents have remained unaltered since at least the 1820s.

Also on view are the sizeable, airy dining room, a large kitchen with a huge stock of utensils, and the Museum of Curiosities – a small room filled to the rafters with artifacts collected from 1790 onwards by Cobbe family members on their foreign travels. Housed in cabinets, some of which date back to the late 1700s, are unusual and bizarre items such as delicately carved ostrich eggs, snakeskins and stuffed animals.

The cobbled courtyard has been restored and now has displays of aspects of late 18th-century life, including dairy production, carpentry and forging. This and the playground make it a popular spot with families. It also houses rare goat and pony breeds, including the native Connemara pony, as well as a pleasant tea room. The Lord Chancellor's intricately detailed ceremonial carriage, which is on loan from the National Museum (see pp44–5), is an incongruous exhibit but considered to be one of the best examples of carriagework in existence.

Footpaths wind through the woodland, and the elegant, rolling grounds of Newbridge, which are attractively landscaped in the style of an English estate.

Ardgillan Demesne ⑰

Balbriggan, Co Dublin. **Tel** 849 2212.
🚌 33 via Skerries to Balbriggan.
Castle ⭕ Apr–Sep: 11am–6pm Tue–
Sun & public hols (Jul–Aug: daily);
Oct–Mar: 11am–4:30pm Tue–Sun &
public hols. ⬤ 23 Dec–1 Jan. 📷 ♿
except kitchen. **Park and Gardens**
⭕ daily. **www**.fingalcoco.ie

In between the very likeable resort towns of Skerries and Balbriggan, the Ardgillan Demesne is set on a high stretch of coastline and offers

The elegant façade of Newbridge House

Stately drawing room in Ardgillan Castle

a particularly pleasant vantage point for stunning views over Drogheda Bay. Its sweeping and expansive grounds, which cover 78 ha (194 acres), incorporate various ornamental gardens, including a rose garden and a walled kitchen garden, as well as rolling pasture and dense woodland (the name Ardgillan means "high wooded area").

In the grounds stands Ardgillan Castle, which was built in 1737 by the Reverend Robert Taylor. The rooms on the ground floor are all furnished in Georgian and Victorian styles and the basement kitchen also retains its original decor. Upstairs there is an exhibition space which houses a permanent collection of old maps.

Gramophone in the Millmount Museum

Drogheda ⓲

Co Louth. 🏛 28,000. 🚌 🚍
ℹ️ Bus Station, Donore Rd, 041 9837070, 9am–5pm Mon–Fri, 9am–4:30pm Sat. 🛍 Sat.

In the 14th century, this historic Norman port near the mouth of the River Boyne was one of Ireland's most important towns. It was first captured

by the Danes in AD 911 and later heavily fortified by the Normans. However, the place seems never to have fully recovered from a vicious attack by the English general Oliver Cromwell in 1649, during which 3,000 citizens were killed after refusing to surrender. Although it looks rather dilapidated today, the town has retained its original street plan and has a rich medieval heritage. Little is left of Drogheda's Norman defences but **St Lawrence Gate**, a fine 13th-century barbican, has survived. The **Butter Gate** is the only other surviving gate. Near St Lawrence Gate there are two churches called **St Peter's**. The one belonging to the Church of Ireland, built in 1753, is the more striking and has some splendid gravestones. The Catholic church, on West Street and dating from 1791, is worth visiting just to see the embalmed head of Oliver Plunkett, an archbishop who was martyred in 1681. It is displayed in an elaborate glass case beside its certificate of authenticity, dated 1682.

South of the river you can climb Millmount, a Norman motte that is topped by a Martello tower. As well as providing a good view, this is the site of the **Millmount Museum**, which contains an interesting display of artifacts relating to the town and its history, as well as a number of craft workshops.

🏛 **Millmount Museum**
Millmount Square. **Tel** 041 983 3097.
◐ daily. ● 10 days at Christmas.
📷 📹 ♿ www.millmount.net

Monasterboice ⓳

Co Louth. 🚌 to Drogheda. ◐ daily.

Founded in the 5th century by an obscure disciple of St Patrick called St Buite, this monastic settlement is one of the most famous religious sites in Ireland. The ruins of the medieval monastery are enclosed within a graveyard in a lovely secluded spot to the north of Drogheda. The site includes a roofless round tower and two churches, but Monasterboice's greatest treasures are its 10th-century High Crosses, carved to help educate an illiterate populace.

Muiredach's High Cross is the finest of its kind in Ireland, and its sculpted biblical scenes are still remarkably fresh. They depict the life of Christ on the west face, while the east face features mainly Old Testament scenes. These include Moses striking the rock to get water for the Israelites and David struggling with Goliath. The cross is named after an inscription on the base which reads: "A prayer for Muiredach by whom this cross was made", which, it is thought, may refer to the abbot of Monasterboice.

The 6.5-m (21-ft) West Cross, also known as the Tall Cross, is one of the largest in Ireland. The carving has not lasted as well as on Muiredach's Cross, but scenes from the Death of Christ can still be made out. The North Cross, which is the least notable of the three, features a Crucifixion illustration and a carved spiral pattern.

Round tower and West High Cross at Monasterboice

Thatched cottage in Carlingford on the mountainous Cooley Peninsula

Carlingford ⓴

Co Louth. 🏃 650. 🚌
ℹ️ **Holy Trinity Heritage Centre**
Churchyard Rd, 042 9373454.
🕐 *10am–12:30pm, 2–4pm Mon–Fri.*
www.carlingfordheritagecentre.com
Carlingford Adventure Centre
Tholsel St. **Tel** *042 9373100.*
🕐 *9am–5:30pm daily.* 🔴 *two weeks at Christmas.* **www**.
carlingfordadventure.com

This is a picturesque fishing village, located between the mountains of the Cooley Peninsula and the waters of Carlingford Lough. The border with Northern Ireland runs right through the centre of this drowned river valley, and from the village you can look across to the Mountains of Mourne on the Ulster side. Carlingford is an interesting place, with its pretty whitewashed cottages and ancient buildings clustered along medieval alleyways. The ruins of **King John's Castle**, built by the Normans to protect the entrance to the lough, still dominate the village. The **Holy Trinity Heritage Centre**, which is housed in a medieval church, tells the history of the port from Anglo-Norman times.

Carlingford is the country's oyster capital, and its oyster festival in August draws large crowds. The lough is popular for watersports and in summer cruises leave from the quay.

Carlingford is well placed for hikes on the Cooley Peninsula. The **Carlingford Adventure Centre** provides information on walking and water activities.

Environs
A scenic route weaves around the **Cooley Peninsula**, skirting the coast and then cutting

through the mountains. The section along the north coast is the most dramatic: just 3 km (2 miles) northwest of Carlingford, in the **Slieve Foye Forest Park**, a road climbs to give a breathtaking view over the hills and lough.

The Táin Trail, which you can join at Carlingford, is a 30-km (19-mile) circuit through some of the peninsula's most rugged scenery, with cairns and other prehistoric sites dotted over the moorland. Keen hikers can walk it in a day.

Glazed tiles at Old Mellifont Abbey

Dundalk ⓴

Co Louth. 🏃 30,000. 🚌 🚉
ℹ️ *Jocelyn St, 042 9335484.* 🛒 *Thu.*

Dundalk once marked the northernmost point of the Pale, the area controlled by the English during the Middle Ages *(see p108)*. Now, lying midway between Dublin and Belfast, it is the last major town before you reach the Northern Ireland border.

Dundalk is the gateway to the Cooley Peninsula, but there is little worth stopping for in the town itself. However, the fine **County Museum**, which is housed in an 18th-century distillery, gives an insight into some of Louth's traditional industries, such as beer-making.

🏛 **County Museum**
Jocelyn St. **Tel** *042 9327056.*
🕐 *10am–5pm Tue–Sat.*
🔴 *public hols.* 📷 ♿
www.dundalkmuseum.ie

Old Mellifont Abbey ⓶

Cullen, Co Louth. **Tel** *041 9826459.*
🚉 *to Drogheda.* 🚌 *to Drogheda or Slane.* 🕐 *May–Oct: 10am–6pm daily (last adm 5:15pm).* 📷
www.heritageireland.ie

On the banks of the River Mattock, 10 km (6 miles) west of Drogheda, lies the first Cistercian monastery built in Ireland. Mellifont was founded in 1142 on the orders of St Malachy, the Archbishop of Armagh. Influenced by St Bernard, who was behind the rise of the Cistercian Order in Europe, St Malachy brought Cistercian rigour to Mellifont, as well as the formal style of monastic architecture used on the continent. In 1539, the abbey was closed and turned into a fortified house. William of Orange used it as his headquarters during the Battle of the Boyne in 1690. It is now a ruin, but it is still possible to appreciate the scale of the original complex. Little survives of the abbey church but, to the south of it, enclosed by what is left of the Romanesque cloister, is a 13th-century lavabo where monks washed their hands before meals. Four

Ruined lavabo at Old Mellifont Abbey

THE BATTLE OF THE BOYNE

In 1688, the Catholic King of England, James II, was deposed from his throne, to be replaced by his Protestant daughter, Mary, and her husband, William of Orange. Determined to win back the crown, James sought the support of Irish Catholics, and challenged William at Oldbridge by the River Boyne west of Drogheda. The Battle of the Boyne took place on 12 July 1690, with James's poorly trained force of 25,000 French and Irish Catholics facing William's hardened army of 36,000 French Huguenots, Dutch, English and Scots. The Protestants triumphed and James fled to France, after a battle that signalled the beginning of total Protestant power over Ireland. It ushered in the confiscation of Catholic lands and the suppression of Catholic interests, sealing the country's fate for the next 300 years.

William of Orange leading his troops at the Battle of the Boyne, 12 July 1690

of the building's original eight sides survive, each with a graceful Romanesque arch. On the eastern side of the cloister stands the 14th-century chapter house. It has an impressive vaulted ceiling and a floor laid with glazed medieval tiles taken from the abbey church.

The Boyne Valley ㉓

Co Meath. 🚂 to Drogheda.
🚌 to Slane or Drogheda. 🛈 Brú
na Bóinne interpretive centre, 041
9880300. 🕐 9:30am–5:30pm (May–
Sep: to 6:30pm; Nov–Feb: to 5pm).
www.heritageireland.ie

Known as Brú na Bóinne, the "Palace of the Boyne", this river valley was the cradle of Irish civilization. The fertile soil supported a sophisticated society in Neolithic times. Much evidence survives, in the form of ring forts, passage graves and sacred enclosures. The most important Neolithic monuments in the valley are three passage graves: supreme among these is **Newgrange** (see pp120–21), but **Dowth** and **Knowth** are significant too. The Boyne Valley also encompasses the Hill of Slane and the Hill of Tara (see p122), both major sites in Celtic lore.

With monuments pre-dating Egypt's pyramids, the Boyne Valley has been dubbed the Irish "Valley of the Kings".

Knowth and Newgrange can only be seen on a tour run by the interpretive centre near Newgrange, which also details the area's Stone Age heritage.

🛖 Dowth

Off N51, 3 km (2 miles) E of
Newgrange. ⬤ to the public.
This passage grave was plundered in Victorian times by souvenir hunters and has not been fully excavated since. Visitors cannot approach the tomb, but may walk around the outside of the monument.

🛖 Knowth

1.5 km (1 mile) NW of Newgrange.
◻ as Newgrange (see pp120–21).
Knowth outdoes Newgrange in several respects, above all in the quantity of its treasures – Europe's greatest concentration of megalithic art. In addition, the site was occupied for a much longer period – from Neolithic times to about 1400.

Unusually, Knowth has two passage tombs rather than one. The excavations begun in 1962 are now complete and the site is open. The tombs can only be viewed externally to prevent further decay and visitors must sign up for tours via Brú na Bóinne (see p120).

River Boyne near the site of the Battle of the Boyne

Newgrange ㉔

Tri-spiral carving in chamber

The origins of Newgrange, one of the most important passage graves in Europe, are steeped in mystery. According to Celtic lore, the legendary kings of Tara *(see p122)* were buried here, but Newgrange predates them. Built in around 3200 BC, the grave was left untouched by all invaders (though not by tomb robbers) and was eventually excavated in the 1960s. Archaeologists then discovered that on the winter solstice (21 December), rays of sun enter the tomb and light up the burial chamber – making it the oldest solar observatory in the world. All visitors to Newgrange and Knowth are admitted through the visitors' centre *(see p119)* from where tours of the historic sight are taken; early arrival is advised in summer to avoid long queues.

Basin stone
The chiselled stones, found in each recess, would have once contained funerary offerings and the bones of the dead.

The chamber has three recesses or side chambers: the north recess is the one struck by sunlight on the winter solstice.

Chamber ceiling
The burial chamber's intricate corbelled ceiling, which reaches a height of 6 m (20 ft) above the floor, has survived intact. The overlapping slabs form a conical hollow, topped by a single capstone.

CONSTRUCTION OF NEWGRANGE

The tomb at Newgrange was designed by people with clearly exceptional artistic and engineering skills, who had use of neither the wheel nor metal tools. About 200,000 tonnes of loose stones were transported to build the mound, or cairn, which protects the passage grave. Larger slabs were used to make the circle around the cairn (12 out of a probable 35 stones have survived), the kerb and the tomb itself. Many of the kerbstones and the slabs lining the passage, the chamber and its recesses are decorated with zigzags, spirals and other geometric motifs. The grave's corbelled ceiling consists of smaller, unadorned slabs and has proved almost completely waterproof for the last 5,000 years.

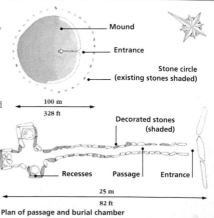

Mound

Entrance

Stone circle (existing stones shaded)

100 m
328 ft

Decorated stones (shaded)

Recesses Passage Entrance

25 m
82 ft
Plan of passage and burial chamber

Restoration of Newgrange
*Located on a low ridge north of the Boyne, Newgrange
took more than 70 years to build. Between 1962
and 1975 the passage grave and mound were
restored as closely as possible to their original state.*

The standing stones in
the passage are slabs of
slate which would have
been collected locally.

Passage
*At dawn on
21 December, a beam of
sunlight shines through
the roof box (a feature
unique to Newgrange),
travels along the 19-m
(62-ft) passage and hits
the central recess in the
burial chamber.*

**The retaining
wall** around the
front of the cairn
was rebuilt using
the white quartz
and granite
stones found
scattered around
the site during
excavations.

Roof box

Entrance
*Newgrange's most elaborately
carved kerbstone stands just
in front of the entrance,
forming part of the kerb of
huge slabs around the cairn.*

Trim Castle, set in water meadows beside the River Boyne

Slane ㉕

Co Meath. 🏃 950. 🚌 ℹ️ 041 988 0305. www.eastcoastmidlands.ie

Slane is an attractive estate village, centred on a quartet of Georgian houses. The Boyne river flows through it and skirts around **Slane Castle Demesne**, set in glorious grounds laid out in the 18th century by the renowned landscape gardener, Capability Brown. The castle, dating from 1785, incorporates the designs of James Wyatt, Francis Johnson and James Gandon and is famous for its Gothic Revival ballroom designed by Thomas Hopper. The castle was badly damaged by fire in 1991 but reopened in 2001 after a decade of restoration. Just to the north rises the **Hill of Slane** where, in AD 433, St Patrick is said to have lit a Paschal (Easter) fire as a challenge to the pagan High King of Tara. The local priest still marks this event by the lighting of a fire at Easter.

Hill of Tara ㉖

Nr Killmessan Village, Co Meath. *Tel May–Oct: 046 25903; Nov–Apr: Brú na Bóinne 041 9880300.* 🚌 *to Navan.* ⏰ *May–Oct: 10am–6pm daily (last adm: 5:15pm).* 🎟️ *for interpretive centre.* 📷 **www**.heritageireland.ie

A site of mythic importance, Tara was the political and spiritual centre of Celtic Ireland and the seat of the High Kings until the 11th century. The spread of Christianity, which eroded the importance of Tara, is marked by a statue of St Patrick. Tara's symbolism was not lost on Daniel O'Connell *(see p16)*, who chose the site for a rally in 1843, attended by more than a million people.

Tours from the interpretive centre point out a Stone Age passage grave and Iron Age hill forts though, to the untutored eye, these look like mere hollows and grassy mounds. Clearest is the Royal Enclosure, an oval fort, in the centre of which is Cormac's House containing the "stone of destiny" *(Liath Fáil)*, an ancient fertility symbol and inauguration stone of the High Kings. However, all this is secondary to the views over the Boyne Valley and the site's sense of history.

Trim ㉗

Co Meath. 🏃 6,500. 🚌 ℹ️ *Mill St, 046 9437111 or 046 9437227.* 🚌 *Fri.* **www** eastcoastmidlands ireland.ie

Trim is one of the most pleasing Midlands market towns. A Norman stronghold on the River Boyne, it marked a boundary of the Pale *(see p108)*. Trim runs efficient heritage and genealogy centres, including a visitors' centre next door to the tourist office.

Trim Castle was founded in 1173 by Hugh de Lacy, a Norman knight, and is one of the largest medieval castles in Europe. It makes a spectacular backdrop so is often used as a film set, famously seen in Mel Gibson's *Braveheart* (1995).

Over the river is **Talbot Castle**, an Augustinian abbey converted to a manor house in the 15th century. Just north of the abbey, **St Patrick's Cathedral** incorporates part of a medieval church with a

Aerial view of Iron Age forts on the Hill of Tara

15th-century tower and sections of the original chancel.

During the Easter Bank Holiday weekend, Trim hosts the colourful Hot Air Balloon Fiesta, featuring Easter egg hunts, market stalls, banquets and other activities. Early July sees the Trim Swift Festival, celebrating the poet and satirist Jonathan Swift, who lived in this market town for a significant part of his life.

⋔ Trim Castle
Tel 046 9438619. ☐ *Apr–Oct:*
10am–6pm daily; Nov–Jan: 9am–
5pm Sat & Sun; Feb & Mar: 9:30am–
5:30pm Sat & Sun (last adm 1hr
before closing). ◒ *1 & 2 Jan, 25 &*
26 Dec. ☑ *compulsory.* ♿ *limited.*
www.heritageireland.ie

Mullingar ㉘

Co Westmeath. 👥 *14,000.* 🚃 🚌
ℹ *Market Sq, 044 9348650.* 🛒 *Sat.*

The county town of Westmeath is a prosperous market town encircled by the Royal Canal *(see p85)*, which links Dublin with the River Shannon. Although Mullingar's main appeal is as a base to explore the surrounding area, pubs such as Con's and cheery Canton Casey's can make a pleasant interlude. In addition, the 20th-century cathedral features unusual mosaics of St Anne and St Patrick.

Environs
Restoration of the Dublin to Mullingar stretch of the Royal Canal has resulted in attractive towpaths for canal-side walks, as well as good angling

The remains of the Jealous Wall at Belvedere House, near Mullingar

Lighting votive candles in Mullingar Cathedral

facilities. South of Mullingar, just off the road to Kilbeggan, stands **Belvedere House**, a romantic Palladian villa overlooking Lough Ennel. Built in 1740 by architect Richard Castle, Belvedere is decorated with Rococo plasterwork and set in wonderful gardens. Shortly after the house was built, the first Earl of Belvedere accused his wife of having an affair with his brother, and imprisoned her for 31 years in a neighbouring house. He sued the brother and had him jailed for life. In 1760, the Earl built a Gothic folly – the Jealous Wall – in order to block the view from another brother's more opulent mansion. The Jealous Wall still remains, as does an octagonal gazebo and other follies.

Miniature whiskey bottles at Locke's Distillery in Kilbeggan

Charming terraces, framed by urns and yews, descend to the lake; on the other side of the house is a pretty walled garden, enclosed by an arboretum and rolling parkland. There is also an animal sanctuary next to the visitor centre.

♨ Belvedere House
6 km (4 miles) S of Mullingar. *Tel*
044 9349060. **Gardens** ☐ *daily.*
May, Apr, Sep–Feb: 10:30am–
7pm (Nov–Feb: to 4:30pm); May–
Aug: 9:30am–9pm (last adm 1hr
before closing). 🎦 ☑ *of estate*
by tram. ♿ *visitor centre only.*
🅿 ☐ www.belvedere-house.ie

Kilbeggan ㉙

Co Westmeath. 👥 *600.* 🚌

Situated between Mullingar and Tullamore, this pleasant village has a small harbour on the Grand Canal. However, the main point of interest is **Locke's Distillery.** Founded in 1757, it claims to be the oldest licensed pot still distillery in the world. Unable to compete with Scotch whisky manufacturers, the company went bankrupt in 1954, but the aroma hung in the warehouses for years and was known as "the angels' share". The distillery was reopened as a museum in 1987. The building is authentic, a solid structure complete with a water wheel and an indoor steam engine. A tour traces the process of Irish whiskey-making, from the mash tuns through to the fermentation vats and creation of wash (rough beer) to the distillation and maturation stages. At the tasting stage, workers would sample the whiskey in the can pit room. Visitors can still taste whiskeys in the bar but, unlike the original workers, cannot bathe in the whiskey vats.

🏛 Locke's Distillery
Museum Main St. *Tel* 057 933
2134. ☐ *Apr–Oct: 9am–6pm daily;*
Nov–Mar: 10am–4pm daily. 🎦 🍴
www.lockesdistillerymuseum.ie

TRAVELLERS'
NEEDS

WHERE TO STAY

Whether you are staying in exclusive luxury or modest bed-and-breakfast accommodation, one thing you can be certain of in Dublin is that you will receive a warm welcome. The Irish are renowned for their friendliness and even in big corporate hotels, where you might expect the reception to be more impersonal, the staff go out of their way to be hospitable. The choice is enormous: you can stay in an elegant, refurbished Georgian house, a comfortable bed-and-breakfast, a Victorian

Doorman at the Conrad Hotel

townhouse, an old-fashioned commercial hotel or a cosy pub. Details are given here of the various types of accommodation available. The listings on pages 128–33 recommend around 60 hotels in both central Dublin and outside the city – all places of quality, ranging from basic to luxury – and should help you decide upon your choice of accommodation. Fáilte Ireland (the Irish Tourist Board) and Dublin Tourism also publish comprehensive guides to recommended accommodation in the area.

Main entrance to the fashionable Clarence Hotel *(see p131)*

HOTELS

At the top of the price range there are quite a few expensive, luxury hotels in the heart of Dublin. Magnificently furnished and run, they offer maximum comfort, delicious food and often have indoor facilities, such as a gym and swimming pool. As well as luxurious individual hotels, there are also the modern chains, such as **Bewleys Hotels** and **Maldron Hotels**, which offer a high standard of accommodation. However, these establishments can lack the charm and individuality of privately run hotels.

There are also numerous very moderate hotels in the centre of Dublin, providing a good standard of accommodation.

If you prefer to stay outside Dublin, there are some wonderful castles and stately homes which offer the same standards as the top city hotels but which have the bonus of being set in beautiful countryside. They can often also arrange outdoor pursuits such as fishing, riding and golf.

The shamrock symbol of Fáilte Ireland is displayed by hotels (and other forms of accommodation) that have been inspected and approved.

BED-AND-BREAKFAST ACCOMMODATION

Ireland has a reputation for the best B&Bs in Europe. Your welcome will always be friendly and the food and company excellent. Even if the house is no architectural

The entrance to the grand Shelbourne Hotel *(see p130)* on St Stephen's Green

A contemporary deluxe bedroom in the Brooks Hotel *(see p130)*

beauty, the comfort and atmosphere will more than compensate. Not all of the bedrooms have bathrooms *en suite*. When one is available, you may possibly have to pay a little extra but, considering the generally cheap rates, the surcharge is negligible.

The Irish swear by their B&Bs and many stay in them by choice rather than paying to stay in the luxurious surroundings of some of the big hotels. **B&B Ireland** will provide details of bed-and-breakfast accommodation throughout Ireland.

GUESTHOUSES

Most guesthouses are found in cities and large towns. They are usually converted family homes and have an atmosphere all of their own. Most offer a good-value evening meal and all give you a delicious full Irish breakfast *(see p136)*. Top-of-the-range guesthouses can be just as good, and sometimes even better, than hotels. You will see a much more personal side of a town or city while

◁ View of Ha'Penny Bridge from O'Connell Bridge

staying at a guesthouse. There are plenty to choose from in the Dublin area and the prices are usually reasonable. The **Irish Hotels Federation** publishes a useful booklet with guesthouse listings that cover the whole of Ireland, including Dublin and its environs.

PRICES

Room rates advertised are inclusive of service and tax. Hotel rates can vary by as much as 40 per cent depending on the time of year. Prices in guesthouses are influenced more by their proximity to tourist sights and public transport. Dublin offers a complete range of accommodation, from youth hostels through very reasonably priced bed-and-breakfasts to lavish five-star hotels such as the Merrion, Morrison and the Clarence.

TIPPING

Tipping in Dublin is a matter of personal discretion but is not common practice, even at the larger hotels. Tasks performed by staff are considered part of the service. Tipping is not expected for carrying bags to your room or for serving drinks. However, it is usual to tip the waiting staff in hotel restaurants: the standard tip is around 10–15 per cent of the bill – anything in excess of that would be considered particularly generous.

The elegant and modern reception at The Morrison hotel *(see p131)*

BOOKING

It is wise to reserve your accommodation during the peak season and public holidays *(see p29)*, particularly if your visit coincides with a local festival such as the St Patrick's Day celebrations *(see p26)* when the city can get booked up. Dublin Tourism *(see p164)* can offer advice and make reservations through its accommodation service. Central reservation facilities are available at the hotel chains listed here.

Fáilte Ireland accommodation sign

YOUTH HOSTELS

There are 31 youth hostels registered with **An Óige** (the Irish Youth Hostel Association), with one in the Dublin area. Accommodation is provided in dormitories

with comfortable beds and basic cooking facilities. You can only use these hostels if you are a member of An Óige or another organization affiliated to the International Youth Hostel Federation.

There are also independent hostels, and places such as universities that offer similar inexpensive accommodation in Dublin. The tourist board has listings of those places that are recommended.

DISABLED TRAVELLERS

A fact sheet for disabled visitors is produced by Fáilte Ireland and their accommodation guide indicates wheelchair accessibility. Dublin Tourism and **Citizens Information Board** are also helpful. *Accommodation for Disabled Persons* and *Dublin: A Guide for Disabled Persons* are useful leaflets which are available at the tourist office.

DIRECTORY

CHAIN HOTELS

Bewleys Hotels
Tel 1890 798 999
(central reservations).
www.bewleyshotels.com

Maldron Hotels
Tel 1850 885 885
(central reservations).
www.maldronhotels.com

OTHER USEFUL ADDRESSES

An Óige (Irish Youth Hostel Association)
61 Mountjoy St, Dublin 7.
Tel 830 4555. Fax 830 5808.
www.anoige.ie

B&B Ireland
Beleek Rd, Ballyshannon, Co Donegal. *Tel 071 982 2222.*
www.bandbireland.com

Citizens Information Board
George's Quay House,
43 Townsend St, Dublin 2.
Tel 1890 777 121.
www.citizensinformation.ie

Irish Hotels Federation
13 Northbrook Rd, Dublin 6.
Tel 808 4419. Fax 497 4613.
www.irelandhotels.com

The stately charm of Dunbrody Country House *(see p133)*

Choosing a Hotel

The hotels in this guide have been selected across a wide price range for their good value, facilities and location. These listings highlight some of the factors that may influence your choice. Hotels are listed by area, beginning with the Southeast. For information on restaurants in the area, see pages 138–145.

PRICE CATEGORIES
For a standard double room per night, including tax, service charges and breakfast.

€ Under €120
€€ €120–€160
€€€ €160–€190
€€€€ €190–€250
€€€€€ Over €250

SOUTHEAST DUBLIN

Baggot Court Townhouse   🍴   €

92 Lower Baggot Street, Dublin 2 **Tel** *01 661 0246* **Fax** *01 661 0253* **Rooms** *17*   **Map** *F5*

A comfortable and relaxing stay is guaranteed at this historical Georgian townhouse, which is renowned for its friendly and helpful service and for its excellent cooked breakfasts. Baggot Court is a short walk from Grafton Street. Complimentary Wi-Fi and parking are included. **www.baggotcourt.com**

Harcourt Hotel   📺 🍴 🏃   €

60 Harcourt Street, Dublin 2 **Tel** *01 478 3677* **Fax** *01 478 1577* **Rooms** *104*   **Map** *D5*

Just off St Stephen's Green, the Harcourt boasts a beautifully central location. Although the interior is fairly unremarkable, bedrooms are modern and well equipped. A popular nightclub, D-Two, is situated in the basement of the hotel and is a draw for late-night revellers. **www.harcourthotel.ie**

Kilronan House   🏃   €

70 Adelaide Road, Dublin 2 **Tel** *01 475 5266* **Fax** *01 478 2841* **Rooms** *12*

Situated on a leafy street near St Stephen's Green, around the corner from the National Concert Hall, this listed townhouse dates back to 1834. Although it retains its Georgian character, it boasts all modern comforts, including orthopaedic beds. Delicious breakfasts and friendly hosts. **www.dublinn.com**

Leeson Court Hotel   📺 🏃   €

27 Leeson Street Lower, Dublin 2 **Tel** *01 676 3380* **Fax** *01 661 8273* **Rooms** *20*   **Map** *E5*

Close to St Stephen's Green, this cheerfully decorated hotel is spread across two Georgian buildings. The ambience is relaxed and informal, but the service is of a high quality. The hotel bar, Kobra, is elegant, with wood furnishings. Bedrooms are tidy and comfortable, if somewhat on the small side. **www.theleesonhotel.com**

Russell Court   📺 🍴 🏃   €

21–25 Harcourt Street, Dublin 2 **Tel** *01 478 4066* **Fax** *01 478 1576* **Rooms** *42*   **Map** *D5*

Lively and welcoming, the Russell Court is a good choice for younger visitors. The hotel's main attraction lies in its upbeat nightclubs: Bojangles for the 30-plus set and Krystle for a younger crowd. At the rear, Dicey's Garden is a popular beer garden. Bedrooms are neat and tidy, and trams stop near the front. **www.russellcourthotel.ie**

Stauntons on the Green   €

83 St Stephen's Green, Dublin 2 **Tel** *01 478 2300* **Rooms** *57*   **Map** *D5*

Located beside the Ministry of Foreign Affairs, this guesthouse offers comfortable and modest accommodation in three terraced Georgian houses. While bedrooms are reasonably equipped and en suite, those to the rear are quieter, with views of the private garden and Iveagh Gardens. Valet parking is available. **www.thecastlehotelgroup.com**

Temple Bar Hotel   📺 🍴 🏃   €

Fleet Street, Dublin 2 **Tel** *01 612 9200* **Fax** *01 677 3088* **Rooms** *129*   **Map** *D3*

Its location in the heart of Temple Bar – a lively area with several pubs and restaurants – makes this modern hotel popular for stag and hen parties. Bedrooms are clean and adequate, if a little on the small side and lacking in character. A multi-storey car park is available nearby. **www.templebarhotel.com**

Trinity Lodge   🍴   €

12 South Frederick Street, Dublin 2 **Tel** *01 617 0900* **Fax** *01 617 0999* **Rooms** *23*   **Map** *E4*

Close to Grafton Street and Trinity College, this Georgian townhouse enjoys one of the best locations in town. Though traditional in style, it is furnished with all modern conveniences, and the warmly coloured en-suite bedrooms are well maintained. Spend some time at Georges, the in-house bistro and wine bar. **www.trinitylodge.com**

Buswell's   📺 🍴 🍽   €€

25 Molesworth Street, Dublin 2 **Tel** *01 614 6500* **Fax** *01 676 2090* **Rooms** *67*   **Map** *E4*

Comprising five Georgian townhouses, this slightly old-fashioned hotel has been in operation since 1882. It is frequented by political figures, perhaps due to its location beside the government buildings, on a street renowned for commercial art galleries. The sophisticated interior is decorated in warm colours. **www.buswellshotel.com**

Key to Symbols *see back cover flap*

Davenport

Merrion Square, Dublin 2 **Tel** *01 607 3500* **Fax** *01 661 5663* **Rooms** *114* **Map** *F4*

This hotel lies in the heart of Georgian Dublin, and its Neo-Classical façade dates from 1863. Mahogany, brass and marble furnishings give the Davenport the feel of a gentleman's club. The ample bedrooms are well appointed, with a warmly coloured decor. A fitness suite and a business centre are available. **www.ocallaghanhotels.com**

Maldron Hotel

Sir John Rogerson's Quay, Cardiff Lane, Dublin 2 **Tel** *643 9500* **Fax** *643 9510* **Rooms** *304*

The Maldron is housed in a modern building in the Docklands, overlooking the magnificent Grand Canal Theatre. Its leisure centre offers a pool, sauna and spa therapies. Rooms are clean, modern and spacious. The hotel's affordability makes up for the 15-minute walk into the city centre. **www.maldronhotels.com**

Mont Clare

Merrion Square, Dublin 2 **Tel** *01 607 3800* **Fax** *01 661 5663* **Rooms** *74* **Map** *F4*

Though not as grand as its sister hotel the Davenport *(see above)*, Mont Clare is traditionally furnished in mahogany and brass. The well-appointed bedrooms are air conditioned and tastefully decorated. The popular bar serves food and the restaurant serves carvery lunches. Guests may use the gym across the road for free. **www.ocallaghanhotels.com**

Morgan Hotel

10 Fleet Street, Dublin 2 **Tel** *01 643 7000* **Fax** *01 643 7060* **Rooms** *121* **Map** *D3*

In the heart of Temple Bar, this self-styled boutique hotel is contemporary in design, with clean lines and uncluttered public spaces. The minimalistic bedrooms have beech furnishings, cotton linen and CD systems. The ambience is relaxing, though the rooms overlooking the street can be noisy. There is a fine bar on site. **www.themorgan.com**

St Stephen's Green Hotel

St Stephen's Green, Dublin 2 **Tel** *01 607 3600* **Fax** *01 661 5663* **Rooms** *99* **Map** *D4*

Warm and friendly, this hotel is superbly located on the southwest corner of St Stephen's Green. It consists of two splendid Georgian townhouses with a modern glass atrium. The spacious bedrooms are clean and well equipped, with comfortable beds and nice views of the green. **www.ocallaghanhotels.com**

Stephen's Hall Hotel

14–17 Leeson Street Lower, Dublin 2 **Tel** *01 638 1111* **Fax** *01 638 1122* **Rooms** *30* **Map** *E5*

Situated close to St Stephen's Green, Stephen's Hall Hotel provides suites that include an attached kitchen. Its proximity to the vibrant city centre makes this hotel a very good-value family option. Underground parking is available. **www.stephens-hall.com**

Alexander Hotel

Fenian Street, off Merrion Square, Dublin 2 **Tel** *607 3700* **Fax** *661 5663* **Rooms** *102* **Map** *F4*

Located beside the National Gallery, the Alexander is a modern build that is tastefully sympathetic to the Georgian surroundings of Merrion Square. Modern rooms have climate control, wireless Internet access and large beds. Residents can use the facilities of three sister hotels nearby. **www.ocallaghanhotels.com**

The Cliff Town House

22 St Stephen's Green, Dublin 2 **Tel** *01 638 3939* **Fax** *01 638 3900* **Rooms** *10* **Map** *D4*

Set in a Georgian house overlooking St Stephen's Green, this charming and intimate boutique hotel is stylishly furnished with antiques. Each of the bedrooms is individually designed with comfort and character in mind. The sophisticated Oyster Bar restaurant serves outstanding food. **www.theclifftownhouse.com**

Harrington Hall Guesthouse

70 Harcourt Street, Dublin 2 **Tel** *475 3497* **Fax** *475 4544* **Rooms** *28* **Map** *D5*

Just off St Stephen's Green, this hotel is housed in two adjoining Georgian buildings. Careful restoration has retained many original features, including high ornamental ceilings and marble bathrooms. Guests can relax in the elegant drawing room, which has an open fire and comfy armchairs. Good breakfast. **www.harringtonhall.com**

Molesworth Court Suites

Molesworth Court, Schoolhouse Lane, Dublin 2 **Tel** *01 676 4799* **Fax** *01 676 4982* **Rooms** *12* **Map** *E4*

Tucked away in a quiet lane off Molesworth Street, this four-star hotel comprises 12 self-contained apartments and penthouses. Equipped with modern conveniences, the lodgings are stylish and cosy, making this establishment ideal for business people and families alike. Enclosed parking is provided. **www.molesworthcourt.ie**

Number 31

31 Leeson Close, Leeson Street Lower, Dublin 2 **Tel** *01 676 5011* **Fax** *01 676 2929* **Rooms** *21* **Map** *E5*

Reputedly the most stylish guesthouse in the city, this elegant establishment is more of a boutique hotel than a B&B, with individually decorated, luxurious bedrooms in two houses. The Coach House is decorated in contemporary style and the Georgian house is grand and formal. Delicious breakfasts are served in the plant-filled conservatory. **www.number31.ie**

Fitzwilliam Hotel

St Stephen's Green, Dublin 2 **Tel** *478 7000* **Fax** *478 7878* **Rooms** *139* **Map** *D4*

This five-star hotel features a fresh contemporary design by Sir Terence Conran, including a glass drawbridge in the entrance hall. Rooms are modern and unfussy, except for the penthouse, which boasts a grand piano. Voted one of the Top 20 Hottest Hotels in the World by *Condé Nast Traveller* magazine. **www.fitzwilliamhotel.com**

Shelbourne Renaissance Hotel   €€€€   Map D4

27 St Stephen's Green, Dublin 2 **Tel** *01 663 4500* **Fax** *01 661 6006* **Rooms** *265*

The five-star Shelbourne, part of the Marriott empire, has been the city's most distinguished hotel since it first opened in 1824. Now extensively restored, the Shelbourne remains a haven of sophistication, featuring Egyptian-cotton bedding, flat-screen TVs and marble bathrooms. **www.theshelbourne.ie**

Westbury Hotel   €€€€   Map D4

Grafton Street, Dublin 2 **Tel** *01 679 1122* **Fax** *01 679 7078* **Rooms** *205*

Enjoying possibly the most convenient location in the city, the Westbury is only seconds from Dublin's main shopping street. The first floor lobby of this smart, ritzy, yet traditionally styled hotel, is a popular meeting place for afternoon tea. Underground parking comes with free valet service. There is also a small gymnasium. **www.doylecollection.com**

Conrad Hotel   €€€€€   Map D5

Earlsfort Terrace, Dublin 2 **Tel** *01 602 8900* **Fax** *01 676 5424* **Rooms** *192*

Opposite the National Concert Hall, this international-style hotel is geared towards business people. The decor is tasteful and the atmosphere airy. Bedrooms are fitted out in a contemporary style with light wood furnishings and comfortable beds. The higher floors have good views. Professional service. **www.conraddublin.com**

Merrion   €€€€€   Map E4

Merrion Street Upper, Dublin 2 **Tel** *01 603 0600* **Fax** *01 603 0700* **Rooms** *143*

In the heart of Georgian Dublin, the Merrion is an elegant and stylish oasis, with open log fires, opulent interiors and a collection of Irish art and antiques. It is a landmark hotel, comprising four listed townhouses from the 1760s, all sensitively restored to their original grandeur. Guests can use the excellent Tethra Spa. **www.merrionhotel.com**

Westin Hotel   €€€€   Map D3

College Green, Dublin 2 **Tel** *01 645 1000* **Fax** *01 645 1234* **Rooms** *163*

Two 19th-century landmark buildings and part of the former Allied Irish Bank were reconstructed to create this sizeable hotel, across the street from Trinity College. The well-appointed bedrooms are furnished to a high standard; the beds are particularly comfortable. The former vaults of the bank are now a bar, The Mint. **www.westin.com/dublin**

SOUTHWEST DUBLIN

Avalon House   €   Map C4

55 Aungier Street, Dublin 2 **Tel** *01 475 0001* **Fax** *01 475 0303* **Rooms** *70*

One of the longest established hostels in the city, the centrally located Avalon House provides cheap and cheerful accommodation in a restored red brick Victorian building. Rooms are clean, with pine and tile floors, high ceilings and an open fire. Popular with young travellers, Avalon House also has a café. **www.avalon-house.ie**

Barnacles Hostel   €   Map C3

Temple Lane, Temple Bar, Dublin 2 **Tel** *01 671 6277* **Fax** *01 671 6591* **Rooms** *32*

Directly in the middle of Temple Bar, this award-winning hostel is bright, spacious, lively and clean, with a sunny lounge and a self-catering kitchen. There is a variety of rooms, including doubles, twins and dormitories sleeping from four to 12 people. All rooms are en suite. Staff are friendly and helpful. Open 24 hours. **www.barnacles.ie**

Blooms Hotel   €   Map D3

Anglesea Street, Dublin 2 **Tel** *01 671 5622* **Fax** *01 671 5997* **Rooms** *100*

The location – on the fringes of Temple Bar and close to Trinity College – is the main selling point of the Blooms. The hotel has an appealing modern exterior, and its compact bedrooms are adequate, if bland – the ones at the front are preferable. There is live music in the busy Vat House Bar, while Club M is a popular nightclub. **www.blooms.ie**

Central Hotel   €   Map D5

1–5 Exchequer Street, Dublin 2 **Tel** *01 679 7302* **Fax** *01 679 7303* **Rooms** *70*

Established in 1887, this three-star hotel is aptly named, given its convenient location, very close to Grafton Street. Featuring modern facilities, the Central retains a somewhat old-fashioned atmosphere, with traditional yet cosy decor. Bedrooms are neat, functional and reasonably priced. **www.centralhotel.ie**

Jury's Inn Christchurch   €€   Map B4

Christchurch Place, Dublin 8 **Tel** *01 454 0000* **Fax** *01 454 0012* **Rooms** *182*

Opposite Christ Church Cathedral, in the old Viking centre of Dublin, this modern hotel lies within easy walking distance of the Temple Bar area. Rooms are neat and well equipped. Bathrooms are adequate, if a little on the small side. Prices per room are particularly good value for families. **www.jurysinns.com**

Brooks   €€€   Map D4

59–62 Drury Street, Dublin 2 **Tel** *01 670 4000* **Fax** *01 670 4455* **Rooms** *98*

This immaculately maintained boutique hotel, located just minutes from Grafton Street, has a club-like feel and a welcoming ambience. Some rooms have their own DVD player and sound system, in addition to power showers and king-size beds. Brooks enjoys a great reputation. **www.brookshotel.ie**

Key to Price Guide *see p128* **Key to Symbols** *see back cover flap*

Clarence Hotel

6–8 Wellington Quay, Dublin 2 **Tel** *01 407 0800* **Fax** *01 407 0820* **Rooms** *49* **Map** *C3*

Overlooking the Liffey, this 1852 Dublin landmark was bought by the rock band U2 in 1992. Extensively refurbished, it has now acquired cult status. With original wood panelling in the Arts and Crafts style, and luxuriously furnished rooms, this establishment successfully combines contemporary cool and old-style comfort. **www.theclarence.ie**

Mercer Hotel

Lower Mercer Street, Dublin 2 **Tel** *01 478 2179* **Fax** *01 475 6524* **Rooms** *41* **Map** *C5*

Well located in the city centre, this three-star hotel combines the traditional with the contemporary, as witnessed in its wooden floors, subtle colour scheme and modern furnishings. Bedrooms are clean and comfortable and include all modern conveniences. There is a cosy bar, as well as a restaurant, Cusacks. **www.mercerhotel.ie**

NORTH OF THE LIFFEY

Cassidy's Hotel

Cavendish Row, Upper O'Connell Street, Dublin 1 **Tel** *01 878 0555* **Fax** *01 878 0687* **Rooms** *113* **Map** *D2*

This hotel is conveniently located at the top of O'Connell Street, opposite the Gate Theatre, in three adjoining red brick Georgian townhouses. The generously proportioned rooms have been modernized, but they retain some period features. Spacious bedrooms are all en suite, with contemporary furnishings. **www.cassidyshotel.com**

Clifden Guest House

32 Gardiners Place, Dublin 1 **Tel** *01 874 6364* **Fax** *01 874 6122* **Rooms** *15*

This three-star family-run guesthouse is set in a four-storey Georgian townhouse, just a few minutes' walk from the centre of the city. The high-ceilinged rooms are functional, yet comfortably furnished and cheerfully decorated. They come in varying sizes – one accommodating up to five people. **www.clifdenhouse.com**

Harvey's Hotel

11 Upper Gardiner Street, Dublin 1 **Tel** *01 874 8384* **Fax** *01 874 5510* **Rooms** *16*

This hospitable family-run Georgian townhouse, north of the Liffey, is ten minutes' walk from the top of O'Connell Street. Rooms are clean and pleasant; while some are a little jaded, most are nicely decorated. Those at the back are quieter. The atmosphere is friendly and relaxed. **www.harveysguesthouse.com**

The Gibson Hotel

Point Village, Dublin 1 **Tel** *01 681 5000* **Fax** *01 681 5001* **Rooms** *252* **Map** *D1*

Dublin's most fashionable hotel exudes rock 'n' roll – its name calls to mind a famous guitar; its location is just steps away from the O2 Arena; and its bars and restaurants have musical names. Rooms come with complimentary Wi-Fi. The area around Point Village has a great buzz about it. **www.thegibsonhotel.ie**

The Morrison

Ormond Quay, Dublin 1 **Tel** *01 887 2400* **Fax** *01 874 4039* **Rooms** *138* **Map** *C3*

Located on the quay overlooking the river, this luxurious hotel had John Rocha as design consultant. The interior is a mix of high ceilings, dark woods, pale walls, dim lighting, handcrafted Irish carpets and original art. Bedrooms have a modern design. There is also a stylish restaurant, Halo. **www.morrisonhotel.ie**

Gresham Hotel

23 Upper O'Connell Street, Dublin 1 **Tel** *01 874 6881* **Fax** *01 878 7175* **Rooms** *288* **Map** *D1*

One of Dublin's oldest and best known hotels, the Gresham is a popular rendezvous spot with ever-lively public areas. It has pleasant furnishings that combine classic and contemporary styles. The well-equipped bedrooms are cheerfully decorated. A good business hotel. **www.gresham-hotels.com**

Clarion IFSC

International Financial Service Centre, North Wall Quay, Dublin 1 **Tel** *01 433 8800* **Rooms** *163* **Map** *F2*

A short stroll from the centre, the Clarion IFSC offers well-designed and comfortable accommodation overlooking the River Liffey, in the heart of the financial district. This hotel is as popular with tourists as it is with business travellers. Public spaces are bright, airy and minimalist in style. **www.clarionhotelifsc.com**

FURTHER AFIELD

Butlers Town House

44 Landsdowne Road, Ballsbridge, Dublin 4 **Tel** *01 667 4022* **Fax** *01 667 3960* **Rooms** *20*

Furnished in a country-house style, this Georgian guesthouse offers four-star accommodation in individually designed bedrooms with Egyptian cotton sheets. Good breakfasts are served in the Conservatory Restaurant, which features an all-day menu, making this more of a small hotel than a B&B. **www.butlers-hotel.com**

Clara House

23 Leinster Road, Rathmines, Dublin 6 **Tel** *01 497 5904* **Fax** *01 497 5580* **Rooms** *13*

Built in 1840, this listed red brick Georgian house is a favoured B&B. It is a 15-minute walk from the city centre, and there is also a good bus route into town. The atmosphere is relaxed and friendly. Secure private car park is available at the rear. The pleasant waterside walks along the canal are an added attraction.

Crowne Plaza Hotel

Northwood Park, Santry Demesne, Santry, Dublin 9 **Tel** *01 862 8888* **Fax** *01 862 8800* **Rooms** *204*

Set in mature parkland, just five minutes from Dublin Airport and 15 minutes from the city centre, the Crowne Plaza offers all modern comforts. Rooms are well equipped, and there is an on-site fitness centre. A 24-hour courtesy coach for the airport is available. Located close to the M1 and M50 motorways. **www.cpdublin-airport.com**

Donnybrook Hall

6 Belmont Avenue, Donnybrook, Dublin 4 **Tel** *01 269 1633* **Fax** *01 269 2649* **Rooms** *10*

This family-run guesthouse is located on a quiet residential street near the Royal Dublin Society showgrounds and Landsdowne Road stadium. The interior is light and elegant, and all rooms have orthopaedic mattresses. Three of them open on to a garden. Great breakfasts include pancakes, French toast and fresh fruit. **www.donnybrookhall.com**

Druid Lodge

Killiney Hill Road, Killiney, Co Dublin **Tel** *01 285 1632* **Fax** *01 285 8504* **Rooms** *4*

Situated on picturesque Killiney Hill, overlooking the bay, Druid Lodge is 11 km (7 miles) south of Dublin city centre. A charming ivy-clad guesthouse, it was built in 1832 and named after the adjoining sacred site of Druid's Chair. Exuding a peaceful, old-world charm, it is well furnished and comfortable. **www.druidlodge.com**

Glenogra Guesthouse

64 Merrion Road, Ballsbridge, Dublin 4 **Tel** *01 668 3661* **Fax** *01 668 3698* **Rooms** *12*

This stylish and award-winning guesthouse provides pleasant and good value B&B accommodation in a leafy, upmarket area of Dublin. The owners create a welcoming atmosphere for their guests: bedrooms are pleasantly appointed, and the breakfast is good. **www.glenogra.com**

Grand Canal Hotel

Grand Canal Street, Ballsbridge, Dublin 4 **Tel** *01 646 1000* **Fax** *01 646 1001* **Rooms** *142*

Spacious and modern, with a friendly staff, the Grand Canal offers comfortable accommodation. The on-site pub, Kitty O'Sheas, is one of the best in town. There is also a restaurant, Epic. It is conveniently located between Trinity College and Landsdowne Road. **www.grandcanalhotel.com**

Marble Hall Guest Accommodation

81 Marlborough Road, Donnybrook, Dublin 4 **Tel** *01 497 7350 or 086 370 769* **Rooms** *3*

This much-loved guesthouse is set in a leafy residential area, 20 minutes' walk from town and on a well-serviced bus route. Victorian in style, it is meticulously maintained by Shelagh Conway, who is renowned for her excellent breakfasts. Bedrooms are spacious and tastefully decorated with antique furniture. **www.marblehall.net**

Portmarnock Hotel & Golf Links

Portmarnock, Co Dublin **Tel** *01 846 0611* **Fax** *01 846 2422* **Rooms** *135*

Famous for their Irish whiskey, the Jameson family originally owned this house with a lovely beachside location. Close to Dublin Airport, the Portmarnock is tastefully decorated, with bright public spaces. Rooms are excellently furnished, with views of the sea or the championship golf course. There is also a spa. **www.portmarnock.com**

Sandymount Hotel

7 Herbert Road, Ballsbridge, Dublin 4 **Tel** *01 668 4321* **Fax** *01 660 7077* **Rooms** *168*

Formerly named the Mount Herbert Hotel, Sandymount Hotel is located in a residential area close to the Aviva Stadium. It consists of a terrace of interconnecting houses decorated with modern furnishings. The en-suite bedrooms are equipped with good facilities. There is free access to a nearby gym. **www.sandymounthotel.ie**

Tara Towers Hotel

Merrion Road, Booterstown, Dublin 4 **Tel** *01 269 4666* **Fax** *01 269 1027* **Rooms** *111*

South of the city centre, this three-star hotel is situated on the coastal road. Dun Laoghaire is a 15-minute drive away, and there is a well-serviced bus route and a DART station nearby. The ambience is relaxed, and bedrooms are comfortable and spacious, if rather basic in decor. There is a traditional restaurant on site. **www.taratowers.com**

Ballsbridge Court

Landsdowne Road, Ballsbridge, Dublin 4 **Tel** *01 668 4468* **Rooms** *188*

In the heart of the embassy belt, this five-star hotel is conveniently located for the Royal Dublin Society showground and Aviva Stadium. Beyond the unappealing exterior, the chandeliered lobby sets the tone for a plush ambience. Rooms are well appointed and there is a jazz bar and bistro. **www.d4hotels.com**

The Burlington

Upper Leeson Street, Dublin 4 **Tel** *01 618 5600* **Fax** *01 660 8086* **Rooms** *500*

This four-star hotel is a genuine Dublin institution at the heart of the city's south side. The rooms are smartly appointed, and there is a choice of two restaurants, The Sussex or The Diplomat. Bellini's bar is contemporary and stylish and has a relaxed atmosphere for an afternoon drink. **www.burlingtonhotel.ie**

Key to Price Guide *see p128* **Key to Symbols** *see back cover flap*

Clontarf Castle Hotel  €€

Castle Avenue, Clontarf, Dublin 3 **Tel** *01 833 2321* **Fax** *01 833 0418* **Rooms** *111*

The luxurious Clontarf Castle Hotel is just ten minutes' drive from the city centre, in the elegant suburb of Clontarf. This is the heart of golf country, and the hotel would make a good base for visitors keen to try out a few of the renowned courses in the area, such as The Royal or Portmarnock. **www.clontarfcastle.ie**

Herbert Park Hotel €€

Ballsbridge, Dublin 4 **Tel** *01 667 2200* **Fax** *01 667 2595* **Rooms** *153*

Overlooking the park after which it is named, this big contemporary hotel is bright and airy. Materials used to enliven the interiors include polished granite, Irish abstract art, Irish furniture and glass walls. Bedrooms are well appointed and stylishly designed. **www.herbertparkhotel.ie**

The Red Bank €€

6–7 Church Street, Skerries, Co Dublin **Tel** *01 849 1005* **Fax** *01 849 1598* **Rooms** *18*

On the premises of a former bank, in the heart of the village of Skerries, this guesthouse offers comfortably furnished rooms with good facilities. The award-winning Red Bank Restaurant has great character and specializes in seafood. Warm hospitality is guaranteed. Dublin Airport is just a short drive away. **www.redbank.ie**

Waterloo House €€

8–10 Waterloo Road, Ballsbridge, Dublin 4 **Tel** *01 660 1888* **Fax** *01 667 1955* **Rooms** *17*

A short walk from St Stephen's Green, this lovely guesthouse comprises two adjoining Georgian buildings on a tree-lined road, away from the bustle of the city. The ambience is informal, and the bedrooms cosy. A good, hearty breakfast is served in a cheerful dining room. Off-street parking is available. **www.waterloohouse.ie**

Dylan €€€€€

Eastmoreland Place, Dublin 4 **Tel** *01 660 3000* **Fax** *01 660 3005* **Rooms** *44*

A very stylish boutique hotel, the Dylan boasts a plush interior with sumptuous rooms, each of which has been individually designed. Special touches include rainfall showerheads and Italian marble in the bathrooms, and iPods in the rooms. Dine in the hotel's elegant but informal restaurant, or sip cocktails in the bar. **www.dylan.ie**

Four Seasons €€€€€

Simmonscourt Road, Ballsbridge, Dublin 4 **Tel** *01 665 4000* **Fax** *01 665 4099* **Rooms** *196*

The luxurious Four Seasons combines period-style elegance with contemporary comfort. The large public spaces are opulently decorated with deep-pile rugs and rich furnishings. Bedrooms are large and lavish, and service is exceptional. The Ice Bar is a magnet for fashionistas. There are also 25 apartments. **www.fourseasons.com**

BEYOND DUBLIN

Smarmore Castle €

Ardee, Co Louth **Tel** *041 685 7167* **Fax** *041 685 7650* **Rooms** *5*

This 1320 castle-mansion is a hidden gem. The Mullen family offer a warm welcome and impeccable service, then leave you to enjoy the peaceful garden, rooms – all different – and the drawing room. The spa offers massages, Jacuzzi and sauna. Smarmore Castle is one hour from Dublin, close to Newgrange. **www.smarmorecastle.com**

Beaufort House €€

Ghan Road, Carlingford, Co Louth **Tel** *042 937 3879* **Rooms** *6*

Michael Caine (not the film star) is a fantastic chef. Along with their core business of sailing courses and yacht charter, he and wife Glynis run this award-winning guesthouse in medieval Carlingford, halfway between Dublin and Belfast. En-suite rooms enjoy sea and mountain views. Great breakfasts. **www.beauforthouse.net**

Castle Leslie Estate  €€€

Glaslough, Co Monaghan **Tel** *047 88 100* **Fax** *047 88 256* **Rooms** *50*

Located within a thousand acres of rolling countryside, this castle is owned and run by the colourful Leslie family. The castle and a hunting lodge provide accommodation for 50, and two self-catering apartments and five houses in the village are also available. The Organic Spa and equestrian centre are open to visitors. **www.castleleslie.com**

Brooklodge Hotel €€€€

Macreddin Village, Co Wicklow **Tel** *0402 36444* **Fax** *0402 36580* **Rooms** *90*

Not so much a hotel as a village complex. Standard rooms have four-poster beds; the suites are even more luxurious. The renowned spa offers a flotation tank and hammam massages. There is an equestrian centre, an organic food fair on Sundays and live jazz on Saturday nights. **www.brooklodge.com**

Dunbrody Country House Hotel €€€€€

Arthurstown, Co Wexford **Tel** *051 389 600* **Fax** *051 389 601* **Rooms** *22*

Set in parkland on the dramatic Hook Peninsula, this 1830s Georgian manor (home to the world-renowned Dunbrody cookery school) offers a relaxing, elegant atmosphere complemented by log fires and a luxury spa. Rooms are individually styled. **www.dunbrodyhouse.com**

RESTAURANTS, CAFES AND PUBS

The Dublin of today is a modern, cosmopolitan city, something which is reflected in its vast array of restaurants. The Temple Bar area is good for modern international cuisine, and also has a large number of pubs as well as a few traditional Irish restaurants. There are many Italian, Chinese and Indian, as well as a number of Indonesian, Thai, Japanese, Mexican and Cuban restaurants. Seafood and fish is abundant in Dublin,

The Bad Ass Café, Temple Bar

in particular smoked salmon and oysters; the latter is famously often consumed with Guinness. Popular for a light lunch is smoked salmon on delicious dark rye bread, with a pint of Guinness. Wherever you eat, portions will be generous, especially in pubs, whose platefuls of roast meat and vegetables offer excellent value for money. Takeaway food, from fish and chips to pizzas and kebabs, is also widely available.

IRISH EATING PATTERNS

Traditionally, the Irish have started the day with a huge breakfast: bacon, sausages, black pudding, eggs, tomatoes and brown bread. The main meal, dinner, was served at midday, with a lighter "tea" in the early evening.

Although Continental breakfasts are now available, the traditional breakfast is still included in almost all hotel and B&B rates. Most of the Irish today settle for a light lunch and save their main meal for the evening. Vestiges of the old eating patterns remain in the huge midday meals still served in pubs.

EATING OUT

Elegant dining becomes considerably more affordable when you make lunch your main meal of the day. In many of the top restaurants in Dublin, the fixed-price lunch

and dinner menus offer much the same, but the bill at lunchtime will usually amount to about half the price. If you like wine to accompany your meal, the house wines are quite drinkable in most restaurants and can reduce the total cost of your meal. If you are travelling with children, look out for one of the many restaurants that offer a children's menu. Lunch in Dublin is invariably served between noon and 2:30pm, with dinner between 6:30 and 10pm, although many ethnic and city-centre restaurants stay open later. If you are staying in a bed-and-breakfast, your hosts may provide a home-cooked evening meal if given advance notice. Visa and MasterCard are the most commonly accepted credit cards in Ireland, with American Express and Diners Club also in use.

GOURMET AND ETHNIC DINING

Once considerably lacking in gourmet establishments, Dublin now offers many restaurants that rank among Europe's very best, with chefs trained in outstanding domestic and Continental institutions. Increasingly it is the hotels which house the city's award-winning restaurants. There is an enormous range of cuisines to be found in and around Dublin. Locations vary as widely as the cuisine, from conventional hotel dining rooms, townhouse basements and city mansions to romantic castle hotels and tiny village cafés tucked away by the sea.

An Irish coffee

In the city centre, the eating areas with the widest choice tend to be located in Temple Bar or between St Stephen's Green and Merrion Square and between Grafton Street and South Great Georges Street. Outside the city, Malahide and Howth have a good selection of restaurants, and Dun Laoghaire is worth a special visit for fresh fish and seafood.

BUDGET DINING

It is quite possible to eat well on a moderate budget in Dublin. Both in the city and outside it, there are small

The Mermaid Café, with its floor-to-ceiling windows **(see p142)**

La Stampa's luxurious bar, Samsara (see p140)

cafés, tea rooms and family-style restaurants which offer reasonably priced meals. Sandwiches are usually made with thick, delicious slices of fresh, rather than processed, cheese or meat; salad plates feature chicken, pork, beef and the ever-popular smoked salmon; and hot meals usually come with generous helpings of vegetables, with the beloved potato often showing up in different forms, including roasted and mashed, sometimes all on one plate.

Another cheap alternative is to take picnics when you go out. Farmhouse cheeses and homegrown tomatoes make delicious sandwiches, and the beautiful countryside, fine beaches and breathtaking mountains make ideal locations for a picnic. Phoenix Park and Powerscourt both have their own picnic areas.

Whelan's, renowned for its live music programme (see p155)

PUB FOOD

Ireland's pubs have moved into the food field with a vengeance. In addition to bar snacks (soup, sandwiches and so on), salads and hot meals are served from noon until late. At rock-bottom prices, hot plates all come heaped with mounds of fresh vegetables, potatoes, and good portions of local fish or meat. Particularly good value are the pub carveries that offer a choice of joints, sliced to your preference. The international staples of spaghetti, lasagne and quiche often appear on pub menus, along with more Mediterranean dishes such as *bruschetta* in the trendier pubs. For a list of recommended pubs, see pages 146–7.

PUB OPENING HOURS

Many people come to Dublin for its endless pubs and bars and its excellent stouts and whiskeys. Opening hours are Monday to Wednesday 10:30am until 11:30pm; Thursday to Saturday 10:30am until 12:30pm. Sunday opening times have changed to become more flexible. Pubs used to close for "holy hour" between 2pm and 4pm. Now most pubs are open on a Sunday from 12:30pm until 11pm. Late bars tend to stay open until 1am or 2am, the nightclubs even later. Alcohol is not served past 2am, however, and off-licences must close at 10pm.

FISH AND CHIPS AND OTHER FAST FOODS

The Irish, from peasant to parliamentarian, love their "chippers", immortalized in Roddy Doyle's novel *The Van*, and any good pub night will often end with a visit to the nearest fish-and-chip shop. At virtually any time of day, however, if you pass by Leo Burdock's in Dublin, there will be a long queue for this international institution (see p141). With Ireland's long coastline, wherever you choose, the fish will usually be the freshest catch of the day – plaice, cod, haddock, whiting or ray (a delicacy). As an alternative to fish and chips, there are numerous good pasta and pizza restaurants around the city, including the Steps of Rome, Pasta Fresca and Milano, which also does takeaways (see p147). In addition, ubiquitous burger chains can be found in Dublin, including McDonald's, as well as other forms of fast food outlets such as KFC.

Picnickers enjoying the sunshine outside at Dublin Zoo (see p81)

VEGETARIAN FOOD

As with most western European cities, there is plenty of scope for vegetarians to eat well in Dublin. Although much traditional Irish food is meat-based, most restaurants will have vegetarian dishes on the menu, particularly in the modern international and Italian restaurants, but there are also some excellent exclusively vegetarian restaurants in the city. If you happen to go somewhere to eat and realize that there is no vegetarian option, most restaurants will be more than happy to make something up for you, such as a salad or a vegetable stir fry.

The Flavours of Ireland

Boxty, barm brack, champ, coddle, cruibins, colcannon – the basic dishes that have nourished Ireland are spiced with fancy names. But the secret of their success is their ingredients, which are nurtured in a warm, damp climate on lush hills that brings them flavour. Beef and dairy cattle can stay out all year and produce abundant butter, cheese and cream. Pork and pork products, such as ham and bacon, are a mainstay, though lamb is traditional, too. Potatoes, the king of vegetables, turn up in soup, pies, cakes, bread and scones that are piled on breakfast and tea tables. And the rivers, lakes and shores are rich in seafood.

Oysters

Sea trout, plucked fresh from the Atlantic Ocean

THE BASIC DISHES

Irish stews are thick and tasty, traditionally featuring lamb or mutton, onion and potatoes, while beef and Guinness *(see pp82–3)* make a darker casserole, sometimes with the addition of oysters. Carrots and turnips are the first choice of vegetables. Pork is the basis of many dishes. Trotters, called

cruibins or crubeens, are sometimes pickled, while bacon can be especially meaty. Dublin coddle, a fill-me-up after the pub on a Saturday night, relies on sausages and potatoes as well as bacon. Ham is sometimes smoked over peat and, for special occasions, it is baked with cloves and brown sugar and served with buttered cabbage. Cabbage is the basis of colcannon, with

mashed potato and onions, sometimes with butter and milk. Boxty is a bake of raw and cooked potato mashed with butter, buttermilk and flour; champ is potatoes mashed with milk, butter and onions.

FISH AND SEAFOOD

The Atlantic Ocean and Irish Sea have a rich variety of shellfish, from lobsters and Dublin Bay prawns to

Barm brack   White soda bread   Brown soda bread   Potato bread

Potato farls

Wheaten brea

Selection of the many traditional Irish breads

TRADITIONAL IRISH FOOD

Gubbeen cheese

If your heart is up to it, start the day with a "Full Irish Fry". This breakfast fry-up includes thick, tasty bacon, plus black pudding, soda farls and potato cake. A "lady's breakfast" will have one egg, a "gentleman's" two. Gooseberry jam will be spread on fried bread, and mugs of tea will wash it down. Irish stews traditionally use mutton, not so common today, while Spiced Beef uses up brisket, which is covered in a various spices then left for a week before being cooked slowly with Guinness and vegetables. A high tea in the early evening is the major meal in many homes; a main course will be followed by a succession of breads and cakes.

Irish Stew *Traditionally, neck of mutton, potatoes, carrots and onions are slowly cooked together for hours.*

Delivery in time-honoured style at Moore Street Market, Dublin

mussels and oysters, clams, scallops, and razor-shells. Herring, mackerel, plaice and skate are brought in from the sea, while the rivers and lakes offer up salmon, trout and eels, which are often smoked. Galway salmon and oysters are famous and are served throughout the city's restaurants. Salmon is usually smoked in oak wood kilns. Also traditional is a red seaweed called dulse, mixed with potatoes mashed in their skins to make dulse champ.

BAKED GOODS

Bread and cakes make up a large percentage of the Irish diet. Unleaven soda bread is ubiquitous in both white and brown varieties, and is great with Irish cheeses. Potato bread is fried or eaten cold, as cake. Farls ("quarters") are made with wheat flour or oats, bicarbonate of soda and buttermilk, which goes into many recipes. Fruit breads include barm brack, which is traditionally eaten at Hallowe'en and on All Saints' Day, while rich porter cake is made with Guinness or

A range of Ireland's finest farmhouse cheeses

other stout. White, brown and fruit scones will never be far from tea and breakfast tables.

DAIRY PRODUCTS

Creamy butter, usually salted, is applied generously. Cream, too, is used in cooking, stirred into soups and whipped for puddings. The variety and quality of Irish farmhouse cheeses has given them a worldwide reputation, and a farmhouse St Killian took the crown of "Best Irish Cheese" from Irish Cheddar at the 2007 World Cheese Awards. The winner in 2010 was Newmarket Creamery Vintage Red Cheddar.

IRISH CHEESES

Carrigaline Nutty-tasting, Gouda-like cheese from Cork.

Cashel Blue The first Irish blue cheese. Soft and creamy. Unpasteurized; from Tipperary.

Cooleeny Small, Camembert-style unpasteurized cheese from Tipperary.

Durrus Creamy, natural-rind unpasteurized cheese from West Cork. May be smoked.

Gubbeen Semi-soft washed rind cheese. Rich, milky taste.

Mileens Soft, rich rind-washed cheese. Unpasteurized; from the Beara peninsula, Cork.

St Killian Hexagonal Brie-like creamy cheese from Wexford.

Dublin Coddle *This is a comforting mixture of sausages, bacon, potatoes and onions, stewed in ham stock.*

Galway Salmon *Top quality fish can be simply served with an Irish butter sauce, watercress and colcannon.*

Irish Coffee *This is a chilled soufflé of coffee, cream and Irish whiskey, topped with crushed walnuts.*

Choosing a Restaurant

The restaurants in this guide have been selected across a wide range of price categories for their good value, exceptional food or interesting location. These listings highlight some of the factors that may influence your choice, such as whether you can eat outdoors or if the venue offers live music. Entries are listed by area.

PRICE CATEGORIES
For a three-course evening meal for one including a half bottle of house wine, service and taxes.

€ Under €25
€€ €25–€35
€€€ €35–€45
€€€€ €45–€55
€€€€€ Over €55

SOUTHEAST DUBLIN

Avoca Café
11–13 Suffolk Street, Dublin 2 **Tel** *01 672 6019* €€
Map D3

Climb to the top floor of the renowned Irish craft shop Avoca, and you will be rewarded with creative, wholesome and colourful cooking in a bright and airy room. The queues get longer during lunch hour. Such popularity is testament to the delicious salads, panini, hot dishes and wonderful desserts on offer. Open daytime only.

Cornucopia
19 Wicklow Street, Dublin 2 **Tel** *01 677 7583* €€
Map D3

Small and often crowded, Cornucopia is one of the few exclusively vegetarian restaurants in the city, open for breakfast, lunch and dinner. It serves delicious, cheap and wholesome food – such as salads, soups, pasta dishes, casseroles and quiches – to an army of bookworm bachelors and earthy students. Open until 8pm (9pm on Thursdays and 7pm Sundays).

Dunne & Crescenzi
14 South Frederick Street, Dublin 2 **Tel** *01 677 3815* €€
Map E4

This delightful Italian wine bar serves authentic food and wine in a stylishly rustic atmosphere. Enjoy the excellent minestrone, antipasti platters, bruschettas, panini, pasta dishes, delicious fruit tartlets and excellent coffee. There is also a superb collection of wines, many of them served by the glass, too. Open all day and into the evening.

Good World Chinese Restaurant
18 South Great George's Street, Dublin 2 **Tel** *01 677 5373* €€
Map C4

This restaurant's popularity with the Chinese community is witness to the superlative and authentic quality of the food on offer. The dim sum selection is a popular choice. Authentic beef, chicken and fish dishes are also on the menu, along with the standard range of Westernized dishes. Friendly and efficient service.

Kilkenny Restaurant and Café
5–6 Nassau Street, Dublin 2 **Tel** *01 677 7066* €€
Map E4

Situated on the first floor of a high quality craft shop, the Kilkenny overlooks the grounds of Trinity College. Wholesome, freshly prepared soups, sandwiches, panini, salads, quiches, hot casseroles and pies are available in this self-service restaurant. Lovely desserts include baked cheesecake, carrot cake and fruit tarts.

Nude
21 Suffolk Street, Dublin 2 **Tel** *01 677 4804* €€
Map D3

Bono's brother, Norman Hewson, has created a very successful, hip and intimate restaurant that serves freshly prepared food, organic where possible. Soups, panini, wraps, salads and freshly squeezed juices are ordered at the counter. Then, take a seat at the long wooden tables and enjoy these colourful snacks in an upbeat atmosphere.

Steps of Rome
1 Chatham Street, Dublin 2 **Tel** *01 670 5630* €€
Map D4

This tiny Italian café, selling great coffee, is always abuzz with people coming and going to collect tasty slices of pizza. The reasonably priced menu includes pasta dishes and bruschettas. Service is brisk, if a little brusque. Steps of Rome is popular with students and fast-moving shoppers pausing for breath. Open all day and into the evening.

Yamamori Noodles
71 South Great George's Street, Dublin 2 **Tel** *01 475 5001* €€
Map C4

Very popular with the young crowd, this lively and informal Japanese restaurant specializes in *yamamori ramen* (a noodle dish with meat and vegetables), sushi and sashimi. Try the interesting bento box for variety. Dishes are good value, service is prompt, and the atmosphere is friendly. Evenings are very busy. Open for lunch and dinner.

The Cedar Tree
118 South Andrew Street, Dublin 2 **Tel** *01 677 2121* €€€
Map D3

Dublin's longest established Lebanese restaurant serves authentic Lebanese dishes. There is a wide *meze* selection, including hummus, mussels, quails, prawns, *baba ganoush*, *tabbouleh* and spiced potatoes. Belly dancing shows take place on Friday and Saturday evenings. The ground floor restaurant, Byblos, serves lighter fare.

Key to Symbols *see back cover flap*

Chilli Club €€€

Anne's Lane, South Anne Street, Dublin 2 **Tel** *01 677 3721*   **Map** *D4*

Knock on the door to be let into this award-winning Thai restaurant just off Grafton Street. Do not let the very small, intimate setting and simple decor put you off: the standard of cooking is very high, and the service is great. Thai curries are particularly tasty and the set lunches are good value. AmEx is not accepted.

Gotham Café €€€

8 South Anne Street, Dublin 2 **Tel** *01 679 5266*   **Map** *D4*

Always abuzz with activity, this lively and colourful spot offers bistro-style food at affordable prices. With covers of *Rolling Stone* magazine lining the walls, it is popular with the young – and the young-at-heart. Gotham Café is renowned for its tasty and imaginative pizzas, but it also serves delectable pasta dishes and salads.

Il Posto €€€

10 St Stephen's Green, Dublin 2 **Tel** *01 679 4769*   **Map** *D4*

Il Posto is an oasis of calm from the bustle of Stephen's Green. Although the atmosphere is relaxed, this restaurant offers very formal dining. The food is of the highest standard, a mix of traditional and contemporary Italian, coupled with excellent service. In summer, try to get one of the tables on the terrace, with views of St Stephen's Green.

Nico's €€€

53 Dame Street, Dublin 2 **Tel** *01 677 3062*   **Map** *D3*

Traditional Italian fare from a restaurant that has maintained a quiet, dignified presence on the scene for more than 30 years. Plush red drapes set the tone for the decor and for the traditional menu. For dessert, try the Italian *cassata* with Galliano. A piano player performs Tuesday to Saturday evenings, and there is an excellent wine list.

Trocadero €€€

3–4 St Andrew Street, Dublin 2 **Tel** *01 677 5545*   **Map** *D3*

This much-loved restaurant has been in operation since 1956. A favourite haunt of actors and the literati, it has deep red walls lined with black and white images of the notables who have passed through its doors. Traditional classics include rack of lamb, steak, Dublin Bay prawns and tempting desserts. The service is intimate and welcoming.

Diep le Shaker €€€€

55 Pembroke Lane, Dublin 2 **Tel** *01 661 1829*   **Map** *E5*

Superb food and efficient service await at this bright, cheery Asian diner. Try prawn red curry served in the shell of a baby coconut, or the popular spicy beef curry. The layout is open-plan, and you can eat on the balcony overlooking the lower floor. Excellent exotic cocktails can be enjoyed at the bar. Live jazz Tuesdays and Wednesdays.

Dobbins Wine Bistro €€€€

15 Stephen's Lane, Dublin 2 **Tel** *01 661 9536*   **Map** *F5*

Popular since 1978, this cheerful bistro has a sleek, modern look, with leather banquettes and cool lighting. Given the good and extensive wine list, Dobbins is a popular spot for a leisurely liquid lunch. Among the highlights on the menu are Dublin Bay prawns and organic pork served with crackling.

Ely Wine Bar and Café €€€€

22 Ely Place, Dublin 2 **Tel** *01 676 8986*   **Map** *E5*

Erik and Michelle Robson's unusual wine bar and café, just off St Stephen's Green, has been stylishly converted. The menu features delicious cheese dishes, fish cakes, Kilkee oysters, lamb stew and home-made sausages. The atmosphere is cosy and lively, and the imaginative wine list features some truly exceptional labels.

FXB €€€€

Pembroke Street, Dublin 2 **Tel** *01 676 4606*   **Map** *E5*

This quality traditional steakhouse and seafood chain enjoys a long-standing reputation of excellence. Meat is supplied by reliable butchers in Offaly. Sip a bubbly champagne cocktails as you wait for your meaty order to arrive. The popularity of this restaurant has led to other branches being opened in Temple Bar and Christchurch.

Jaipur €€€€

41–46 South Great George's Street, Dublin 2 **Tel** *01 677 0999*   **Map** *C4*

Often acclaimed as the best Indian restaurant in the city, Jaipur offers high-quality, innovative dishes. The decor, stylish and with a contemporary feel, features warm, tasteful colours. The restaurant is superbly managed by a well-informed and charming staff. Vegetarians are well catered for. There are branches in Malahide and Dalkey also.

La Cave €€€€

28 South Anne Street, Dublin 2 **Tel** *01 679 4409*   **Map** *D4*

Descend the stairs from street level into a tiny cavernous wine bar that is also a restaurant offering French food of a high standard, sometimes with a North African flavour. The owner, Margaret, is one of Ireland's leading wine experts and offers an impressively extensive wine list, sourced everywhere from France to Uruguay. The wine bar is open late.

La Maison €€€€

15 Castle Market Street, Dublin 2 **Tel** *01 672 7258*   **Map** *D4*

This former boulangerie is now a restaurant serving classic French cuisine. The menu includes dishes such as *magret de canard* (roast duck breast) and the veggie-friendly *tarte provençal*. In fine weather you can sit on the terrace by the pretty sky-blue shopfront, beneath the candy-cane canopy, and enjoy some people-watching.

La Peniche   €€€€
Grand Canal, Mespil Road, Dublin 4 **Tel** *087 790 00 77*

This floating French/Italian bistro and wine bar is moored on a lovely stretch of the Grand Canal. Each table has an attention light that you can switch on, rather than having to catch the waiter's eye. Every Tuesday, Wednesday and Thursday, cruise dinners are available for an extra €10 – be sure to book early. La Peniche can also be chartered privately.

La Stampa   €€€€
35 Dawson Street, Dublin 2 **Tel** *01 677 4444*   **Map** *D4*

The main attraction of the brasserie-style La Stampa is its dining room, arguably the most romantic in the city, set in a charming 19th-century mirrored ballroom. Given the food's modest quality, the experience is rather pricey. However, the pleasing ambience and cordial staff more than make up for any shortcomings on your plate.

L'Gueuleton   €€€€
1 Fade Street, Dublin 2 **Tel** *01 675 3708*   **Map** *C4*

Come to this popular French bistro for everything from snail and Roquefort Pithivier to duck with sweetened chicory, all accompanied by smooth jazz music in the background. Although it is not possible to make reservations in advance, there is a bar area where you can wait for a table. AmEx and Diner cards not accepted.

Pearl Brasserie   €€€€
20 Merrion Street Upper, Dublin 2 **Tel** *01 661 3572*   **Map** *D4*

This basement brasserie exudes a cool, contemporary French ethos. It combines charming service with good food at affordable prices. Lunch is particularly good value. Seafood features prominently on the menu, and the impressive wine list is heavy on French labels. The separate Oyster Bar offers lighter fare, including a fish platter.

Rustic Stone   €€€€
South Great George's Street, Dublin 2 **Tel** *01 707 9596* **Map** *C4*

Run by renowned chef Dylan McGrath, Rustic Stone serves quality fare made with seasonal and local produce, with an emphasis on nutrition and affordability. Diners are served their meat or fish dishes on a hot volcanic stone, a Spanish technique that enables the ingredients to be cooked to taste. The steak dishes are firm favourites.

Bang Café   €€€€€
11 Merrion Row, Dublin 2 **Tel** *01 400 4229*   **Map** *E5*

This hip restaurant has been restyled – gone is the stark minimalism, to be replaced by warm colours and art on the walls. The menu, however, has maintained its elegant connotations. Contemporary fare includes great fish dishes, mouthwatering steaks and an excellent choice of game. The service is highly professional.

The Cliff Town House   €€€€€
22 St Stephen's Green, Dublin 2 **Tel** *01 638 3939*   **Map** *D4*

Twinned with the Michelin-starred Cliff House Hotel in Ardmore, County Waterford, this restaurant has a menu that relies heavily on locally sourced, seasonal ingredients. Seafood is their strongest suit, and there is a fantastic wine list, too. It's relatively expensive, but the surroundings are exquisite and the service superlative.

L'Ecrivain   €€€€€
109a Lower Baggot Street, Dublin 2 **Tel** *01 661 1919* **Map** *F5*

One of the best restaurants in Dublin, L'Ecrivain combines classic formality with contemporary cool. Authentic French cuisine with an Irish flavour includes delicacies such as Galway Bay oysters and caviar. Seasonal game and seafood, as well as tasty desserts and cheeses, also figure prominently on the menu. The service is highly polished and efficient.

Peploe's Wine Bistro   €€€€€
16 St Stephen's Green, Dublin 2 **Tel** *01 676 3144*   **Map** *D4*

Located in the basement of a Georgian building, Peploe's is a glamorous, cosy and immensely popular restaurant. It is also always rushed, due to the consistently high-quality food available. It provides an extensive wine list – more than 30 varieties of wine are served by the glass. Book in advance.

Shanahan's on the Green   €€€€€
119 St Stephen's Street, Dublin 2 **Tel** *01 407 0939*   **Map** *D5*

The most succulent steaks in Dublin are found at this renowned steakhouse, set in an elegantly furnished Georgian house. Though steeply priced, the food is consistently of the highest quality. The portions are gargantuan, so it is wise to skip the starter if you hope to finish your main. Seafood, too, is available at this superbly managed establishment.

Thorntons   €€€€€
128 St Stephen's Green, Dublin 2 **Tel** *01 478 7008*   **Map** *D4*

Haute cuisine is on the menu at this Michelin-starred restaurant in the Fitzwilliam Hotel *(see p129)*. Its small dining room gives it a sense of privacy, while the cream and gold decor adds to the cosy, bright atmosphere. Chef Kevin Thornton offers signature dishes such as braised suckling pig, loin of venison or roast quail with brioche.

Unicorn   €€€€€
12B Merrion Court, Dublin 2 **Tel** *01 662 4757*   **Map** *E4*

Situated around the corner from St Stephen's Green, Unicorn has maintained an excellent standard since it first opened in 1938. Its casual atmosphere is unparalleled and enhanced by the friendly waiting staff. The Italian-Mediterranean food served here is utterly delicious, and the veal is particularly appetizing.

Key to Price Guide *see p138* **Key to Symbols** *see back cover flap*

SOUTHWEST DUBLIN

Govinda's €
4 Aungier Street, Dublin 2 **Tel** *01 475 0309* **Map** *C4*

Bright, cheerful and bustling with energy, Govinda's is run by Hare Krishnas and offers filling and tasty vegetarian fare, such as samosas, pizzas and moussaka, not to mention vegan options. For dessert, try the upside-down pineapple cake. Sinead O'Connor is a regular here. Another branch can be found at 83 Middle Abbey Street, and a third on Merrion Row.

Gruel €€
68a Dame Street, Dublin 2 **Tel** *01 670 7119* **Map** *C3*

This tiny, quirky café blends the rustic with the innovative in its light snacks, soups and hot specials. The "roast in a roll" is delicious and a firm favourite among the colourful patrons. Good pizzas and tasty sweet dishes make it an ideal spot for a quick bite at affordable prices. Eat in or take away.

Leo Burdock's €€
2 Werburgh Street, Dublin 8 **Tel** *01 454 0306* **Map** *B4*

The patrons of Leo Burdock's, the oldest fish-and-chip takeaway in Dublin, include the ordinary folk of Dublin, as well as the stars. The chips are made from top-grade Irish potatoes, and there is a wide choice of fish, including smoked cod, haddock and lemon-sole goujon. Service is efficient. There is another branch on Liffey Street.

Mongolian Barbecue €€
7 Anglesea Street, Dublin 2 **Tel** *01 670 4154* **Map** *D3*

Mix your own meat and spices, and bring the resulting patty to a shared, massive, hot metal plate to sizzle to your satisfaction. And go back for seconds, thirds and fourths. Veggies follow the same steps using tofu instead of meat – they also get a free starter of samosa or a spring roll. Excellent value.

Queen of Tarts €€
4 Cork Hill, Dame Street, Dublin 2 **Tel** *01 670 7499* **Map** *C3*

Opposite Dublin Castle and Dublin City Hall, this charming little café is cosy and welcoming. In addition to freshly prepared soups, sandwiches and hot savoury tarts, there is a dazzling array of mouth-watering desserts, including chocolate fudge cake, fruit tarts and home-made biscuits. A roomier branch can be found on Cow's Lane.

Buenos Aires Grill €€€€
Unit 2, Castle Way, Golden Lane, Dublin 2 **Tel** *01 475 9616* **Map** *C4*

This authentic Argentinian restaurant has floor to ceiling windows, an open kitchen and contemporary decor in cool, neutral tones. There are good lunch deals and an evening menu specialising in beef, but also offering pork and chicken dishes, and good vegetarian and seafood options. Popular with people working in the area and tourists.

Chez Max €€€€
1 Palace Street, Dublin 2 **Tel** *01 633 7215* **Map** *C3*

This cosy French diner at the gates of Dublin Castle is so authentic that it is hard to get a seat on account of all the French clients who come here for lunch. There is a covered back garden and a little terrace out front for alfresco dining. The good, simple French cuisine is classic; the signature dish is *boeuf bourguignon*.

Darwin's €€€€
80 Aungier Street, Dublin 2 **Tel** *01 475 7511* **Map** *C4*

Specializing in steaks made from certified organic meat from the proprietor's own butcher shop, this is a carnivore's dream. The menu also includes crab cakes and duck spring rolls, not to mention some vegetarian options. Dishes are prepared using quality ingredients and presented with flair. Unpretentious ambience, with warm, friendly service.

Les Frères Jacques €€€€
74 Dame Street, Dublin 2 **Tel** *01 679 4555* **Map** *C3*

This elegant restaurant is French in style, cuisine, atmosphere and service. Seafood and game feature prominently on the balanced seasonal menus. Try the grilled lobster fresh from the tank, or the roast lamb casserole with courgette, aubergine (eggplant) and thyme. Classic desserts are also on the menu. The good wine list favours French labels.

Monty's of Kathmandu €€€€
28 Eustace Street, Dublin 2 **Tel** *01 670 4911* **Map** *C3*

This friendly Nepalese restaurant serves tasty and interesting fish, chicken and lamb dishes at affordable prices. Vegetarians are also well catered for. Try the dumplings or the tandoori butter chicken in a deliciously creamy sauce. Upstairs is more cheerful than the basement dining room. The service is good and the atmosphere relaxed.

Saba   €€€€
26–28 Clarendon Street, Dublin 2 **Tel** *01 679 2000* **Map** *D4*

This slick Thai/Vietnamese eatery is a cut above the norm. Chef Trakoolwattana has previously cooked for the Thai royal family. Herbs, vegetables and fruit arrive weekly from Bangkok, ensuring fresh authentic flavours. The extensive menu features hake and banana leaf, red curry sauce, and crispy whole sea bass. Good vegetarian selection, too.

Eden

Meeting House Square, Temple Bar, Dublin 2 **Tel** *01 670 5372* **Map** *C3*

Featuring an outside terrace on the square, this split-level restaurant is bright and modern in design, with cool blue tiled walls and an open kitchen. Eden is famed for its sirloin steaks, cleverly arranged fish dishes and imaginative use of seasonal vegetables. The early evening menu provides excellent value for money.

Elephant & Castle

18 Temple Bar, Dublin 2 **Tel** *01 679 3121* **Map** *D3*

Very lively, this American-style brasserie in the heart of Temple Bar is invariably crowded. Have the mouth-watering chicken wings to start, and continue with the good omelettes, steaks, hamburgers and salads, all available at affordable prices. Weekend brunches are also popular. Telephone bookings are not accepted.

Fallon & Byrne

11–17 Exchequer Street, Dublin 2 **Tel** *01 472 1010* **Map** *D3*

A New York-style food hall combined with a French restaurant and a superlative wine cellar. There is also a food shop on the ground floor and a restaurant upstairs. The restaurant is open, spacious and bright, and serves particularly tasty breads. The wines are incredible, but beware – you can pay in excess of €1,000 a bottle here.

Lord Edward

23 Christchurch Place, Dublin 8 **Tel** *01 454 2420* **Map** *B4*

The oldest seafood restaurant in the city, Lord Edward is located above a cosy and traditional pub that serves lunch downstairs. It has changed little over the years and maintains an authentic, old-fashioned feel. The long-established waiters are renowned for their charming service.

The Mermaid Café

69–70 Dame Street, Dublin 2 **Tel** *01 670 8236* **Map** *C3*

A bright, contemporary restaurant with large windows and wooden furniture, The Mermaid Café is a firm favourite for weekend brunches. There is a certain American East Coast ambience about it, which is also evident in specialities such as New England crab cakes. The chef makes creative use of high quality Irish artisanal produce.

The Tea Room

The Clarence Hotel, 6–8 Wellington Quay, Dublin 2 **Tel** *01 407 0800* **Map** *C3*

The Clarence Hotel is owned by rock band U2. Come in by the Essex Street entrance, opposite the Project Theatre, and savour excellent cuisine served in a stylish dining room. High ceilings and large windows create a bright and airy atmosphere. The food is innovative and seasonal, and the lunch menu is particularly good value.

NORTH OF THE LIFFEY

The Cobalt Café

16 North Great George's Street, Dublin 1 **Tel** *01 873 0313* **Map** *D3*

This daytime café offers a range of home-made soups, sandwiches and cakes, as well as the delicious signature dish, Chicken Cobalt. The café doubles as a gallery exhibiting the works of up-and-coming Irish artists; as a result, it is a popular venue for art lovers.

Epicurean Food Hall

Lower Liffey Street, Dublin 1 **Map** *D2*

This food hall comprises a number of outlets serving international light meals and snacks. There is a communal dining area in the centre, or you can take your food away and enjoy it on a seat on the boardwalk overlooking the Liffey. Itsabagel's snacks and Burdock's fish and chips are on offer, as well as Turkish, Italian and Mexican cuisines.

Kingfisher Restaurant

166 Parnell Street, Dublin 1 **Tel** *01 872 8732* **Map** *C2*

Modestly decorated but immaculately maintained, Kingfisher Grill is a no-frills diner. Prompt service and cheap prices make it a good spot for the simple dishes many of us long for. Potato wedges and prawn cocktail are two of the more popular starters. Finish your meal with jelly or ice cream.

Panem

Ha'penny Bridge House, 21 Lower Ormond Quay, Dublin 1 **Tel** *01 872 8510* **Map** *C3*

This tiny café and bakery offers Italian and French food, freshly prepared using only high quality ingredients. The menu includes delicious croissants and focaccia with savoury fillings, sweet brioches with chocolate, home-baked biscuits and good coffee. The mouth-watering hot chocolate is made from dark Belgian chocolate. Friendly staff.

Bar Italia

Quartier Bloom, Lower Ormond Quay, Dublin 1 **Tel** *01 874 1000* **Map** *C3*

The popular Bar Italia, specializing in Italian fare, is always a hive of activity around lunchtime, when patrons stream in for freshly prepared antipasti, risottos, grilled vegetables or the pasta specials. Desserts are also an attraction, as is the excellent – and strong! – espresso.

Key to Price Guide *see p138* **Key to Symbols** *see back cover flap*

Kimchi at The Hop House

*160 Parnell Street, Dublin 1 **Tel** 01 872 8318*
Map *C2*

Tasty Korean food is on the menu at this restaurant with a warm, informal atmosphere. Kimchi offers a great variety of traditional Asian dishes, with sushi a house speciality. Prices are keen. Come here for a bite to eat, then spend the rest of the evening in the lively, adjoining Hop House bar.

101 Talbot

*100–102 Talbot Street, Dublin 2 **Tel** 01 874 5011*
Map *E2*

A Mediterranean approach is reflected in the decor as much as the cuisine at 101 Talbot, livening up the rather drab street on which it is located. The early-bird menu is good value and attracts many theatre-goers. Vegetarians are spoiled for choice at this restaurant, which will also do its utmost to meet any other dietary requirements.

The Still Room Restaurant

*Old Jameson Distillery, Bow Street, Dublin 1 **Tel** 01 807 2355*
Map *A2*

This restaurant is part of the Old Jameson Distillery complex, which lies on the site of the original 18th-century distillery. At lunchtime the legal eagles from the nearby Courts swoop in here to savour the comfort food on offer. Traditional dishes include a daily roast, as well as delicious sandwiches and soups.

Cactus Jacks

*Millennium Walkway, Middle Abbey Street, Dublin 1 **Tel** 01 874 6198*
Map *C3*

Part of the popular chain begun in Galway, this restaurant is modern and slick, with a low-lit setting. As well as authentic delicious Mexican food, Cactus Jacks serves simple but tasty steak, fish and vegetarian dishes that are lighter versions of traditional Mexican recipes. Nice frozen margaritas, too.

Koh

*6–7 Jervis Street, Millennium Walkway, Dublin 1 **Tel** 01 814 6777/6212*
Map *C2*

Koh offers elegant Asian dining in smart, ultra-modern surroundings on the bustling Millennium Walkway. It has an enjoyable night-time ambience, with potent cocktails, but it's also a good place for lunch, with its lively outdoor terrace providing a great place to stop between shops.

Milano

*Unit 6, Excise Walk, Clarion Quay, Dublin 1 **Tel** 01 611 9012*
Map *F2*

Milano is the chain run by the popular British eatery Pizza Express in Ireland. It is family-friendly, with a play area and face painter on Sundays, and features mainly Italian fare such as pizzas, pastas, and chicken dishes. Lunchtime is buzzing, and evenings see concert goers to the nearby O2 area stopping in.

Nancy Hands

*30–32 Parkgate Street, Dublin 8 **Tel** 01 677 0149*

Traditional Irish cuisine is on the menu at this restaurant next to Phoenix Park and the zoo. The open fireplace and wood and stone decor give an old-world atmosphere to this pub. The fare is of a good standard, a mix of traditional bar food, carvery and more international offerings. The chowder is particularly good.

Chapter One

*18–19 Parnell Square, Dublin 1 **Tel** 01 873 2266*
Map *C1*

In the basement of the Dublin Writers' Museum, Chapter One is often cited by critics as the best restaurant north of the Liffey. Relish the imaginative European cuisine, with an Irish twist, in a dining room of great character and comfort. The pre-theatre menu is a favourite among regulars who frequent the nearby Gate Theatre.

Ely chq

*Stack A, Mayor Street, IFSC, Dublin 1 **Tel** 01 672 0010*
Map *F2*

This offshoot of the Ely Wine Bar *(see p139)* boasts a stylish and contemporary decor. The food – whether from the bar or à la carte menu – is fresh and tasty, and there is an exceptional wine list, with almost 100 wines by the glass. Eat alfresco on the covered terrace, in the cavernous basement or in the spacious, ground floor interior.

Winding Stair

*40 Ormond Quay, Dublin 1 **Tel** 01 872 7320*
Map *D3*

At this slick and popular contemporary Irish restaurant, dishes include smoked haddock poached in milk with onions and white cheddar mash, or boiled Irish bacon collar with buttered new-season organic cabbage, mash and parsley sauce. Ingredients are organic and local where possible – even the chorizo is made in Ireland. No Diner or AmEx.

FURTHER AFIELD

Abbey Tavern

*Abbey Street, Howth, Co Dublin **Tel** 01 839 0307*

Open fires, linen-clad tables, fresh flowers and a slightly old-fashioned atmosphere define this restaurant on the first floor of a characteristic pub. Good, uncomplicated fish and meat dishes are served. The traditional Irish evening downstairs, featuring set dinners, is popular with visitors.

Angler's Rest

Knockmaroon Hill, Strawberry Beds, Chapelizod, Dublin 20 **Tel** *01 820 4351*

Long known as a watering hole for fishermen along the river, the Angler's Rest has an open fire, timber ceilings and floors, and comfortable seating. Specials include seafood chowder and platter – fish is delivered daily from Howth. At weekends there is live music, featuring a mix of artists. Michael Collins used to be a regular in the Salmon Bar.

Dali's Restaurant

63–65 Main Street, Blackrock, Co Dublin **Tel** *01 278 0660*

At this chic, small restaurant with a distinctive contemporary feel, menus are appealingly light and colourful. High-lights include variations on classic themes, such as seared scallops and Dublin Bay prawns. The set lunch menus offer particularly good value for money. There is also a good wine list and a varied cheese selection.

Expresso Bar Café

1 St Mary's Road, Ballsbridge, Dublin 4 **Tel** *01 660 0585*

This restaurant is decorated in a contemporary, minimalist style. Open from breakfast, it is popular for lunch and weekend brunches. The traditional Irish fare, featuring chicken, fish, steaks and Irish beefburgers, uses high quality ingredients. The bread-and-butter pudding makes a perfect dessert. The service could be friendlier, though.

Hartley's

1 Harbour Road, Dun Laoghaire, Co Dublin **Tel** *01 280 6767*

Conveniently located beside the harbour, ferry terminal and DART station, this welcoming restaurant is housed in a graceful period building. Seafood is a speciality, but the extensive menu makes room for steaks and a variety of pasta dishes too. The home-made desserts are delicious.

Independent Pizza

28 Lower Drumcondra Road, Dublin 7 **Tel** *01 830 2044*

This pizza house, owned by Gotham Café crew *(see p139)*, serves delicious, surprising and light American-style pizza, said to be the best in Dublin. Try the Texas Chicken, the Thai Spice or the Pizza of the Month. A good wine list is also available. Book ahead if you can: the place is extremely popular and always busy.

Johnnie Fox's

Glencullen, Co Dublin **Tel** *01 295 5647*

About 30 minutes' drive south of the city, on the way up to the Dublin Mountains, this friendly pub has good Irish food, open fires, traditional music and dancing. Pan-seared scallops, crab salad, smoked salmon and sirloin steak are on the menu. The "Hooley Night", featuring dinner and a traditional show, attracts overseas visitors. Book ahead.

Nosh

111 Coliemore Road, Dalkey, Co Dublin **Tel** *01 284 0666*

Nosh is contemporary in style, with light wood furniture. The well-balanced menus feature good fish and vegetarian dishes, as well as succulent steaks. Cod and chips, pea and asparagus risotto, and seared scallops also make appearances. The home-made desserts are good. The weekend brunch is very popular, as is the early-bird menu.

The Queens

Castle Street, Dalkey **Tel** *01 285 4569*

Established in 1745, The Queens is one of Ireland's oldest hostelries, right in the centre of Dalkey. It has grown into an award-winning restaurant serving everything from hamburgers to steamed mussels, or bacon and cabbage. The most pleasant tables are those located out front, with a view of the battlements of Goat's Castle, next door.

The Washerwoman's Hill Café

62a Glasnevin Hill, Dublin 9 **Tel** *01 837 9199*

A short stroll from the Botanic Gardens, this cosy restaurant is housed in an 18th-century building, one of the oldest in Glasnevin. It serves traditional food made from locally sourced ingredients. Try the pork belly with cider sauce, and the delicious chocolate brownies. While you eat, enjoy the original artworks on the walls – they are all for sale.

Beaufield Mews Restaurant, Gardens & Antiques

Woodlands Ave, Stillorgan, Co Dublin **Tel** *01 288 0375*

One of County Dublin's oldest restaurants, Beaufield Mews is beautifully set in an 18th-century cobbled courtyard with a rose garden to the rear. Good modern European food is served in an elegant dining room decorated with Irish art and antiques. An inviting atmosphere prevails throughout.

Caviston's Seafood Restaurant

59 Glasthule Road, Dun Laoghaire, Sandycove, Co Dublin **Tel** *01 280 9245*

Stunning seafood, prepared with simple flair, is on the menu at Caviston's. Sadly, this culinary cult address is only open for lunch, so be sure to book early and reserve the last sitting so that you can enjoy a leisurely afternoon lingering over coffee and dessert. The adjoining delicatessen sells delectable fare great for a picnic.

Eatery 120

120 Ranelagh Village, Dublin 6 **Tel** *01 470 4120*

A little gem in the heart of pretty Ranelagh Village, on Dublin's southside. Locals and visitors come for the delicious brasserie-style food, such as slow-cooked pork belly and pan-fried cod. Eatery 120's delightful decor (colourful tiles, stacked bookshelves and cosy seats), its excellent wine bar and friendly service are just some of the draws.

Key to Price Guide *see p138* **Key to Symbols** *see back cover flap*

The Forty Foot

Pavilion Centre, Dun Laoghaire, Co Dublin **Tel** *01 284 2982*

After a walk on the pier, relax in this very modern upstairs restaurant and watch the day fade over Dublin Bay. The views are the main attraction at The Forty Foot, but the food is also appealing. Try the tian of crab and salmon with crème fraîche. Pleasant and competent staff.

King Sitric Fish Restaurant and Accommodation

East Pier, Howth, Co Dublin **Tel** *01 832 5235*

Named after the medieval Norse king of Dublin, this restaurant is acclaimed for good seafood and game. The dining room is stylishly modern, with scenic views. Specialities include crab bisque, Balscadden Bay lobster, black sole meunière and fillet steak with forest mushrooms. Excellent wine cellar.

The Lobster Pot

9 Ballsbridge Terrace, Ballsbridge, Dublin 4 **Tel** *01 660 9170*

This long-established upstairs restaurant deservedly commands a loyal following. High-quality food is well presented and served by professional, charming waiters. Specialities feature dressed Kilmore crab, Dublin Bay prawns in Provençal sauce, generously sized sole on the bone, delicious steaks, and chicken and game dishes.

Aqua Restaurant

1 West Pier, Howth, Co Dublin **Tel** *01 832 0690*

This first floor restaurant, with lovely sea and harbour views, was formerly a yacht club and has been converted into a bright contemporary space. The cuisine betrays a Californian-Italian influence, prominent on the menu are steaks, as well as fish and chicken dishes. The set menus are good value. Sunday brunch is accompanied by live jazz.

Bon Appetit

9 St James Terrace, Malahide, Co Dublin **Tel** *01 845 0314*

Under the direction of chef-patron Oliver Dunne, this restaurant has retained its reputation as Malahide's fine dining choice. With a smart reception area and basement bistro, the restaurant takes a sophisticated, modern approach. Dishes include Aberdeen Angus beef with slow-roasted tomato and Bordelaise onion pomme purée.

Roly's Bistro

7 Ballsbridge Terrace, Ballsbridge, Dublin 4 **Tel** *01 668 2611*

In the heart of Ballsbridge, this lively, bustling bistro offers reliable, colourful and delicious food. Try the Kerry lamb pie or the Dublin Bay prawns Provençal. Other delicacies include fish and game dishes and succulent steaks. Sit upstairs, if possible, and take home the delicious home-made breads, which are for sale. Reservations are advised.

BEYOND DUBLIN

Franzini O'Briens

French's Lane, by Trim Castle, Co Meath **Tel** *046 943 1002*

Modern and crisp in both decor and cuisine, this restaurant beside Trim Castle offers contemporary European cuisine. Food is prepared simply but to a high standard, and includes chicken and pasta dishes, pizzas and steaks. Vegetarians will have plenty of choice, too. The staff are very welcoming, and there is a good wine list.

O'Brien's Good Food and Drink House

The Village, Johnstown, Navan, Co Meath **Tel** *046 902 0555*

The menu at this award-winning gastropub with wood panelling, brick walls and a rustic feel includes spring rolls and pizzas. Seafood dishes are a speciality: try the Seafood Surprise, a pie dish full of prawns, salmon, monkfish and other sea creatures. Leave some room for the ginger and honeycomb pudding. Live music on Friday nights.

Wineport Lodge

Glasson, Athlone, Co Westmeath **Tel** *090 643 9010*

Ireland's first wine hotel is housed in a modern, cedar-clad structure on the shores of Lough Ree – you can even arrive by boat if you wish. The mission statement says they believe in good food, great wine and relaxation, and they certainly deliver on all three. Seasonal local food is creatively mastered. The wine list is extensive.

The Harvest Room

Arthurstown, Co Wexford **Tel** *051 389 600*

TV chef Kevin Dundon, one of Ireland's best, runs a cookery school at this award-winning restaurant at the Dunbrody Country House Hotel. The understated dishes rely on the freshness and quality of locally sourced seasonal ingredients – some from the kitchen garden and orchard. The airy dining room overlooks the garden. No children after 8pm.

The Strawberry Tree

Brooklodge Hotel, Macreddin Village, Co Wicklow **Tel** *0402 36444*

Ireland's only certified organic restaurant, at the Brooklodge Hotel, serves only wild and organic foods sourced from local artisan suppliers. Large feasts can be arranged for parties of eight or more. Try the wild wood pigeon terrine with strawberry and green pepper jam, or the carrot and orange sorbet, described by critics as "a slice of heaven".

Pubs, Bars and Cafés

Dublin's pubs are a slice of living history, famous as the haunts of literary figures, politicans and rock stars alike. Today, as well as the memorabilia on the walls, it is the singing, dancing, talk and laughter that make a pub tour of Dublin a necessity *(see p156)*.

There are nearly 1,000 pubs inside the city limits. Some excel in entertainment, others in the quality of their Guinness and their pub food, but there are also many modern bars to match the best in Europe.

Dublin is very cosmopolitan and, as well as the pubs, there is a wide range of cafés offering quick and inexpensive food. The ones listed here are good for those on a busy sightseeing schedule.

TRADITIONAL PUBS

Each Dublin pub has its own character and, while many of them are rather touristy, they retain a trademark clientèle: **Doheny & Nesbitt** and the **Horseshoe Bar** attract politi-cians, journalists and lawyers, while **Neary's** pulls in a theatrical crowd. Others have a strong literary connection; Brendan Behan drank at **McDaid's** while **Davy Byrne's** was featured in Joyce's *Ulysses*. Some of the best and most ornate interiors include **The Brazen Head**, the **Stag's Head**, **The Long Hall** and **John Kehoe's** with its great snugs. **Mulligan's**, founded in 1782, claims to have the best Guin-ness. If you fancy something different, **Porter House** in Parliament Street brews its own, including an excellent oyster stout.

MUSIC PUBS

Regular traditional music sessions take place all over Dublin. **The Brazen Head** *(see Traditional Pubs)*, **O'Donoghue's** and the **Cobblestone** are popular venues. The **International Bar** focuses on singers and comedians, while **Whelan's** has a proper venue room next door with an eclectic range of acts for a cover charge of under 10 euros.

MODERN BARS

A number of Continental-style bars cater to a young and fashionable crowd. **Hogan's** and **The Globe** are on the edge of Temple Bar. The **Octagon Bar** at the Clarence Hotel does great cocktails. Inventive drinks are also on the menu at the trendy **Tripod**. **Café en Seine** near Trinity College has a wide choice of food and offers a live jazz brunch on Sunday.

PUB FOOD

Many of Dublin's grand old pubs offer tasty and good-value pub lunches. Just off Grafton Street are **O'Neill's** and the very traditional **The Old Stand**. In Temple Bar, **Oliver St John Gogarty** is probably the best option.

MUSEUM AND SHOP CAFES

Many of Dublin's tourist attractions offer good-quality cafés and snack bars. One of the best is at the **National Gallery**: it serves mainly Mediterranean food and is operated by the Fitzer's chain. Food at the **National Museum** has more of a traditional Irish choice while the **Irish Film Institute** offers an eclectic range. Food at **Avoca Café** is modern and delicious: go early if you want to get in. For a unique place to eat, try the upstairs café at the **Winding Stair Bookshop**.

BREAKFAST

Most hotels and B&Bs in the city serve reasonable breakfasts, an essential start to a full day's sightseeing. A particular favourite of Dubliners is **Café Java**, while **Odessa** is the place to visit for fancy breakfasts and brunches. **Café Kylemore** also makes a good breakfast.

COFFEE AND CAKES

In an attractive setting among the stalls at Powerscourt Townhouse, **Mimo** offers coffee, fresh food and a good wine selection in a relaxed, spacious environment.

PIZZA AND PASTA

Irish-Italian cafés and restaurants offer some of the best-value meals in the city. Two very popular ones, the family-oriented **Little Caesar's Palace** and the tiny **Steps of Rome**, lie off Grafton Street, as does the excellent **Pasta Fresca**. Temple Bar's **Bad Ass Café** has a youthful feel and serves pizza, pasta and salads. Sinéad O'Connor worked here before making it in music. **Milano**, currently with two branches in the city, is a branch of the popular British chain Pizza Express.

TRADITIONAL FOOD

For traditional food with a modern slant, **Gallagher's Boxty House**, specializing in Irish pancakes, is a popular choice. However, some might prefer the even simpler fare at **Café Kylemore** *(see Breakfast)*, which is run by a major city bakery. For good, honest fish and chips, try the venerable **Leo Burdock's** or **Beshoff's**.

VEGETARIAN

One of the great favourites is the long-running café, **Cornucopia**, also open for breakfast and lunch. **Café Fresh** is a fun place to eat in the Powerscourt Townhouse while **Juice** offers a cool, modern feel. The **Alamo Café** is the pick of the city's Mexican restaurants and offers lots of choice for vegetarians but also serves meat dishes. Temple Bar's Saturday market has a good organic selection.

DIRECTORY

TRADITIONAL PUBS

The Brazen Head
20 Bridge St Lower.
Map A3.
Tel 679 5186.

Davy Byrne's
21 Duke St.
Map D4.
Tel 677 5217.

Doheny & Nesbitt
5 Lower Baggot St.
Map F5.
Tel 676 2945.

Horseshoe Bar
Shelbourne Hotel,
27 St Stephen's Green.
Map E4.
Tel 663 4500.

John Kehoe's
9 Anne St South.
Map D4.
Tel 677 8312.

The Long Hall
51 South Great George's
St. Map C4.
Tel 475 1590.

McDaid's
3 Harry St.
Map D4.
Tel 679 4395.

Mulligan's
8 Poolbeg St.
Map E3.
Tel 677 5582.

Neary's
1 Chatham St.
Map D4.
Tel 677 8596.

Porter House
16–18 Parliament St.
Map C3.
Tel 679 8847.

Stag's Head
1 Dame Court,
off Dame St. Map C3.
Tel 679 3687.

MUSIC BARS

Cobblestone
77 North King St.
Map A2.
Tel 872 1799.

International Bar
23 Wicklow St.
Map D3.
Tel 677 9250.

O'Donoghue's
15 Merrion Row.
Map E5.
Tel 676 2807.

Whelan's
25 Wexford St.
Map C5.
Tel 478 0766.

MODERN BARS

Café en Seine
40 Dawson St.
Map D4.
Tel 677 4567.

The Globe
11 South Great
George's St. Map C4.
Tel 671 1220.

Hogan's
35 South Great
George's St. Map C4.
Tel 677 5904.

Octagon Bar
Clarence Hotel,
6–8 Wellington Quay.
Map C3.
Tel 670 9000.

Tripod
Harcourt St, at Hatch St
Lower. Map D5.
Tel 476 3374.

PUB FOOD

The Old Stand
37 Exchequer St.
Map D3.
Tel 677 7220.

**Oliver St John
Gogarty**
57 Fleet St.
Map D3.
Tel 671 1822.

O'Neill's
2 Suffolk St.
Map D3.
Tel 679 3656.

MUSEUM AND SHOP CAFÉS

Avoca Café
11–13 Suffolk St.
Map D3.
Tel 286 7466.

Irish Film Institute
6 Eustace St,
Temple Bar.
Map C3.
Tel 679 3477.

National Gallery
Merrion Square West.
Map E4.
Tel 661 5133.

National Museum
Kildare St.
Map E4.
Tel 677 7444.

**Winding Stair
Bookshop**
40 Ormond Quay Lower.
Map C3.
Tel 872 7320.

BREAKFAST

Café Java
145 Leeson St.
Map E5.
Tel 660 0675.

Café Kylemore
O'Connell St.
Map D2.
Tel 872 2138.

Odessa
14 Dame Court.
Map C3.
Tel 670 4195.

COFFEE AND CAKES

Mimo
Powerscourt Townhouse,
South William St.
Map D4.
Tel 679 4160.

PIZZA AND PASTA

Bad Ass Café
9 Crown Alley,
Temple Bar.
Map D3.
Tel 671 2596.

**Little Caesar's
Palace**
1–3 Balfe St. Map D4.
Tel 670 4534.

Milano
38 Dawson St.
Map D4.
Tel 670 7744.
19 Essex St East.
Map C3.
Tel 670 3384.

Pasta Fresca
4 Chatham St.
Map D4.
Tel 679 2402.

Steps of Rome
Unit 1, Chatham Court,
Chatham St.
Map D4.
Tel 670 5630.

TRADITIONAL FOOD

Beshoff's
O'Connell St.
Map D2.
Tel 462 4181.

**Gallagher's
Boxty House**
Temple Bar.
Map D3.
Tel 677 2762.

Leo Burdock's
2 Werburgh St.
Map C4.
Tel 454 0306.

VEGETARIAN

Alamo Café
22 Temple Bar.
Map C3.
Tel 677 6546.

Café Fresh
Powerscourt Townhouse,
South William St.
Map D4.
Tel 671 9669.

Cornucopia
19 Wicklow St.
Map D3.
Tel 677 7583.

Juice
9 Castlehouse
South Great George's St.
Map C4.
Tel 475 7856.

SHOPS AND MARKETS

Dublin is a paradise for shoppers, with its wide streets, indoor markets, craft stores and out-of-town shopping centres. Popular buys include chunky Aran sweaters, Waterford crystal, Irish linen, hand-loomed tweed from Donegal and tasty farmhouse cheeses. The thriving crafts industry is based on traditional products with an innovative twist. Typical of contemporary Irish crafts are good design, quality craftsmanship and a range spanning

Modern Irish pottery

Celtic brooches and bone china, knitwear and designer fashion, carved bogwood and books of Irish poetry. Kitsch souvenirs also abound, from leprechauns and shamrock emblems to Guinness tankards and garish religious memorabilia. Irish whiskeys and liqueurs are always popular and very reasonable to buy in Dublin.

In the directory on page 151, a map reference is given for each address that features on the Dublin Street Finder map on pages 180–81.

Johnson's Court alley behind Grafton Street in southwest Dublin

WHERE TO SHOP

There are two major shopping quarters in Dublin. The north side of the Liffey, centred on O'Connell and Henry streets, has several shopping centres and department stores. The famous Moore Street fruit and vegetable market is held Monday to Saturday just off Grafton Street. More upmarket shops can be found on the south side, around Grafton and Nassau streets. The Temple Bar area contains a number of trendy craft shops.

WHEN TO SHOP

Most shops are open from Monday to Saturday, 9am to 5:30 or 6pm. Shops open late on Thursday nights. Shops are closed at Easter and Christmas and on St Patrick's Day but are open on most other public holidays.

HOW TO PAY

Major credit cards such as VISA and MasterCard are accepted in most large stores, but smaller shops may prefer cash. Traveller's cheques are accepted in major stores with a passport as identification. Eurocheques are generally no longer acceptable.

SALES TAX AND REFUNDS

Most purchases are subject to VAT (sales tax) at 21 per cent, a sum included in the sales price. However, visitors from outside the European Union (EU) can reclaim VAT prior to departure. If you are shipping goods overseas, refunds can be claimed at the point of purchase. If taking your goods with you, look for the CashBack logo in shops, fill in the special voucher, then visit the CashBack offices at Dublin airport.

SHOPPING CENTRES

Dublin has several large shopping centres, including the **Dundrum Shopping Centre**, voted the best in Ireland in 2009. The **Dun Laoghaire Shopping Centre** is on several floors and has a huge range of clothes shops, bookshops and electronics shops. In central Dublin are the **St Stephen's Green Shopping Centre** and the **Jervis Shopping Centre**, both offering the comfort of covered shopping. A more unusual centre is the **Powerscourt Townhouse** (see p60), more an indoor market than a shopping centre, selling various Irish crafts. **Kildare Village**, on the outskirts of town, is good for outlet shopping.

BOOKS

Bookshops abound in Dublin. **Eason and Son**, on O'Connell Street, is the biggest bookseller in the city with a wide

The Ha'penny Bridge Galleries on Bachelors Walk

Brown Thomas department store on Grafton Street

range of Irish literature and national and international newspapers. For antiquarian books, **Cathach Books** on Duke Street is excellent.

Foreign-language books are available in Dublin – try **International Books** for the best range. **Hodges Figgis** specializes in Irish literature and academic publications. They also have a coffee shop in the store. One of the best for general books is the **Dublin Book-shop** on Grafton Street (part of the Dubray Books chain). On two floors, they have an extensive Irish section and a good range of tourist guides as well as general fiction and children's books. **Chapters** and **Hughes & Hughes** are also both good general booksellers.

Sign outside Eason and Son

MUSIC

Traditional musical instruments are made in many regions of Ireland, but Dublin has a history of specializing in hand-made harps. Several shops sell musical instruments, such as hand-crafted bodhráns (traditional goatskin hand-held drums) and uilleann pipes (bagpipes). **Waltons** sells traditional instruments and sheet music, while **Claddagh Records** is a specialist folk shop, selling Irish folk and ethnic music. For a standard range of pop and classical music there are two branches of the **HMV** music store in Dublin.

ANTIQUES

Dublin has its own antiques centre, in the form of Francis Street in the south west of the city. **Lantern Antiques** specializes in old pub fittings such as mirrors and old advertisements. For rugs and carpets try **Forsyth Antiques**. For 20th-century decorative arts visit **Johnston Antiques. The Ha'penny Bridge Galleries** sell everything from furniture through to cast iron and marble. **Courtville Antiques** in the Powerscourt Townhouse has a beautiful collection of antique jewellery, silver, paintings and objets d'art. On Grafton Street, **McCormack** is particularly good for antique jewellery.

CRAFTS

Whichcraft at the Designyard Gallery on Nassau Street and the **Irish Celtic Craftshop** in Lord Edward Street have a

great range of contemporary Irish crafts. The Crafts Council also recommends other good outlets for Irish crafts, and the tourist offices have lists of local workshops, where you can often watch the production process. **The Kilkenny Shop** sells tiles, rugs, metal-, leather- and woodwork.

JEWELLERY

In its golden age, Celtic metalwork was the pride of Ireland. Many contemporary craftspeople are still inspired by traditional designs on Celtic chalices and ornaments. Silver and gold jewellery is made all over Ireland in many designs and widely available in Dublin. The Claddagh ring is the most famous of all – the lovers' symbol of two hands cradling a heart with a crown. In the Powerscourt Town-house, shops have handmade and antique jewellery on display and gold- and silver-smiths can be seen at work. **McDowell** jewellers specialize in handcrafted gold and silver Irish jewellery.

CHINA, CRYSTAL AND GLASSWARE

Ireland's most famous make of crystalware is Waterford Crystal. Still made today in the town of Waterford, south of Dublin, this beautiful crystal and glassware is known all over the world for its outstanding quality.

Dublin Crystal, in Blackrock, south of the city, makes and sells on the premises fine-quality hand-cut crystal.

There are many producers of fine china in Ireland. Royal Tara China in Galway is Ireland's leading fine bone china manufacturer, with designs incorporating Celtic themes. The best place to buy china and glassware is in department stores, such as Clery's and Brown Thomas.

Bodhráns of perfect pitch for sale in Dublin

LINEN

Damask linen was brought to Armagh in Northern Ireland by Huguenot refugees fleeing French persecution. Linen is widely available all over Ireland today, and fine Irish linen can be bought at many outlets in Dublin, including the **Brown Thomas** department store, which has an excellent linen shop. Another good supplier is **Murphy, Sheehy and Co**, who are located behind the Powercourt Townhouse. As well as being famous for fine-quality Irish linen, they also sell tweeds.

Sign for the linen department at Brown Thomas store

KNITWEAR AND TWEED

Aran sweaters are sold all over Ireland, but originate in County Galway and the Aran Islands themselves, off the west coast of Ireland. One of Dublin's best buys, these oiled, off-white sweaters used to be handed down through generations of Aran fishermen. Legend has it that each family used its own motifs so that, if a fisherman were lost at sea and his body unidentifiable, his family could recognize him by his sweater. Warm and rain-resistant clothes are generally of good quality, from waxed jackets and duffel coats to sheepskin jackets. **House of Ireland** offer an excellent selection of quality Irish clothing. Knitwear is sold everywhere in Dublin.

Good buys include embroidered waistcoats and handwoven scarves. **The Sweater Shop** has woollens and tweeds at reasonable prices. The Suffolk Street branch of **Avoca** has a good mix of traditional and trendy.

Donegal tweed is noted for its texture and subtle colours (originally produced by local plant and mineral dyes). Tweed caps, scarves, ties, jackets and suits are sold in outlets such as **Kevin & Howlin** in Dublin. For menswear specialists, try **Kennedy & McSharry**.

FASHION

Inspired by a predominantly young population, Ireland is fast acquiring a name for fashion. Conservatively cut tweed and linen suits continue to be models of classic good taste, while younger designers are increasingly experimental, using bold lines and mixing traditional fabrics. **A-Wear** is an Irish chain store with branches in Dublin. The Design Centre in Powerscourt Townhouse Shopping Centre features the best Irish designers including Paul Costelloe, Louise Kennedy, Quin and Donnelly and Mariad Whisker. The Loft Market at Powerscourt showcases up-and-coming design talent (Thu, Sat, Sun). The department stores **Brown Thomas** and **Clery's** have an excellent selection of men's, women's and children's clothing.

Fresh cheeses in Meetinghouse Square

FOOD AND DRINK

Smoked salmon, home-cured bacon, farmhouse cheeses, preserves, soda bread and handmade chocolates make perfect last-minute gifts. **Butlers Chocolate Café**, sells particularly delicious handmade Irish chocolates. Several shops will package and send Irish salmon overseas.

Bewley's teas and coffees are sold in supermarkets like Tescos, **Dunnes** and Super Value all over Ireland. Guinness travels less well and is best drunk in Ireland. Irish whiskey is hard to beat as a gift or souvenir. Apart from the cheaper Power and Paddy brands, the big names are Bushmills and Jameson. Irish liqueurs to enjoy include Irish Mist and Bailey's Irish Cream.

Fresh fruit stall off O'Connell Street

DIRECTORY

SHOPPING CENTRES

Dun Laoghaire Shopping Centre
Marine Rd, Dun Laoghaire.
Tel 280 2981.

Dundrum Shopping Centre
Sandyford Rd, Dundrum, Dublin 16.
Tel 299 1700.
www.dundrum.ie

Jervis Shopping Centre
125 Abbey St Upper.
Map C2.
Tel 878 1323.

Kildare Village
Nurney Rd, Kildare Town, Co. Kildare.
Tel 455 20501.

Powerscourt Townhouse
South William St.
Map D4.
Tel 671 7000.
www.powerscourtcentre.com

St Stephen's Green Shopping Centre
St Stephen's Green West.
Map D4.
Tel 478 0888.

BOOKS

Cathach Books
10 Duke St.
Map D4.
Tel 671 8676.
www.rarebooks.ie

Chapters Bookstore
Ivy Exchange, Parnell Street, Dublin 1.
Map C1.
Tel 872 3297.

Dublin Bookshop
36 Grafton St.
Map D4.
Tel 677 5568.

Eason and Son
80 Middle Abbey St.
Map D2.
Tel 858 3881.
www.eason.ie

Hodges Figgis
56–58 Dawson St.
Map D4.
Tel 677 4754.

Hughes & Hughes
St Stephen's Green Shopping Centre.
Map D4.
Tel 478 3060.
Also at Dublin Airport.
Tel 704 4034.

International Books
18 Frederick St South.
Map E4.
Tel 679 9375.
www.internationalbooks.ie

MUSIC

Claddagh Records
2 Cecilia St, Temple Bar.
Map C3.
Tel 677 0262.

HMV
18 Henry St. **Map** D2.
Tel 873 2899.
Also at Grafton St.
Map D4.
Tel 679 5334.

Waltons
3–5 Frederick St North.
Map C1.
Tel 874 7805.

ANTIQUES

Courtville Antiques
Powerscourt Townhouse Shopping Centre.
Map D4.
Tel 679 4042.

Forsyth Antiques
108 Francis St.
Map B4.
Tel 473 2148.

The Ha'penny Bridge Galleries
15 Bachelors Walk.
Map D3.
Tel 872 3950.

Johnston Antiques
69–70 Francis St.
Map B4.
Tel 473 2384.
www.johnstonantiques.net

Lantern Antiques
56 Francis St
Map B4.
Tel 453 4593.

McCormack
51 Grafton St.
Map D4.
Tel 677 3737.

CRAFTS

Irish Celtic Craftshop
10–12 Lord Edward St.
Map C3.
Tel 679 9912.

The Kilkenny Shop
6 Nassau St. **Map** E4.
Tel 677 7066.
www.kilkennygroup.com

Whichcraft
Designyard Gallery, 48–49 Nassau St.
Map D3.
Tel 474 1011.
www.whichcraft.com

JEWELLERY

McDowell
3 Upper O'Connell St.
Map D2.
Tel 874 4961.

CERAMICS, CHINA AND CRYSTAL

Dublin Crystal
Dundrum Shopping Centre.
Tel 298 7302.
www.dublincrystal.com

LINENS

Brown Thomas (Linen Department)
Grafton St. **Map** D4.
Tel 605 6666.
www.brownthomas.com

Murphy, Sheehy and Co
14 Castle Market.
Map D4
Tel 677 0316.
www.murphysheehyfabrics.com

KNITWEAR AND TWEED

Avoca
11–13 Suffolk St.
Map D3.
Tel 677 4215.
www.avoca.ie

House of Ireland
37–38 Nassau St.
Map D4.
Tel 671 1111.
www.houseofireland.com

Kennedy & McSharry
39 Nassau St.
Map D3.
Tel 677 8770.

Kevin & Howlin
31 Nassau St.
Map D3.
Tel 677 0257.

The Sweater Shop
9 Wicklow St.
Map D3.
Tel 671 3270.
www.sweatershop.ie

FASHION

A-Wear
26 Grafton St.
Map D4.
Tel 671 7200.
www.awear.ie

Brown Thomas
88–95 Grafton St.
Map D4.
Tel 605 6666.

Clery's
18–27 O'Connell St Lower.
Map D2.
Tel 878 6000.
www.clerys.ie

FOOD AND DRINK

Butlers Chocolate Café
51a Grafton St.
Map D4.
Tel 671 0599.

Dunnes
Henry St.
Map D2.
Tel 671 4629.

What to Buy in Dublin

St Brigid's cross

The many gift and craft shops scattered throughout Dublin make it easy to find Irish specialities to suit all budgets. The best buys include linen, tweeds and lead crystal. Local crafts make unique souvenirs, from delicate handmade silver jewellery and hand-thrown ceramics to traditional musical instruments. Religious artifacts are also widely available. Irish food and drink, especially whiskey, are evocative reminders of your trip.

Traditional hand-held drum (*bodhrán*) and beater

Connemara marble "worry stone"

Traditional Claddagh ring

Modern jewellery and metalwork *draw on a long and varied tradition. Craftspeople continue to base their designs on sources such as the* Book of Kells *(see p40) and Celtic myths. Local plants and wildlife are also an inspiration. Claddagh rings – traditional betrothal rings – originated in County Galway but are widely available in Dublin.*

Enamel brooch

Fuchsia earring from Dingle

Celtic design enamel brooch

Celtic design silver pendant

Donegal tweed jacket and waistcoat

Tweed jacket and skirt

Clothing *made in Ireland is usually of excellent quality. Tweed-making still flourishes in Donegal where tweed can be bought ready-made as clothing or hats or as lengths of cloth. Knitwear is widely available throughout Dublin in department stores and local craft shops. The many hand-knitted items on sale, including Aran jumpers, are not cheap but should give years of wear.*

Tweed cap

Tweed fisherman's hat

Aran jumper

Irish linen *is world-famous and the range unparalleled. There is a huge choice of table and bed linen, including extravagant bedspreads and crisp, formal tablecloths. On a smaller scale, tiny, intricately embroidered handkerchiefs make lovely gifts as do linen table napkins. Tea towels printed with colourful designs are widely available. You can also buy linen goods trimmed with fine lace, which is still handmade in many parts of the country.*

Set of linen placemats and napkins

Nicholas Mosse plate

Belleek teapot

Nicholas Mosse cup

Fine linen handkerchiefs

Irish ceramics *come in traditional and modern designs. You can buy anything from a full dinner service by established factories, such as Royal Tara China or the Belleek Pottery, to a one-off contemporary piece from a local potter's studio.*

Irish crystal, *hand-blown and hand-cut, can be ordered or bought in many shops in Dublin. Pieces from the principal manufacturers, such as Waterford Crystal, Tyrone Crystal and Jerpoint Glass, from glasses and decanters to elaborate chandeliers, are widely sold.*

·IRISH· PROVERBS

ILLUSTRATED BY KAREN BAILEY

Book of Irish Proverbs

Books and stationery *are often beautifully illustrated. Museums and bookshops stock a wide range.*

Celtic design cards

Waterford crystal tumbler and decanter

Food and drink *will keep the distinctive tastes of Dublin fresh long after you arrive home. Whiskey connoisseurs should visit the Old Jameson Distillery (see p75) to sample their choice of whiskeys. The Guinness Storehouse (see p82) is a must for aficionados of the dark stout. Good regional food can be found all over the Dublin area.*

| Jameson whiskey | Bushmills whiskey | Fruit cake made with Guinness | Jar of Irish marmalade | Packet of dried seaweed |

ENTERTAINMENT IN DUBLIN

Although Dublin is well served by theatres, cinemas, night-clubs and rock venues, what sets the city apart from other European capitals is its pubs. Lively banter, impromptu music sessions and great Guinness are the essential ingredients for an enjoyable night in any one of dozens of lively, atmospheric hostelries in Dublin.

One of the most popular entertainment districts is the Temple Bar area. Along this narrow network of cobbled streets you can find everything from traditional music in grand old pubs to the latest dance tracks in a post-industrial setting. The variety of venues makes the centre south of the Liffey the place to be at night, although the north side does boast the two most illustrious theatres, the largest cinemas and the 7,000-seater Point Theatre, a converted 19th-century rail terminal beside the docks. It is now the venue for all major rock concerts and stage musicals as well as some classical music performances.

Traditional Irish dancer

ENTERTAINMENT LISTINGS

Entertainment listings can be found in the online directory www.dublin.ie. *The Dubliner* magazine also reviews bars and restaurants.

Hot Press, a national bimonthly newspaper, covers rock and traditional music, and it has comprehensive listings for Dublin. The *Dublin Event Guide* is a free sheet available from pubs, cafés, restaurants and record shops. Published every two weeks, it is particularly strong on the city's music and nightclub scene.

Listings are also available in the free morning paper *Metro Herald* and in *Totally Dublin* magazine.

BOOKING TICKETS

Tickets for many events are available on the night, but it is safer to book in advance. The main venues accept payment over the telephone by all major credit cards. **Ticketmaster** accepts phone bookings by credit card for many of the major shows in and around Dublin, while **HMV** and Dublin Tourism in Suffolk Street *(see p165)* sell tickets for theatres and gigs.

NIGHTCLUBS

Dublin's nightclub scene offers plenty of choice. **POD** (Place of Dance) has renowned DJs performing, while the decadent vibe of **Lillie's Bordello** is a magnet for celebrities and visiting stars. **Krystle** is a glitzy club frequented by Dublin's glamorous model set. The more laid-back **Rí-Rá** (Gaelic for "uproar") is at the cutting edge of R&B and dance music.

For a lounge atmosphere, head for **The Sugar Club**, which offers live music and potent cocktails.

Club M, in the basement of Bloom's Hotel, plays chart, dance and R&B hits. Another popular basement club is **Boomerang**, with three bars, a state-of-the-art sound system and a different music mix each night.

Nightclubs in Dublin are being replaced by "super pubs" with dance floors. This has led to the rise of the "club night", which hosts a particular DJ or music genre

The decadent interior of Lillie's Bordello, reminiscent of a boudoir

on a given night of the week. Check out the club nights at POD, named Crawdaddy and Tripod, which involve a mix of electro, break beats, house and hip hop.

Copper Face Jack's is a lively and popular nightclub known to Dubliners simply as Coppers. It has DJs playing chart music late into the night all week long, attracting a young, unpretentious and fun-loving crowd. At **The Village**, DJs take to the decks every night, and there is karaoke on Sundays. The music at **Thinktank** covers everything from retro grooves to contemporary house.

The Academy is a live music venue and club, playing mainly indie, alternative and

Street entertainer in central Dublin

Buskers playing on Grafton Street in Southeast Dublin

legendary Dubliners started out in the early 1960s. The long-established **Auld Dubliner** and **Cobblestone** are also renowned venues for local and foreign bands. **The Merry Ploughboy** hosts traditional nights with an exciting mix of music and dancing involving many of Ireland's finest talents. **The Farmhouse Bar** and the **Castle Inn** stage Irish cabaret featuring dancing, singing and lively, toe-tapping music.

electro. Fridays at **The Vaults** see a mix of electro house, progressive and techno trance, while Saturdays host R&B, hip hop, soul and funk.

The George, a gay pub and club that has been running since 1985, stages popular drag shows, as well as Irish and international acts.

South William is a chic retro cocktail bar with a cool crowd and eclectic music. Tuesdays are devoted to Brazilian music and food, and the monthly programme also features Caribbean parties and swing jive cabaret nights. Friday's Sub Zero is a mix of indie, ska, alternative and funk downstairs in **Thomas Reads** pub.

CLASSICAL MUSIC, OPERA AND DANCE

Dublin has a great venue in the **National Concert Hall**, a 19th-century exhibition hall that was redesigned and acoustically adapted in the 1980s. This is where the National Symphony Orchestra plays most Friday evenings. The programme also includes jazz, dance, opera, chamber music and some traditional Irish music.

The **Hugh Lane Municipal Gallery of Modern Art** *(see p73)* has regular Sunday lunchtime concerts. Other classical venues include the **Royal Hospital Kilmainham** *(see p84)* and the **Royal Dublin Society (RDS)**. Irish National Opera performs every April and November at the **Gaiety Theatre** on King Street South.

COMEDY

The Laughter Lounge is one of Dublin's top comedy venues, attracting big names from the world of stand-up comedy. Other venues include the **Olympia Theatre** for international stars and **The Ha'penny Bridge Inn**, Tuesday to Thursday, for local talent. The Ha'Penny Laugh is a comedy improvisation show on Thursday nights.

The Laughter Lounge

TRADITIONAL MUSIC AND DANCE

To many Irish people, the standard of music in a pub is just as important as the quality of the Guinness. Central Dublin has a host of pubs reverberating to the sound of bodhráns, fiddles and uilleann pipes. One of the most famous is **O'Donoghue's**, where the

ROCK, JAZZ, BLUES, SALSA AND COUNTRY

Dublin has had a thriving rock scene ever since local band Thin Lizzy made it big in the early 1970s. U2's success acted as a further catalyst for local bands, and there is a gig somewhere in the city on most nights. **Whelan's** features the best new Irish bands nightly; the **International Bar** caters mostly for acoustic acts and singer-songwriters; and **The Ha'penny Bridge Inn** *(see Comedy)* has folk and blues on Fridays and Saturdays. Big names play at either **The O2** or, in summer, local sports stadia. **Slane Castle** often hosts a big rock event in summer.

The Button Factory and **The Sugar Club** *(see Nightclubs)* offer jazz, blues, salsa, swing and latin throughout the year, while **Heineken Green Spheres** organizes gigs and events all year round, attracting artists such as Goldfrapp. Country music also has a big following.

Crowds dancing at The Sugar Club

The glamorous Horseshoe Bar in the Shelbourne Hotel

HOTEL BARS

The hotel bars are the city's sophisticated watering holes, appealing to those who wish to escape the raucous "craic" of the more traditional pubs.

The **Inn on the Green**, located in the Fitzwilliam Hotel, features Nineties cool metal decor. At the Merrion Hotel, you can hide from the hubbub of the city in the **Cellar Bar**. Trendy media types hang out at the mellow **Octagon Bar** at The Clarence Hotel, or at the **Lobo Bar** at the Morrison. However, if it is undiluted glamour you seek, head for a shot of whiskey in **The Horseshoe Bar**, located within the renowned Shelbourne Hotel.

PUB CRAWLS AND TOURS

There are a number of organized pub crawls in Dublin, most of which cover the character pubs and those with a long and colourful history. The **Dublin Literary Pub Crawl**, which starts in The Duke pub on Duke Street, is perhaps the most famous of these. The

two-and-a-half-hour tours feature pubs once frequented by Ireland's most famous authors and playwrights, including Oscar Wilde, Samuel Beckett and Brendan Behan.

Viking Splash Tours operate a land-and-water sightseeing tour of Dublin. This tour departs from St Stephen's Green North (opposite Dawson Street) and is carried out in an amphibious military vehicle decorated as a Viking ship and complete with Viking costumed driver.

A handful of tours around the city offer an insight into Dublin's dark and spooky history. **The Walk Macabre**, for example, visits scenes of murder and intrigue in the city. If you prefer to be driven around, the **Dublin Ghost Bus Tour** offers on-board entertainment as well as lessons in bodysnatching and the story behind Bram Stoker's *Dracula*.

If tracing Dublin's musical heritage is of more interest to you, join the **Music Hall of Fame**. This tour takes you to the sites where bands such as U2 and Thin Lizzy first found fame. The **Musical Pub Crawl** is another tour that traces the history of Irish music, with musicians performing from pub to pub.

The **Historical Walking Tour** of Dublin takes in many of the significant locations of the city's colourful past.

For more guided tours of Dublin, see p175.

One of the amphibious vehicles used by Viking Splash Tours

Record shop and ticket office in Crown Alley, Temple Bar

CINEMA

Dublin's cinemas have had a boost thanks to the success of Dublin-based films such as *My Left Foot* (1989), *The Commitments* (1991) and *Michael Collins* (1996) and a subsequent growth in the country's movie production industry. The **Irish Film Institute** (see p58) opened its doors in 1992 and was a most welcome addition to the city's entertainment scene. Housed in an original 17th-century building in Temple Bar, the centre shows mostly independent and foreign films,

"Mr Screen" cinema sign

along with a programme of lectures, seminars and masterclasses. It boasts two screens, a bar, a restaurant and an archive of old film material.

Another two cinemas with repertoires of mostly art house are the **Screen** and **Lighthouse**. The large first-run cinemas, such as the **Savoy** and the multiplex **Cineworld**, are all located on the north side of the river. These usually offer reduced prices for their afternoon screenings and show late-night movies at the weekend.

Temple Bar Cultural Trust Summer Programme (see p159) offers free outdoor screenings of Irish and international films at Meeting House Square. Tickets are available from Temple Bar Information Centre.

DIRECTORY

BOOKING TICKETS

HMV
18 Henry St. **Map** D2.
Tel 872 2095.
65 Grafton St. **Map** D4.
Tel 679 5334.

Ticketmaster
www.ticketmaster.ie

NIGHTCLUBS

The Academy
57 Middle Abbey St.
Map D2. *Tel 877 9999.*
www.theacademydublin.
com

Boomerang
Fleet Street. **Map** D3.
Tel 677 3333. www.
boomerangniteclub.com

Club M
Bloom's Hotel, Cope St.
Map D3. *Tel 671 5622.*
www.clubm.ie

Copper Face Jack's
Jackson Court Hotel,
29–30 Harcourt St.
Map D5.
Tel 475 8777. www.
copperfacejacks.com

The George
South Great George's St.
Map C3. *Tel 478 2983.*

Krystle
21–25 Harcourt St.
Map D5.
Tel 086 306 8081. www.
krystlenightclub.com

Lillie's Bordello
Adam Court, off Grafton
St. **Map** D4. *Tel 679 9204.*

POD
Old Harcourt St train
station, Harcourt St.
Map D5. *Tel 478 0225.*
www.pod.ie

Rí-Rá
11 South Great George's
St. **Map** C3. *Tel 671 1220.*

South William
52 South William St.
Map D4. *Tel 672 5946.*
www.southwilliam.ie

The Sugar Club
8 Lower Leeson St.
Map E5. *Tel 678 7188.*

Thinktank
23–24 Eustace St.
Map C3. *Tel 670 7655.*

Thomas Reads
Parliament Street.
Map C3. *Tel 677 1487.*

The Vaults
Harbourmaster Place.
Map F2. *Tel 605 4700.*
www.thevaults.ie

The Village
26 Wexford St. **Map** C5.
Tel 475 8555.
www.thevillagevenue.com

CLASSICAL MUSIC, OPERA AND DANCE

Gaiety Theatre
South King St. **Map** D4.
Tel 677 1717.
www.gaietytheatre.ie

Hugh Lane Municipal Gallery of Modern Art
Charlemont House,
Parnell Sq North. **Map** C1.
Tel 222 5550.
www.hughlane.ie.

National Concert Hall
Earlsfort Terrace. **Map** D5.
Tel 417 0077.
www.nch.ie

Royal Dublin Society (RDS)
Ballsbridge. *Tel 668 0866.*
www.rds.ie

Royal Hospital Kilmainham
Kilmainham, Dublin 8.
Tel 612 9900.
www.modernart.ie

COMEDY

The Ha'penny Bridge Inn
Wellington Quay.
Map C3. *Tel 677 0616.*

The Laughter Lounge
4–6 Eden Quay. **Map** D2.
Tel 874 4611.

Olympia Theatre
Dame St. **Map** C3.
Tel 679 3323.

TRADITIONAL MUSIC & DANCE

Auld Dubliner
24–25 Temple Bar.
Map D3. *Tel 677 0527.*

Castle Inn
5–7 Lord Edward St.
Map C3. *Tel 475 1122.*

Cobblestone
77 King St North.
Map A2. *Tel 872 1799.*

The Farmhouse Bar
Rathfarnham, Dublin 16.
Tel 494 2311.

The Merry Ploughboy
Rockbrook, Rathfarnham,
Dublin 16.
Tel 493 1495.

O'Donoghue's
15 Merrion Row.
Map E5. *Tel 676 2807.*

ROCK, JAZZ, BLUES, SALSA AND COUNTRY

The Button Factory
Curved St, Temple Bar.
Map E4. *Tel 670 9202.*
www.buttonfactory.ie

Heineken Green Spheres
Tel 284 1747.
www.mcd.ie

International Bar
23 Wicklow St.
Map D3. *Tel 677 9250.*

The O2 Dublin
North Wall Quay. **Map** F2.
Tel 819 8888.
www.theO2.ie

Slane Castle
Co Meath.
Tel 041 988 4400.
www.slanecastle.ie

Whelan's
25 Wexford St.
Map C5. *Tel 478 0766.*
www.whelanslive.com

HOTEL BARS

Cellar Bar
Merrion Hotel,
24 Merrion St Upper.
Map E5. *Tel 603 0600.*

The Horseshoe Bar
Shelbourne Hotel, 27 St
Stephen's Green North.
Map E4. *Tel 663 4500.*

Inn on the Green
Fitzwilliam Hotel, 12 St
Stephen's Green West.
Map D4. *Tel 478 7000.*

Lobo Bar
The Morrison,
Ormond Quay. **Map** C3.
Tel 878 2999

Octagon Bar
The Clarence,
6–8 Wellington Quay.
Map C3. *Tel 407 0800.*

PUB CRAWLS AND TOURS

Dublin Ghost Bus Tour
Tel 873 4222.

Dublin Literary Pub Crawl
Tel 670 5602.
www.dublinpubcrawl.
com

Historical Walking Tour
Tel 878 0227.

Musical Pub Crawl
Tel 475 3313.

Music Hall of Fame
Tel 878 3345.

Viking Splash Tours
Tel 707 6000.
www.vikingsplash.ie

The Walk Macabre
Tel 087 677 1512.

CINEMA

Cineworld
Parnell Centre, Parnell St.
Map C2. *Tel 1520 880
444.* www.cineworld.ie

Irish Film Institute
6 Eustace St. **Map** C3.
Tel 679 5744.
www.irishfilm.ie

Lighthouse Cinema
Market Square, Smithfield.
Map A2. *Tel 679 5744.*

Savoy
O'Connell St. **Map** D2.
Tel 874 8487.
www.savoy.ie

Screen
D'Olier St. **Map** D3.
Tel 672 5500.
www.screencinema.ie

Theatre in Dublin

Dublin is synonymous with theatre, having produced some of the greatest practitioners of the art in both English and Gaelic. It is not surprising, therefore, that with the economic boom of the 1990s, theatre was one of the areas to flourish. These days there is almost always something worth seeing in the capital, whether it is a remake of an old favourite or cutting-edge work from an emerging talent. Productions are usually of a very high standard.

The splendid Victorian interior of the Olympia Theatre

INFORMATION SOURCES

Theatre listings can be found in the *Dublin Event Guide* *(see p154)*. A monthly publication, *The Dubliner*, also has theatre reviews, as do the free daily commuter newspaper *Metro Herald* and the *Irish Times* Friday pullout, The Ticket. Online resources include www.indublin.ie and www.entertainment.ie, which also list music and cinema venues. Visit www.tickets.ie to book tickets in advance.

MAINSTREAM THEATRE

The most famous venue is Ireland's national theatre, the **Abbey** *(see p70)*, which concentrates on new Irish productions, as well as revivals of Irish classics by playwrights such as Brendan Behan, Oscar Wilde, JM Synge and Sean O'Casey. Downstairs in the Abbey Theatre is the smaller Peacock Theatre, which runs more experimental work.

Founded in 1928, the **Gate Theatre** *(see p72)* is still noted for its adventurous interpretations of well-known plays.

The **Gaiety Theatre** stages a mainstream mix of musicals, opera, ballet and plays, emphasizing the work of Irish playwrights. With its Victorian

music-hall interior, the **Olympia Theatre** *(see p60)* stages comedy and popular drama. It is also well known as a music venue.

Other venues include the **Liberty Hall Theatre**, which offers an eclectic mix of drama, musicals and pantomime, and the **Tivoli Theatre**, which focuses on drama.

CONTEMPORARY/ AVANT-GARDE THEATRE

Some of the best fringe theatre in Dublin can be seen at the **Project Arts Centre** in Temple Bar. During the Dublin Fringe *(see Festivals)*, other venues are also used, including Crawdaddy at POD and The Sugar Club *(see p154)* and art galleries.

The **Smock Alley Theatre**, dating from 1662, hosts many dynamic theatre companies, including the acclaimed Rough Magic and Team Theatre.

The small **New Theatre** provides a mix of established and up-and-coming writers and directors, often with an Irish flavour.

New talent can also be found at university theatres.

At the **Samuel Beckett Centre** at Trinity College, the standard is generally higher than you would expect from student theatre. **The Helix** at Dublin City University (DCU), near Glasnevin, has an excellent reputation for cutting-edge and diverse theatre and music. The **Teachers' Club** on Parnell Square is also a good spot to catch emerging talent. The **Axis** in Ballymun has a growing reputation for presenting politically-focused, socially relevant work by emerging Irish playwrights.

Bewley's Café Theatre offers lunchtime performances of one-act plays or cabaret, usually by new writers, with a small cast. The shows cost €15 including lunch.

FESTIVALS

The **Dublin Theatre Festival** runs for two weeks between late September and early October, bringing together Irish and international talents to perform both new and classic works. An integral part of the festival is the Theatre Olympics, a programme of special events, forums, performances, exhibitions and workshops. Booking is highly recommended.

In mid-September, just ahead of the main theatre festival, is the **Dublin Fringe**, one of the country's largest contemporary performing arts festivals. The Fringe includes dance, street theatre, visual arts and comedy, with many performances taking place in the lush, mirrored Spiegeltent. Also in mid-September, puppeteers from across the world come to take part in the **International Puppet Festival**. The **Gay and Lesbian Theatre Festival** held each year in May is a platform for both serious work and outrageous fun, while the vibrant **Festival of World Cultures** (usually late Aug) in Dún Laoghaire features theatre performances from all around the world, as well as music, art and circus.

The Axis theatre in Ballymun

A performance at the Dublin Theatre Festival

The **Temple Bar Cultural Trust Summer Programme**, Dublin's free entertainment festival, includes circus and drama performances.

Free tours of the Abbey and Gate theatres are included in

Culture Night *(see p28)*, one night in September when all cultural organizations open their doors to the public. Visit www.templebar.ie for details.

CHILDREN'S THEATRE

The Ark *(see p59)*, a children's cultural centre in Temple Bar, has a packed programme of events, including drama. It is worth checking out, especially during the Dublin Theatre Festival. Around Christmas, the **Gaiety** *(see Mainstream Theatre)* and the **Olympia** *(see p60)* theatres attempt to outdo each other in lavishly produced pantomimes.

Eugene Lambert, a well loved puppeteer from Irish children's television in the 1980s, gives almost 30 performances a month in his famous **Lambert**

Puppet Theatre and museum in Monkstown.

In mid-June, the Draíocht theatre company runs the annual **Spréacha Festival**, a six-day event of theatre, puppetry, storytelling and visual art for children aged between 3 and 12.

OUT OF TOWN

Outside of town are many more theatres that offer a mix of local amateur drama groups and professional touring companies. They include the **Pavilion** in Dún Laoghaire; **Draíocht** in Blanchardstown; the **Civic Theatre** in Tallaght; the **Millbank Theatre** in Rush; the **Mill Theatre** in Dundrum; and the Axis in Ballymun *(see Contemporary/Avant-Garde Theatre)*.

Outdoor Activities

The city of Dublin is only minutes away from open countryside, and Ireland has many activities to tempt all lovers of the outdoors. The beautiful Wicklow Mountains are within easy reach for scenic walks, and the coastline from Dublin Bay to Dun Laoghaire offers a range of sports including sailing, fishing and windsurfing. There are plenty of opportunities to go horse riding and cycling in the Dublin area. Entire holidays can be based around outdoor activities. In addition to the contacts on page 161, Fáilte Ireland and Dublin Tourism *(see pp164–5)* have information on all sports and recreational activities in and around the city.

Backpackers walking in the Dublin area

Fishing in the canal at Robertstown, County Kildare

The beautiful gardens of Powerscourt House *(see pp114–15)*

WALKING

Walking in Ireland puts you in the very midst of some glorious countryside. The network of waymarked trails takes you to some of the loveliest areas, inaccessible by car. Information on long-distance walks is available from Fáilte Ireland. Routes include the Wicklow Way, which leads from the south of Dublin into the heart of the beautiful Wicklow Mountains *(see p113)*. All the walks may be split into shorter sections for less experienced walkers or those short of time.

Hill walking, rock climbing and mountaineering holidays are also available in Ireland. For specialized information, contact the **Mountaineering Council of Ireland**. When walking or climbing always make sure that you go well-equipped for the notoriously changeable Irish weather.

HORSE RIDING AND PONY TREKKING

A number of riding centres, both residential and non-residential, offer trail riding and trekking along woodland trails, beaches, country lanes and mountain routes. **Equestrian Holidays Ireland** organizes holidays for riders of various abilities. There are two types of trail riding – post-to-post and based. Post-to-post trails follow a series of routes with accommodation in a different place each night. Based trail rides follow different routes in one area and you stay at the same place for the whole holiday. Lessons are available at many centres for beginners to more advanced riders. The **Association of Irish Riding Establishments** has details of riding centres and courses.

Horseriding in Phoenix Park

FISHING

The claim that Ireland is a paradise for anglers is no exaggeration. Coarse, game and sea fishing all enjoy widespread popularity. Coastal rivers yield the famous Irish salmon, and, among other game fish, sea trout and brown trout also offer a real challenge.

Flounder, whiting, mullet, bass and coalfish tempt the sea angler; deep-sea excursions chase abundant supplies of dogfish, shark, skate and ling. You can organize sea-angling trips from many places.

Maps and information on fishing locations are provided by the **Central Fisheries Board** and the **Irish Federation of Sea Anglers**.

CYCLING

Cycling is very popular both in central Dublin and in the countryside. If you prefer to bring your own bike, you can transport it fairly cheaply by train or bus. If not, you can use the Dublinbikes self-service bike-rental scheme *(see p175)*, or rent one from Cycleways or Belfield Bike Shop *(see p177)*. The latter's sister company, **Irish Cycling Safaris**, concentrates on trips outside Dublin, so you can enjoy the quiet country roads. The paths along Dublin Bay offer fun routes with views of the beautiful coastline, while the Wicklow Mountains are more of a challenge.

WATER SPORTS

With a coastline of over 4,800 km (3,000 miles), it is small wonder that water sports are among Ireland's favourite recreational activities. Surfing, windsurfing, water-skiing, scuba-diving and canoeing are the most popular, and there are facilities for all of these along the Dublin coast and in Dublin Bay itself

Windsurfing is a popular sport throughout Ireland and there are a number of clubs and schools operating around Dublin Bay. **Surfdock** at Grand Canal Dock Yard and **Wind & Wave** in Monkstown both offer advice, tuition and the latest equipment.

There is a wide range of diving conditions off the coast of Ireland and the **Irish Underwater Council** will give you details of courses and their facilities.

Dun Laoghaire harbour at dusk

CRUISING AND SAILING

A tranquil cruising holiday is an ideal alternative to the stress and strain of driving, and Ireland's many rivers and lakes offer a huge variety of conditions for those who want a waterborne holiday. Stopping over at waterside towns and villages puts you in touch with the Irish on their home ground. Hiring a boat and drifting down the Grand Canal *(see p85)* from Dublin to the Shannon gives a unique view of the countryside.

Another popular sailing area is the scenic Howth peninsula, and the harbour of Dun Laoghaire southeast of Dublin, where you will find sailing schools offering tuition at all levels. For details of these schools, contact the **Irish Sailing Association**.

SPORTS FOR THE DISABLED

Sports enthusiasts with a disability can obtain details of facilities for the disabled from the **Irish Wheelchair Association**. Central and local tourist boards, and many of the organizations listed in the directory under each sport, will be able to offer facilities for disabled visitors. To be sure of this, it is advisable to call the venue first to check what is available.

Cycling in the Irish countryside

DIRECTORY

WALKING	Equestrian Holidays Ireland	WATER SPORTS	CRUISING AND SAILING
Mountaineering Council of Ireland	www.ehi.ie	**Irish Underwater Council**	**Irish Sailing Association**
House of Sport, 13 Joyce Way, Parkwest Business Park, Dublin 12.	**FISHING**	78a Patrick St, Dun Laoghaire, Co Dublin.	3 Park Rd, Dun Laoghaire, Co Dublin.
Tel 625 1115. www.mountaineering.ie	**Central Fisheries Board** *Tel* 884 2600. www.cfb.ie	*Tel* 284 4601. www.cft.ie	*Tel* 280 0239. www.sailing.ie
HORSE RIDING AND PONY TREKKING	**Irish Federation of Sea Anglers** *Tel* 280 6873. www.ifsa.ie	**Surfdock** Grand Canal Dockyard, South Dock Rd, Ringsend, Dublin 4. *Tel* 668 3945. www.surfdock.ie	**SPORTS FOR THE DISABLED**
Association of Irish Riding Establishments 11 Moore Park, Newbridge, Co Kildare.	**CYCLING**	**Wind & Wave** 16a The Crescent, Monkstown, Co Dublin.	**Irish Wheelchair Association** Áras Chúchulain, Blackheath Drive, Clontarf, Dublin 3.
Tel 045 431584. www.aire.ie	**Irish Cycling Safaris** University College Dublin, Dublin 4. *Tel* 260 0749. www.cyclingsafaris.com	*Tel* 284 4177. www.windandwave.ie	*Tel* 818 6400. www.iwa.ie

SURVIVAL GUIDE

PRACTICAL INFORMATION

Compact and easy to get around, Dublin is a popular tourist destination. Its numerous museums, galleries, other cultural institutions, restaurants and shops, combined with areas such as the vibrant Temple Bar and the rejuvenated Docklands, attract visitors all year round. The best time to visit is probably late spring, before the peak summer season, or autumn. Dublin is generally a safe place, but, as in any busy city, common-sense precautions should be taken to ward against pickpockets and bag-snatchers in crowded areas. Public transport is good, with buses, trams, light rail, taxis and hired bicycles all easily accessible in the city centre. Dublin Tourism offers an extensive information service, and its offices are well organized, with helpful staff who can speak a variety of languages and give practical help and advice.

Dublin Tourism logo

VISAS AND PASSPORTS

US, Canadian, Australian and New Zealand nationals need a valid passport, but not a visa, to enter Ireland. European Union nationals must have a valid passport or identity card. UK nationals do not strictly need a passport, but they are advised to take it, as immigration officers, airlines and ferry companies will ask for official photographic identification. Other visitors, including those who wish to study or work in Ireland, should check with their embassy first.

CUSTOMS INFORMATION AND TAX-FREE GOODS

Travellers from within the EU can bring 800 cigarettes, 200 cigars or 1 kg of tobacco, and 10 litres of spirits, 90 litres of wine or 110 litres of beer into Ireland. The quota for those from outside the EU is 200 cigarettes, 50 cigars or 250 g of tobacco, and 1 litre of spirits, 4 litres of wine or 16 litres of beer. Visitors from outside the EU can also bring goods (such as gifts, perfume and clothing) free of duty if their combined value does not exceed €430 (for those aged over 15) or €215 (under-15s).

There are three customs channels in Ireland: blue for EU travellers; green for passengers from outside the EU with nothing to declare; and red for those who have goods to declare. Certain items – including drugs, plants, bulbs, animals and meat products – are prohibited.

Passengers travelling from Ireland to destinations outside the EU can buy spirits, beers, wines and tobacco products at duty-free prices at the airport.

Non-EU residents can claim back the VAT (Value Added Tax) on a range of goods. Simply ask for a form when making your purchase and take it to the Ireland Tax Free counter at the airport to receive your refund *(see p148)*.

TOURIST INFORMATION

Dublin Tourism is the tourist body for the Dublin area. Its offices provide local information, sell guide books and maps, and can book bus tours, accommodation, car rental and event tickets. Museums and libraries also stock useful tourist literature.

The overseas tourist board for Ireland is **Tourism Ireland**, which has a network of

The office of Dublin Tourism, a converted church in Suffolk Street

offices around the world. Tourism Ireland works in conjunction with both **Fáilte Ireland**, Ireland's tourism authority, and the Northern Ireland Tourist Board.

Heritage Card, giving access to historic sites

ADMISSION CHARGES

Many of Dublin's major sights are free, but some charge an entry fee, usually with discounts for students *(see opposite)* and the elderly. The **Dublin Pass**, available from Dublin Tourism, gives free admission to 31 attractions, as well as discounts at a selection of shops, restaurants and service providers. **Heritage Ireland** issues the Heritage Card, which allows unlimited free access to fee-charging state-managed sites for a year.

OPENING HOURS

Most shops in Dublin are open from 9am to 6pm Monday to Saturday, with city-centre late-night opening until 8pm on Thursdays. Shops in the city centre are also open from noon to 6pm on Sundays. Museums are generally open from 10am to 5pm, but it is advisable to check before you visit. Some museums are closed on Mondays.

◁ **The pedestrianized St Anne Street, just off Grafton Street**

LANGUAGE

Although the day-to-day language is English, the Republic of Ireland's official language is Irish (or Gaelic). Signs and place names are usually in both languages.

TRAVELLERS WITH SPECIAL NEEDS

Most tourist sights in Ireland have access for wheelchairs, but call ahead of your visit to be sure. **Access Matters** has an online directory with information on accessible amenities, from restaurants, bars and shops to hotels and entertainment venues.

STUDENT TRAVELLERS

Holders of an ISIC card (International Student Identity Card) enjoy discounts on travel, as well as reduced entry to museums and concerts. ISIC cards can be obtained from any branch of **USIT**. This agency also supplies non-students under the age of 26 with an EYC or IYC card (European or International Youth Card) for discounts on flights and in restaurants, theatres and shops. In addition, USIT sells ISIC cardholders an Aircoach stamp for a reduced fare on the

Aircoach airport bus *(see p172)*. The **Student Travelcard** allows savings on weekly and monthly travel tickets, as well as train travel and accommodation *(see p176)*. It can be obtained at Dublin Bus (O'Connell Street Upper), at any railway station or by downloading the form online. College ID is necessary.

TIME

Ireland is on Greenwich Mean Time (GMT) – the same time zone as Great Britain. Clocks go forward 1 hour in March to Daylight Saving (summer) Time, which is GMT + 1 hour. They revert back in October.

RESPONSIBLE TOURISM

Dublin is increasingly promoting sustainability and responsible tourism. The city has an extensive recycling scheme, and all light bulbs sold are energy-efficient. **Imaginosity**, a children's museum, is housed in an eco-friendly building that uses wind and solar energy, and **Croke Park Stadium**, famous for Gaelic football matches, sources electricity from a wind farm. Bewley's on Grafton Street *(see p159)* is Ireland's only carbon-neutral café. Farmers' markets are sources

Cruag Massys, one of many nature walks in the Dublin Mountains

of locally grown organic produce – there is a market in Temple Bar every Saturday, and in Point Village every Saturday and Sunday. Visit www.irishfarmersmarkets.ie for more details.

Dublin has many conservation areas. Phoenix Park *(see pp80–81)* is a sanctuary for deer, birds and other wildlife; the **Dublin Mountains**, about 1 hour's drive south of the city centre, offer hiking trails and nature walks; the **Airfield Trust**, which has a working farm, has won awards for its environmental projects; and **North Bull Island** is a UNESCO-listed biosphere reserve and bird sanctuary. Visit www.sustourism.ie for more information.

DIRECTORY

EMBASSIES AND CONSULATES

Australia
7th Floor, Fitzwilton House, Wilton Terrace, Dublin 2. *Tel* 664 5300.
www.ireland.embassy. gov.au

Canada
7–8 Wilton Terrace, Dublin 2. *Tel 234 4000*.
www.canada.ie

UK
29 Merrion Rd, Dublin 4. *Tel 205 3700*.
www.britishembassy.ie

United States
42 Elgin Rd, Ballsbridge, Dublin 4. *Tel 668 8777*.
www.dublin.
usembassy.gov

TOURIST INFORMATION

Dublin Tourism
Suffolk St, Dublin 2. **Map** D3. *Tel* 605 7700.
Also at:
14 O'Connell St Upper, Dublin 1. **Map** D2.
Arrivals Hall, Dublin Airport.
Dun Laoghaire Ferry Terminal, Co Dublin.
www.visitdublin.com

Fáilte Ireland
Tel 1850 230 330.
www.ireland.ie

Tourism Ireland
Tel 0800 039 7000 (UK).
*Tel 800 223 6470
(USA and Canada).*
www.tourismireland.com

ADMISSION CHARGES

Dublin Pass
www.dublinpass.ie

Heritage Ireland
www.heritageireland.ie

TRAVELLERS WITH SPECIAL NEEDS

Access Matters
Tel 222 2194.
www.accessdublin.ie

STUDENT TRAVELLERS

Student Travelcard
www.studenttravelcard.ie

USIT
19–21 Aston Quay, Dublin 2. **Map** D3. *Tel 602 1904*. www.usit.ie

RESPONSIBLE TOURISM

Airfield Trust
Upper Kilmacud Rd, Dundrum, Dublin 14. *Tel 298 4301*.
www.airfield.ie

Croke Park Stadium
Clonliffe Rd, Dublin 3. www.crokepark.ie

Dublin Mountains
www.dublinmountains.ie

Imaginosity
The Plaza, Beacon South Quarter, Sandyford, Dublin 18. *Tel 217 6130*.
www.imaginosity.ie

North Bull Island
Dollymount, Dublin 5. *Tel 833 1859*.

Personal Security and Health

Serious crime is rare in Dublin. However, like many other busy capital cities, it is no stranger to petty, opportunistic crime such as burglaries and car thefts. Taking a few simple precautions will go a long way towards ensuring a trouble-free stay. Always keep an eye on your belongings and watch out for pickpockets and bag-snatchers, especially on public transport and in crowded tourist areas. The banks of the River Liffey are particularly popular with pickpockets. Avoid backstreets and poorly lit areas. For medical needs, pharmacies can provide a wide range of over-the-counter medicines for minor ailments. If you require more serious medical attention, visit a general practitioner or a hospital.

Garda station on Pearse Street, near the centre of Dublin

GARDAI (POLICE)

The police force in Ireland is known as the Garda Síochána, or Gardaí. There are several Garda stations around the city, including one at Store Street (Map E2) and one at Pearse Street (Map E3). You should report any crime and lost or stolen items to the police promptly in person. Note that you will need the Gardaí report if you wish to claim back on your travel insurance.

WHAT TO BE AWARE OF

Visitors to Dublin are advised to take a few simple steps to avoid becoming victims of crime. Pickpocketing and petty theft can be a problem in Dublin as in any other large urban area, so it is best not to carry your passport, travel tickets or large amounts of cash around with you. Most hotels have a safe, so take advantage of this facility and store all essential documents and extra cash here. It is not necessary to carry your passport or ID card with you at all times while in Ireland.

When out and about, always watch your belongings, and do not leave bags and valuables unattended. In pubs and restaurants, keep your bag on your lap, if possible, and do not leave your wallet or mobile phone lying on the table. Watch out for pickpockets and bag-snatchers in crowds – use a money belt or wear a shoulder bag across your chest, and do not draw attention to yourself by wearing flashy jewellery.

Do not leave valuables visible in a car at any time but lock them in the boot. Always lock your car doors. When you arrive at a hotel, ask the receptionist about secure parking in the area. Hotel staff should also be able to help you identify the areas of the city that are best avoided, especially at night. Women should avoid travelling alone after dark.

Always safeguard your PIN when using a cash dispenser and put money away quickly. You may be approached in the street or at cash machines by people asking for money. This rarely develops into a troublesome situation, but it is still best to avoid eye contact and leave the scene as quickly as possible.

In general, safety in the city is about being alert to your surroundings. If you feel uncomfortable anywhere, especially at night, walk away confidently and head for well-lit, populated areas.

IN AN EMERGENCY

In the event of an emergency, you can call the **police** or an **ambulance**. This also alerts the **fire brigade**, **coastguard** and **mountain rescue**.

For medical emergencies that do not require an ambulance, you should visit a general practitioner (GP) or the 24-hour outpatients or casualty department of the nearest public hospital *(see opposite)*. If you have language difficulties, public hospitals are usually able to provide translation services for patients of many nationalities. The **Dublin Dental Hospital** serves emergency dental needs. It is closed at weekends but provides the numbers of dentists on call.

If you become a victim of crime during your time in Dublin, contact the nearest Garda station and the **Irish Tourist Assistance Service (ITAS)**, which offers free support and advice to tourists. The staff at ITAS speak a

Male and female Garda officers in ordinary uniform

variety of languages and can help with everything from translation to cancellation of stolen credit cards, re-issue of stolen travel tickets and liaison with embassies and the Gardaí. In emergencies, they also provide practical assistance, such as help with accommodation, meals and transport.

Rape victims should contact the **Dublin Rape Crisis Centre** for support and guidance by calling the 24-hour helpline.

Dublin ambulance

Dublin fire engine

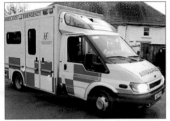
Garda patrol car

HOSPITALS AND PHARMACIES

The main hospitals serving the Dublin area are the **St James's Hospital**, **Beaumont Hospital, Mater Misericordiae Hospital** (all in the north of the city) and **St Vincent's University Hospital** (in the south of the city). All these hospitals have 24-hour walk-in casualty departments that will treat serious injuries. For non-emergencies you should go to a GP. To find one visit www.icgp.ie/go/find_a_gp.

Most pharmacists can give advice on which over-the-counter medicines are suitable for minor ailments. Pharmacies stock a wide range of over-the-counter remedies. However, many medicines can be obtained only with a prescription from a local doctor or hospital. Always obtain a receipt for insurance claims. If you are likely to require specialized drugs during your stay, it is wise to take your own supplies.

There are no 24-hour pharamcies in Dublin. For after-hours medical supplies try **Hickey's Pharmacy**, (open 8am–10pm Monday to Friday;

8:30am–10pm Saturday; and 10am–10pm Sunday). If you are in urgent need of medicines during the night you should visit the nearest hospital with a casualty unit.

TRAVEL AND HEALTH INSURANCE

Before you leave home, make sure that your possessions are insured because it can be expensive and difficult to buy insurance in Ireland. Check that your policy provides adequate cover, including any activities you plan to do.

Visitors from the European Union can claim free emergency medical treatment in Ireland by getting a European Health Insurance Card (EHIC) before setting out; visit www.euhealthcard.org for more details. To avoid having to pay for any treatment, you will need to show your EHIC card and a form of photographic identification, such as a driver's licence or a passport. Also, be sure to let the doctor know that you wish to be treated under the EU's social security regulations. The EHIC is not a substitute for medical or travel insurance. It is advisable to obtain comprehensive travel insurance to cover you for all eventualities

Travellers from outside the EU should either have their own accident and health insurance or be prepared to pay for any treatment received while in Ireland.

DIRECTORY

IN AN EMERGENCY

Police/ Ambulance/ Fire Brigade/ Coastguard/ Mountain Rescue
Tel 999 or 112.

Dublin Dental Hospital
22 Lincoln Place, Dublin 2.
Map E4.
Tel 612 7200.
http:web1.dental.tcd.ie

Dublin Rape Crisis Centre
Tel 1800 778 888.
www.drcc.ie

ITAS
Mon–Fri:
6–7 Hanover St East, Dublin 2. **Map** F3.
Sat & Sun:
Garda Station, Store St, Dublin 2. **Map** E2.
Tel 1890 365 700.
www.itas.ie

HOSPITALS AND PHARMACIES

Beaumont Hospital
Beaumont Rd, Dublin 9.
Tel 809 3000.
www.beaumont.ie

Hickey's Pharmacy
55 O'Connell St, Dublin 1.
Map D2.
Tel 873 0427.
www.hickeys pharmacies.ie

Mater Misericordiae Hospital
Eccles St, Dublin 7.
Tel 803 2000.
www.mater.ie

St James's Hospital
James's St, Dublin 8.
Tel 410 3000.
www.stjames.ie

St Vincent's University Hospital
Elm Park, Dublin 4.
Tel 221 4000.
www.stvincents.ie

Banking and Currency

Banks in Dublin provide a comprehensive service and will change currency at their foreign-exchange counters. Most have a cash dispenser, or automated teller machine (ATM), which can be used outside banking hours. There are ATMs in some convenience stores and petrol stations too. Credit and debit cards are an easy way of withdrawing money and making payments, and are widely accepted in the city. Some banks charge exchange-rate loading fees for foreign transactions and add an additional fee onto cash withdrawals from ATMs. Check with your bank regarding any such fees in advance.

Façade of the Bank of Ireland on College Green, in central Dublin

BANKS AND BUREAUX DE CHANGE

The main retail banks in the Republic of Ireland are **Bank of Ireland**, **Allied Irish Banks (AIB)**, **Ulster Bank**, **National Irish Bank** and **Permanent-TSB**.

Normal banking hours are 10am–4pm Monday to Friday (to 5pm on Thursdays). Small branches outside the city centre may close for lunch. Permanent-TSB is open 10am–5pm Monday to Friday (from 10:30am on Wednesdays), and Ulster Bank is open 9:30am–4:30pm. Some branches also open 10am–1pm on Saturdays. All banks are closed on public holidays (see p29).

Dublin city centre has a number of private bureaux de change, such as **First Rate** and **Joe Walsh Tours Forex**. Foreign-currency exchange outlets and a foreign-currency ATM can also be found at Dublin Airport. Bureaux de change stay open later than banks, but rates of exchange vary and commission charges can be high, so shop around before carrying out any

transactions. Most hotels, some department stores and Dublin Tourism (see p165) also offer currency exchange facilities. Though no longer issued in Ireland, traveller's cheques are still accepted by banks and some retailers – fees vary.

ATMS

ATMs can be found outside banks, in convenience stores and at petrol stations. Most are affiliated to Visa or MasterCard, so if your card bears the Visa, MasterCard, Cirrus, Maestro or Plus logo, you should be able to withdraw cash. A fee may be charged. Be vigilant at ATMs in the city centre, especially at night; shield your PIN and put your cash away quickly.

CREDIT AND DEBIT CARDS

It is possible to pay by credit or debit card in almost all Dublin hotels, in petrol stations and supermarkets and in most shops and restaurants. Most cards operate on a

chip-and-PIN system. VISA and MasterCard are the most widely accepted credit cards; not many businesses will take American Express. Diners Club is generally not accepted. Some small retailers and cafés do not take cards, so have some cash with you at all times.

Before you travel, check with your card issuer that your credit or debit card will work overseas. If your card is lost or stolen, report it to your bank as soon as possible.

WIRING MONEY

Wiring money is another way to transfer funds from home, although it can be expensive. Both **Western Union Ireland** and **MoneyGram** have agents throughout Dublin; the former also has a branch at the General Post Office (see p171).

THE EURO

The Republic of Ireland was one of the 12 countries that adopted the euro in 2002, with the original currency phased out by February of that year. European Union members using the euro as their sole official currency are known as the Eurozone. Several EU members, have opted out of joining this common currency.

Euro notes are identical throughout the Eurozone countries, each one including designs of fictional architectural structures and monuments. The coins have one side identical (the value side) and one side with an image that is unique to each country. Both notes and coins are exchangeable in each of the participating Eurozone countries.

Banknotes

Euro banknotes have seven denominations. The €5 note (grey in colour) is the smallest, followed by the €10 note (pink), €20 note (blue), €50 note (orange), €100 note (green), €200 note (yellow) and €500 note (purple). All notes show the stars of the European Union.

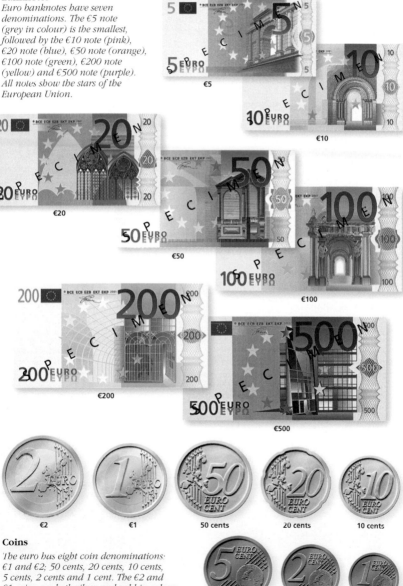

€5

€10

€20

€50

€100

€200

€500

€2

€1

50 cents

20 cents

10 cents

Coins

The euro has eight coin denominations: €1 and €2; 50 cents, 20 cents, 10 cents, 5 cents, 2 cents and 1 cent. The €2 and €1 coins are both silver and gold in colour. The 50-, 20- and 10-cent coins are gold. The 5-, 2- and 1-cent coins are bronze.

5 cents

2 cents

1 cent

Communications and Media

An Post logo

Telephone services in Dublin are good, and there are plenty of mobile-phone providers. Public telephones are not as abundant as they once were, but prepaid phone cards are widely available and are good value. Wi-Fi is found in most hotels and in many cafés. The postal service is reliable; there are two main post offices in Dublin and many smaller branches.

Television and radio are dominated by the state broadcaster RTE, but there are also some privately run TV channels and plenty of independent local radio stations. Ireland is well served for national daily and Sunday newspapers, and there are many Irish magazines.

Public telephone booth in Dublin

INTERNATIONAL AND LOCAL TELEPHONE CALLS

Cheap-rate calls within the Republic of Ireland and cheap-rate international calls can be made from 6pm to 8am on weekdays and all day at weekends. Public telephones are operated by phone companies such as Eircom and Smart Telecom. Most accept both coins and credit cards. It is also possible to buy prepaid international phone cards for cheaper calls from newsagents, convenience stores and on some flights into Ireland. International phone cards can be used in payphones and public phones by keying in a PIN number and access code. Some Internet cafés have facilities for VoIP (Voice over Internet Protocol) calls at cheap rates. Calls from hotels are expensive at all times.

MOBILE PHONES

Mobile-phone usage in Ireland is one of the highest in Europe, and services and coverage are excellent. The main mobile-phone operators are **O2** and **Vodafone**, with **Meteor**, **3**, **Postfone** and **Tesco Mobile** also providing services. Contact your mobile-phone provider before you travel to Ireland to check that your phone will work there – GSM handsets usually do, but if you are travelling from North America you will need a triband or quadband handset.

Before you travel to Ireland it is wise to check that roaming is activated on your handset and to find out how much your service provider will charge you for using your phone abroad. One way to reduce costs is to buy a prepaid SIM card from an Irish mobile-phone operator and use it in your own mobile phone during your visit. In order to do this, you may have to ask your phone provider to unlock your phone before you travel. Mobile-phone shops such as O2 and Vodafone sell prepaid SIM cards and pay-as-you-go mobile phones. You can also rent a mobile phone from a number of providers.

INTERNET ACCESS

Internet access is widely available in Dublin. Most hotels offer free access to the Internet. All public libraries, including the **Central Library**, have computers and free Wi-Fi, but you may have to book a computer in advance. Internet cafés, such as **Central Internet Café**, **Global Internet Café** and **5 Star Internet Café** generally charge by the hour or half-hour for computer use, with a minimum charge, so costs build up quickly. Many cafés and bars, however, offer free Wi-Fi.

USEFUL DIALLING CODES AND TELEPHONE NUMBERS

- To make a call within the Dublin area from a landline, dial the seven-digit number, dropping the Dublin area code (01). If dialling from a mobile phone, include the 01 code.
- To make a call to an area outside Dublin, dial the area code, which always begins with a 0, followed by the number.
- To call Northern Ireland, dial 048, then the area code followed by the number.

- To call other countries, dial 00 followed by the country code (for example, 44 for the UK), then the area code (excluding the leading 0), followed by the number.
- To contact Directory Enquiries, dial 11811 for the Republic and Northern Ireland, and 11818 for Great Britain and for international numbers.

Colourful façade of 5 Star Internet Café in Dublin

POSTAL SERVICES

Postal services in Ireland are run by An Post. The **General Post Office (GPO)** *(see p71)* is open 8:30am–6pm Monday to Saturday. Most other post offices in the city open 9am–5:30pm on weekdays and 9am–1pm on Saturdays. Some smaller post offices close for lunch and on Saturdays. Post office outlets in the suburbs are sometimes incorporated into newsagents and general stores. Standard-value stamps can also be bought from some newsagents.

Ireland has only one class of mail, with most post delivered within the country the next working day. The rate for mail to Great Britain and

Post Office, St Andrew's Street

the rest of Europe is slightly higher. Allow four days when sending a letter to Europe and at least six days for North America and other destinations. All letters destined for outside Ireland should carry a blue *Priority Aerphost* sticker, available at all post offices.

Sending mail by Express or Registered Post costs extra, but delivery is guaranteed in a specified number of days. An Post also runs a Courier Post service.

The easiest way to receive mail in Dublin is to have it sent to your hotel; however, a Poste Restante service is available at major post offices. The GPO on O'Connell Street is the most convenient, and is open from 8am until 8pm Monday to Saturday.

Postboxes in Ireland are green, with the latest collection times displayed on them.

List of the daily collection times

Monogram of Queen Victoria

Standard mailbox   **Rural mailbox**

NEWSPAPERS AND MAGAZINES

The Republic of Ireland has six national daily papers and five Sunday papers. Quality dailies include *The Irish Times*, the *Irish Independent* and the *Irish Examiner*. Dublin's morning freesheet is the *Metro Herald*, while the *Evening Herald* (which is not free) hits the city newsstands in the early afternoon. Ireland's daily tabloid is the *Irish Daily Star*, and Irish editions of British tabloids, such as *The Sun* and the *Daily Mail*, are on sale throughout Dublin, as are imported broadsheets such as *The Times*, the *Guardian* and *USA Today*. Entertainment listings are published in many newspapers and magazines *(see p154)*.

TV AND RADIO

Ireland has five TV channels: RTE 1, RTE 2, TV3, 3e and TG4, which is an Irish-language service. British television channels such as BBC, ITV (UTV), Channel 4 and Sky can be received by cable television subscribers. Other international channels available include CNN, National Geographic and Discovery. Most hotels offer cable or satellite TV.

There are six national radio stations and many local and independent ones. The main national stations are RTE Radio 1 (for news), RTE 2FM (for rock and pop music) and RTE Lyric FM (for classical music and arts programmes).

DIRECTORY

MOBILE PHONES

3
46 Grafton St, Dublin 2.
Map D4. **Tel** 671 8239.
www.three.ie

Meteor
24 Grafton St, Dublin 2.
Map D4. **Tel** 604 0249.
www.meteor.ie

O2
50 Grafton St, Dublin 2.
Map D4. **Tel** 670 5470.
www.o2.ie

Postfone
GPO, O'Connell St Lower,
Dublin 1.
Map D2.
Tel 1850 789 789.
www.postfone.ie

Tesco Mobile
www.tescomobile.ie

Vodafone
48 Grafton St,
Dublin 2. **Map** D4.
Tel 673 0120.
www.vodafone.ie

INTERNET ACCESS

5 Star Internet Café
Talbot St, Dublin 1.
Map D2. **Tel** 855 4009.

Central Internet Café
6 Grafton St, Dublin 2.
Map D4. **Tel** 677 8298.
www.centralinternet
cafe.com

Central Library
Ilac Centre, Henry St,
Dublin 1. **Map** D2.
Tel 873 4333.

Global Internet Café
8 O'Connell St,
Dublin 1. **Map** D3.
Tel 878 0295.

POSTAL SERVICES

General Post Office
O'Connell St Lower,
Dublin 1. **Map** D2.
Tel 705 7000.

19–24 St Andrew's St,
Dublin 2. **Map** D4.
Tel 705 8256.
www.anpost.ie

TRAVEL INFORMATION

Dublin is a popular tourist destination – both in its own right, as a city break, and as a gateway for exploring the rest of Ireland. It is easy to get to the city, with frequent flights from the UK, Europe and the US, good connections from elsewhere in the world and excellent airport facilities. Another way of travelling to Dublin is by ferry from the UK. Ferries dock at Dublin Port or Dun Laoghaire

**Aer Lingus
Airbus in flight**

harbour. From both the airport and the harbours, it is only a short ride by car or bus into the city centre; Dun Laoghaire is also served by a rail link. If you are planning to stay in the city centre, it is not necessary to rent a car – most of the sights are within easy walking distance of one another. You can also easily get around the city by bus, Luas tram, taxi and the bicycles from the Dublinbikes rental scheme.

![The modern exterior of Dublin Airport]

The modern exterior of Dublin Airport

ARRIVING BY AIR

Flights from most of the main cities in Europe arrive at **Dublin Airport**, located 10 miles (16 km) north of the city centre. It is the Republic of Ireland's busiest airport, with two terminals handling more than 60 airlines. Regular flights to Dublin depart from most major airports in Britain, as well as from the Isle of Man and the Channel Islands. The main airlines operating scheduled flights from Europe are **Aer Lingus**, **British Midland** and **Ryanair**. Airlines with direct flights from the United States include Aer Lingus, **American Airlines**, **United Airlines** and **Delta Air Lines**. From the Middle East, **Etihad** operates direct flights to Dublin. There are no direct flights to Ireland from Australia and New Zealand; popular connecting points include London, Singapore and Amsterdam.

There are also internal flights to and from airports in the south, west and northwest of Ireland.

AIR FARES

Airlines offer a wide range of options on air fares to Ireland. Generally speaking, the amount you pay depends on how flexible you are prepared to be and how far in advance you book your flight. The best bargains tend to be found on flights with fixed dates. Fares tend to increase in the summer months and around Christmas, so be sure to book as early as possible for these times. Midweek flights are often cheaper than weekend ones. The budget airlines Aer Lingus and Ryanair fly from many UK airports.

Check airline websites for special offers and seat sales. Travel search engines such as www.kayak.com and www.sky scanner.com can be useful to find comparisons between different airline fares.

Some airlines offer discounts to people aged under 25, while USIT *(see p165)* and other agencies specializing in student travel often have cheaper rates for students and people under 26 years of age.

GETTING TO AND FROM THE AIRPORT

Dublin Bus's 747 and 748 Express Airlink buses run between Dublin Airport and the city's main rail and bus stations from early morning until midnight. The average journey time is 45 minutes, but this is dependent on traffic. Tickets are purchased on board the bus. Another popular service from the airport is the **Aircoach**, which serves the city centre and suburbs south of the city. The 16A and 41 Dublin Bus services are cheaper, if more time-consuming, alternatives to travel to the city centre, while the number 102 bus connects with Sutton DART station. There is a taxi rank outside the airport and a range of car-rental companies inside. The airport has long- and short-term parking facilities.

The frequent-running Express Airlink bus

Irish Ferries ship loading up at Dublin Port

ARRIVING BY SEA

There are ferry services to Dublin from both Holyhead in Wales and Liverpool in England. **Irish Ferries** sails on the Holyhead–Dublin route. In addition to two daily crossings on a conventional ferry that take about 3 hours and 15 minutes to reach Dublin Port, the company operates the Jonathan Swift high-speed service, which crosses in 1 hour and 49 minutes. Irish Ferries also runs regular overnight sailings between northern France (Cherbourg and Roscoff) and Rosslare, on the southeast coast of Ireland.

Stena Line runs a high-speed ferry from Holyhead to Dun Laoghaire; the crossing takes 2 hours. It also operates two conventional ferries to Dublin Port that take 3 hours and

15 minutes. **P&O Irish Sea Ferries** runs ferries from Liverpool to Dublin that take 8 hours. **Norfolk Line** also runs from Liverpool (Birkenhead) to Dublin; the crossing takes 7 hours. The **Isle of Man Steam Packet Company**'s ferry from Douglas, on the Isle of Man, takes 2 hours and 55 minutes.

Passengers requiring special assistance at ports or on board should contact their ferry company at least 24 hours before departure. Most ferries will take bicycles for a small charge – check at the time of reservation. Ferries may not run in rough weather.

PORT CONNECTIONS

From Dublin Port, there are several buses to the city centre. From Dun Laoghaire, DART trains run into Dublin every 10–15 minutes. They depart from the railway

station across the road from the main passenger concourse, and call at Pearse Street, Tara Street and Connolly stations; the journey takes about 20 minutes. There are also buses running from outside Dun Laoghaire DART station to the city centre; however, the journey time is much longer. Taxis can usually be found at each port.

ARRIVING BY COACH AND RAIL

For travellers on a budget, the cheapest way of travelling to Ireland is by coach or train from a range of UK locations, plus ferry. Book your tickets via **SailRail** for direct train-and-ferry routes, or **Eurolines** for coach-and-sail options. To travel out of Ireland, you can book tickets in person at Irish Rail travel centres *(see p177)* or at Busáras bus station on Store Street (map E2).

Stena HSS on the Holyhead to Dun Laoghaire crossing

DIRECTORY

ARRIVING BY AIR

Aer Lingus
*Tel 0818 365 000
or 886 8844.*
Tel 0845 084 4444 (UK).
www.aerlingus.com

American Airlines
Tel 602 0550.
www.aa.com

British Midland
Tel 407 3036.
www.flybmi.com

Delta Air Lines
Tel 1850 882 031.
www.delta.com

Dublin Airport
Tel 814 1111.
www.dublin-airport.com

Etihad
Tel 871 6401.
www.etihadairways.com

Ryanair
*Tel 0818 303 030
or 609 7800.*
Tel 0871 246 0000 (UK).
www.ryanair.com

United Airlines
Tel 1890 925 252.
www.united.com

GETTING TO AND FROM THE AIRPORT

Aircoach
Tel 844 7118.
www.aircoach.ie

Dublin Bus
Tel 873 4222.
www.dublinbus.ie

ARRIVING BY SEA

Irish Ferries
*Tel 1890 31 31 31 or
661 0715.*
Tel 08705 17 17 17 (UK).
www.irishferries.com

Isle of Man Steam Packet Company
Tel 08722 992 992 (UK).
*Tel 01624 661 661
(Isle of Man).*
www.steam-packet.com

Norfolk Line
Tel 819 2999.
www.norfolkline.com

P&O Irish Sea Ferries
Tel 08716 645 645 (UK).
www.poferries.com

Stena Line
Tel 204 7777.
Tel 08705 707070 (UK).
www.stenaline.ie

ARRIVING BY COACH AND RAIL

Eurolines
Tel 836 6111.
www.eurolines.com

SailRail
Tel 703 1884.
www.sailrail.co.uk

Getting Around Dublin

Dublin is fairly easy to get around. The city centre is relatively compact, so most of the sights are within walking distance of one another, and much of it, particularly south of the Liffey, is pedestrianized. If you are travelling in or out of Dublin, there is a wide choice of bus routes, and the DART railway is an efficient service that runs along the coast, stopping at three city-centre stations. The Luas tram line links Dublin's western and southern suburbs with main railway stations and the centre of town. Another way to get around is by bicycle, thanks to the Dublinbikes hire scheme; there are bicycle stands throughout the city centre. There are plenty of taxis in the city but they can be fairly expensive.

Luas tram crossing the modern Dundrum Bridge

GREEN TRAVEL

Ecocabs are passenger tricycles that are emission-free, completely free of charge and a great means for short-distance travel in Dublin. They run 10am–7pm daily from April to December. Another eco-friendly way to get around is to rent a bicycle from **Dublinbikes** *(see also Cycling)*. The **Luas** tram system's website features an eco-calculator that allows passengers to measure the carbon footprint of their journey. A partial restriction on the number of private vehicles in the city has been imposed by the College Green Bus Corridor initiative, which allows only buses, taxis and bikes to pass through the College Green area 7–10am and 4–7pm Monday–Friday.

BUS

Bus services in the city are operated by **Dublin Bus**. Some alterations are being made to the bus network in 2011 and routes and numbers are subject to change. See www.dublinbus.ie for the latest details.

Bus stops are blue or yellow, and the numbers on them indicate which buses stop there. Buses in the city centre run approximately every 10 to 20 minutes from 6am to 11:30pm Monday to Friday (to 11pm Saturday and Sunday), depending on the route. Sunday buses start at 8am.

You will need the exact change for the fare. If you plan on using the bus multiple times during your stay, it might be worth getting a bus pass, available for one day, three days, a week or a month.

Nitelink is the night-bus service, running from midnight until 4am on Friday and Saturday nights. Buses depart from designated stops in the city centre; tickets cost €5.

The main bus station is Busáras in Store Street (map E2). From here, you can also catch the coaches operated by **Bus Éireann** to destinations all over the country *(see p176)*.

LUAS

The Luas is an on-street tram system connecting the city centre with Dublin's southern and western suburbs. It has two lines: the Red Line runs west from The Point through the city, past Heuston Station and to Tallaght; and the Green Line runs from St Stephen's Green to Brides Glen.

The two Luas lines do not intersect, but they will connect with the future Metro North railway line (due to open in 2016) and DART Underground (due in 2018), providing Dublin with a comprehensive transport system.

DART

Run by Irish Rail, the **DART** (Dublin Area Rapid Transit) is a light rail service that stops at 30 stations along the coast between Malahide, in north County Dublin, and Greystones, in County Wicklow, with several stops in Dublin's city centre. There are some spectacular views along the southern section, particularly at Killiney and from Bray to Greystones.

DART logo

TICKETS AND FARES

Dublin Bus operates an exact-change policy; fares depend on age and destination (€1.15–€2.20 per adult for a single ticket). A single DART fare is €1.35–€4.30 and a Luas fare €1.50–€2.30. A one-day rambler ticket (about €10) allows unlimited travel on buses, the DART and local suburban rail.

The Integrated Ticketing Leap Card can be used to pay for travel on most public transport in Dublin. It costs €5 and can be topped up with credit. It can be bought and topped up at Dublin Airport and at over 400 shops displaying the Leap Card sign and at all DART and some Luas ticket machines.

WALKING

Dublin is ideal for exploring on foot as most of the sights are within a fairly short walk of each other. Pedestrianized areas include Grafton Street and Temple Bar, and there are several pedestrian bridges across the River Liffey.

TAXIS

Taxis can be hailed on the street or at designated taxi ranks. They can also be pre-booked by phone *(see City Map)*. Taxis are metered.

DRIVING

To rent a car you must have held a full driver's licence for 2 years without violations. The minimum and upper age limits vary between car hire companies. For a list of rental companies in Dublin, *see p177*.

On-street parking operates on a pay-and-display basis (€1–€2.90 per hour) or by a pre-registered **Parking Tag**. This costs €3.99 and can be topped up at any Payzone retailer. A single yellow line along the edge of the road indicates parking restrictions; double yellow lines mean no parking at any time. Parking is free on some streets after 7pm and on Sundays – check street signs. There are plenty of car parks; many offer special overnight rates.

A Dublinbikes self-service rack

CYCLING

Bicycles can be hired through the **Dublinbikes** scheme, open to everyone from 14 years of age. A three-day rental ticket (€2) is available from bike stations with credit-card terminals. Log in at the terminal using your ticket and the PIN number issued to you with your ticket, select the bike number on screen, and unlock the bike. Each time you rent a bike the first half-hour is free. After that charges range from €0.50 for 1 hour to €6.50 for 4 hours. You can return the bike to any station at the end of your journey. A Long Term Hire Card (for 1 year) can be obtained for €10 by registering online.

Dublin has many cycle lanes, but caution is needed, especially in the city centre; helmets are recommended.

GUIDED TOURS

Dublin has a wide range of guided tours. **Dublin City Bike Tours** and **Dublin by Bike Tours** provide a fun way to see the city on two wheels. Free **iWalks** audio guides can be downloaded from Dublin Tourism's website and allow you to sightsee at your own pace. Hop-on/hop-off bus tours include the **City Sightseeing Dublin** tour, with 25 stops, and the **Dublin City Bus Tour**, which takes in some of the city's less well-known sights, such as Oscar Wilde's home. **Art Impressions** offers tours of art galleries. For more tours of the city, *see page 156*.

Bus Éireann and **Gray Line Wicklow Tours** offer trips to attractions outside Dublin, such as Glendalough and Newgrange; **Dublin Bus** runs tours to the coast. See www.visitdublin.com for a full list of tour providers.

City Sightseeing Dublin tour bus

DIRECTORY

GREEN TRAVEL

Dublinbikes
Tel 1850 777 070.
www.dublinbikes.ie

Ecocabs
www.ecocabs.ie

Luas
Tel 1800 300 604.
www.luas.ie

BUS

Bus Éireann
Tel 836 6111.
www.buscireann.ie

Dublin Bus
Tel 873 4222.
www.dublinbus.ie

DART

DART/Irish Rail
Tel 836 6222.
www.irishrail.ie

DRIVING

Parking Tag
Tel 0818 300 161.
www.parkingtag.ie

GUIDED TOURS

Art Impressions
Book online or in person at a Dublin Tourism office.
Tel 83 375 6668.
www.artimpressions.ie

City Sightseeing Dublin

Dublin Tourism,
Suffolk St, Dublin 2.
Map D3.
Tel 605 7705. www.city-sightseeing.com

Dublin by Bike Tours
Meet outside Mansion House, Dawson St, Dublin 2. **Map** D4.
Tel 086 837 5955.
www.dublinbybike.ie

Dublin City Bike Tours
Tel 087 134 1866.
www.dublincitybiketours.com

Dublin City Bus Tour

59 O'Connell St Upper, Dublin 1.
Map D2.
Tel 873 4222.
www.dublinbus.ie

Gray Line Wicklow Tours
Dublin Tourism,
Suffolk St,
Dublin 2.
Map D3.
Tel 605 7705.
www.irishcitytours.com

iWalks
www.visitdublin.com/iwalks

Travelling Outside Dublin

One of the best ways to see the magnificent country-side around Dublin is by car. However, if you want to venture further out, travelling by train is probably quicker and more convenient. Ireland's national rail network is fast and efficient, and it also provides an ideal way to enjoy the country's dramatic landscape. There are also plenty of bus services and bus tours to towns and tourist destinations outside Dublin. Alternatively, you can tour the countryside on a bicycle, although a certain degree of fitness is advisable if you are going to tackle the beautiful Wicklow Mountains.

Bus Éireann also runs day trips to popular tourist destinations such as Glendalough and Powerscourt Gardens in Wicklow and Newgrange in County Meath.

Logos of popular car rental companies

TRAVELLING BY TRAIN

The train service in the Republic of Ireland is operated by **Irish Rail** (Iarnród Éireann). There are two main railway stations in Dublin. Connolly is close to the city centre (map F1) and has trains going to the north (Belfast), north-west (Sligo) and south (Wexford). Heuston Station is on St John's Road, about 20 minutes' walk southwest of the city centre, and serves destinations to the west (Mayo, Galway), south (Cork), southwest (Limerick) and southeast (Waterford) of Dublin. The Luas Red Line *(see back endpaper)* connects the two stations.

Most trains have both standard and premier (first-class) compartments. Bicycles can be taken on board for a supplement of between €2.50 and €8 one way, depending on distance travelled. Irish Rail often has promotional online fares for certain routes, so keep an eye on its website. Students in possession of a valid Student Travelcard *(see p165)* can also get discounts on train fares. Non-European residents can purchase a **Eurail** Pass that gives unlimited standard-class rail travel for five days within one month.

TRAVELLING BY COACH

The national bus network is operated by Bus Éireann *(see p175)*. Dublin's main bus station is Busáras *(see p174)*, which is served by the Luas Red Line. Bus Éireann and many private operators run buses to main destinations within Ireland from Busáras station.

Long-distance bus fares are usually much cheaper than the equivalent train fares, and travelling during the week tends to be less expensive than at weekends. Bus Éireann issues several types of tourist passes, such as the Open Road Pass, which allows unlimited travel on all Bus Éireann services for between 3 and 15 days; the Irish Rover Bus Only Pass, valid for travel on Bus Éireann and Ulsterbus services for between 3 and 15 days; and the Irish Explorer Bus/Rail Pass, for 8 days' bus and rail travel. Students get fare reductions.

DRIVING

If you wish to drive your own car while in Ireland, check your insurance to make sure you are fully covered. When driving in Ireland, always carry your certificate of motor insurance, proof of ownership of the car, vehicle registration document and driver's licence. If your licence does not include your photograph, carry your passport with you to validate the licence. Inform your insurer that you will be driving in Ireland.

Membership of a reputable breakdown service, such as the **Automobile Association** is advisable. Depending on the type of cover you have, breakdown organizations may offer only limited services in Ireland, so check before you travel. It is possible for non-members to join up only for the duration of their holiday.

If you are renting a car, make sure the insurance cover meets your needs. Car-hire companies in Ireland include all the major names, such as **Avis**, **Budget**, **Hertz**, **Europcar** and **Argus Rentals**.

RULES OF THE ROAD

Driving in Ireland is on the left-hand side of the road. For those unused to this, the most difficult aspect is getting accustomed to passing other vehicles on the right and giving way to traffic on the right at roundabouts. The wearing of safety belts is compulsory for both drivers

Platform of Heuston Station in Dublin

and passengers, whether they are sitting in the front or rear seats. All children must be secured with a suitable restraint system. Motorcyclists and their passengers are obliged by law to wear crash helmets. There is a strict law against drinking and driving. The legal limit for alcohol in your bloodstream whilst driving is below 0.08% and the Gardaí (police) often conduct random breath testing. It is also illegal to use a mobile phone while driving.

Most road signs in Ireland carry information in both Irish (Gaelic) and English. Most are in kilometres, although some older signs may still appear in miles. The sign "Yield" means "give way". Brown signs with white lettering indicate places of historic or cultural interest.

The maximum speed limits in Ireland, which are shown in kilometres, are: 50 km/h (30 mph) in towns, cities and

View of Drogheda, County Louth, on the east coast of Ireland

Junction ahead

Unprotected quay or river ahead

Dangerous bends ahead

Children or school ahead

built-up areas; 100 km/h (60 mph) on national roads and dual carriageways; and 120 km/h (70 mph) on motorways. On certain roads, which are marked, the speed limits are 60 km/h (40 mph) or 80 km/h (50 mph). Where there is no indication, the speed limit is 100 km/h (60 mph). Vehicles towing caravans (trailers) must not exceed 60 km/h (50 mph) on any road. On-the-spot speeding fines can be imposed.

eFlow is a barrier-free tolling system on the M50 motorway running around Dublin, between Junction 6 (N3) and Junction 7 (N4). You must pay this toll (€3 per car) by 8pm the following day. You can do so online, by phone or at a **Payzone** outlet.

There is also a toll of €1.70 per car on the East Link Bridge across the Liffey river. The Dublin Port Tunnel, which connects the M1 motorway (south of Dublin

Airport) to Dublin Port, costs €3 except at the following times, when it costs €10: between 6 and 10am Monday to Friday (southbound) and between 4 and 7pm Monday to Friday (northbound).

CYCLING

The quiet roads of Ireland help to make touring by bike a real joy. **Belfield Bike Shop** and **Cycleways** are good rental outlets in Dublin. The former also organizes cycling safaris around Ireland. If you are venturing further afield, local tourist offices will be able to give you the details of bicycle rentals in their area. You can often rent a bike in one town and drop it off at another for a small charge. You can also take a bike with you on the train. Many rental agents provide safety helmets, but bring your own waterproof clothing to help cope with the weather.

DIRECTORY

Street Finder Index

KEY TO THE STREET FINDER

■ Major sight	▣ Coach station	✝ Church
■ Place of interest	▤ Taxi rank	⊠ Post office
■ Railway station	P Main car park	═ Railway line
▣ DART station	ℹ Tourist information office	One-way street
🚊 Luas stop	✚ Hospital with casualty unit	Pedestrian street
🚌 Main bus stop	▣ Police station	

```
0 metres        200
0 yards         200          1:11,500
```

KEY TO STREET FINDER ABBREVIATIONS

Ave	Avenue	E	East	Pde	Parade	Sth	South
Br	Bridge	La	Lane	Pl	Place	Tce	Terrace
Cl	Close	Lr	Lower	Rd	Road	Up	Upper
Ct	Court	Nth	North	St	Street/Saint	W	West

General Index

Acknowledgments

Dorling Kindersley would like to thank the following people whose contributions and assistance have made the preparation of this book possible.

Main Contributor

Tim Perry, from Dungannon, County Tyrone, writes on travel and popular music for various publishers in North America and the British Isles. He was also a contributor to the *Eyewitness Travel Guide to Ireland.*

Additional Contributor

Yvonne Gordon.

Editorial and Design Assistance

Gillian Allan, Douglas Amrine, Lydia Baillie, Claire Baranowski, Des Berry, Tessa Bindloss, Jo Blackmore, Vivien Crump, Nicola Erdpresser, Fay Franklin, Annette Jacobs, Kathryn Lane, Nonie Luke, Therese McKenna, Caroline Mead, Ian Midson, Christina Park, Victoria Peel, Polly Phillimore, Rada Radojicic, Mani Ramaswamy, Lee Redmond, Sands Publishing Solutions, Andrew Sanger, Meredith Smith, Susana Smith, Rachel Symons.

Maps

Richie Toomey (ERA-Maptec Ltd, Dublin, Ireland) Map Co-ordinator David Pugh

Indexer

Hilary Bird.

Proofreader

Stewart Wild.

Additional Picture Research

Monica Allende, Brigitte Arora, Rachel Barber, Marta Bescos, Rhiannon Furbear, Anna Grapes, Ellen Root.

Additional Illustrations

Joy Fitzsimmons.

Additional Photography

Peter Anderson, Ian O'Leary, Rough Guides/Mark Thomas, Clive Streeter.

Special Assistance

Particular thanks to Niall Kennedy at Dublin Tourism for his invaluable help throughout this project. Thanks also to everyone at the National Museum, especially Dr Felicity Devlin, Damien Debarra and Aoife O'Shea, to Adrian le Harivel at the National Gallery, to Telecom Eireann and the General Post Office.

Photography Permissions

The Publisher would like to thank all those who gave permission to photograph at various cathedrals, churches, museums, restaurants, hotels, shops, galleries and other sights that are too numerous to list individually.

Picture Credits

a = above; b = below/bottom; c = centre; f = far; l = left; r = right; t = top.

The Publisher would like to thank the following individuals, companies and picture libraries for permission to reproduce their photographs:

AER LINGUS/AIRBUS INDUSTRIE: 172t; AKG LONDON: 14cb, 22c; ALAMY IMAGES. AA World Travel Library 9br; Caro/Sorge 167cla; David Sanger Photography 95bc; FMD Stock Photography 58bl; Peter Horree 92bl; irishphoto 93tr; JoeFoxDublin 168cla; Barry Mason 94bl; mediacolor's 137c; nagelestock.com 96bl; Profimedia International s.r.o./Alzbeta Bajgartova 92cl; Robert Harding Picture Library Ltd/G. Richardson 8cl; Neil Setchfield 95ca; Nico Smit 162–163l; Claude Thilbault 170br; Peter Titmuss 137tl, 170cl, 172br; AN POST, THE IRISH POST OFFICE: 170bl; AVIS BUDGET GROUP: 176tr; AXIS ARTS CENTRE: 158cb.

BORD FAILTE/IRISH TOURIST BOARD: 120tr, 120tl; Brian Lynch 19t, 29clb; BRUCE COLEMAN LTD: George McCarthy 112t.

CENTRAL BANK OF IRELAND: 169; CENTRAL CYBER CAFÉ, DUBLIN: Finbarr Clarkson 171br; CHESTER BEATTY LIBRARY, DUBLIN: 57l; COLLECTIONS: Image Ireland 26t, 85b; Slide File 30crb; CORBIS UK LTD: Bettmann/Reuters 19b; Julian Calder 9tr; Marco Cristofori 67tc; Destinations 116cl, 166cl; Jack Fields 136cl; Werner Forman 8tc; Hulton-Deutsch Collection 23t, 23crb; Library of Congress 22bl; National Gallery, London 22t.

DALKEY CASTLE & HERITAGE CENTRE: 97bc; DAVISON & ASSOCIATES LTD, IRELAND: 65cra; DUBLIN AIRPORT AUTHORITY: 172cla; DUBLIN MOUNTAINS PARTNERSHIP: 165tr; DUBLIN THEATRE FESTIVAL: 159tl; DUBLIN TOURISM IMAGE LIBRARY: 164tc; DRTA 2cl, 26bl, 26cl, 52, 175crb; Tony Pleavin 164bc, 164tc; DUNBRODY COUNTRY HOUSE HOTEL & RESTAURANT: 127bl.

EUROPCAR: 176cr; MARY EVANS PICTURE LIBRARY: 7c, 13c, 15c, 17tr, 31c, 57cl, 70b, 125c, 162c.

GUINNESS IRELAND LTD: 82bc, 82br, 83bl, 83tl, 83tr, 83br.

HERTZ: 176cra; HULTON GETTY: 18bc, 38bl, 99t.

THE IRISH ANTIQUE DEALERS FAIR: Louis O'Sullivan 28cr; THE IRISH PICTURE LIBRARY: 15t; IRISH RAIL (IARNROD EIREANN): 174crb, 176bl; IRISH TIMES: 114br.

JAROLD COLOUR PUBLICATIONS: 38bc; JCDECAUX IRELAND: 174cl, 175tc.

LAUGHTER LOUNGE: 155c.

MANSELL/TIME INC: 65bl.

HUGH MCKNIGHT PHOTOGRAPHY: 85t.

JOHN MURPHY: 104cb; JOHN MURRAY: 29c, 80c.

LILLIE'S BORDELLO: 154cr; LONELY PLANET IMAGES: Oliver Strewe 25crb.

THE MERMAID CAFÉ: 134bl; MORRISON HOTEL: 127tc.

Reproduction Courtesy of NATIONAL GALLERY OF IRELAND, DUBLIN: 61tr, 73b, 84cr, 108b; *Argenteuil Basin with a Single Sailboat* 1874, Claude Monet 51cl; For the Road, JB Yeats 48cl; *The Houseless Wanderer*, JH Foley 48tl; Pierrot, Juan Gris 48tr; *Judith with the Head of Holofernes*, Andrea Mantegna 49crb; *The Castle of Bentheim*, Jacob van Ruisdael 49c; *The Sick Call*, Matthew James Lawless 49b; *The Taking of Christ*, Caravaggio 49tr; *Convent Garden, Brittany*, c.1913, William John Leech, ©DACS, London 2011 50ca; *A View of Powerscourt Waterfall*, George Barret the Elder 50bl; *A Group of Cavalry in the Snow*, Ernest Meissonier 51tl; *Virgin and Child* c.1435–1440, Paolo Uccello 51cr; *Peasant Wedding*, Pieter Brueghel the Younger 51br; *Portrait of James Joyce*, Jacques Emile Blanche ©ADAGP, Paris and DACS, London 2011 72bl; NATIONAL MUSEUM OF IRELAND, DUBLIN: 21tl, 35crb, 44tr, 44cl, 44b, 45c, 45tr, 45bc, 45crb, 86clb, 87tl, 87cra, 87cr; NATIONAL LIBRARY OF IRELAND: 6/7, 12, 111t, 119t; NORTON ASSOCIATES: 54clb.

OFFICE OF PUBLIC WORKS, IRELAND: 120cl, 121cr, 121t, 122b; OLYMPIA THEATRE: Linda Farrelly 158cl.

PAPHOTOS: PA Archive/Niall Carson 8br; PHOTOSHOT/NHPA: Jean-Louis Le Moigne 96tr; POWERSCOURT ESTATE: 115tl; PUNCHSTOCK: Brand X Pictures 134c.

RETROGRAPH ARCHIVE LTD: Martin Ranicar-Breese 46c; REX FEATURES: 22b.

SAMSARA CAFE: 135tl; SHELBOURNE HOTEL, DUBLIN 95tr, 156tl; SINNOTT HOTELS: 126cra; SLIDE FILE: 18br, 19cl, 26crb, 27ca, 28cl, 28b, 29b, 62tl, 105c, 112cl, 112b, 118t, 122t, 154t; JENNIFER SMITH-MAYO: www.photographersdirect.com 155tl; STENA LINE: 173cr; STREET PERFORMANCE WORLD CHAMPIONSHIP: 154bc; CINDY STRUNZE: www.photographersdirect.com 97tr; THE SUGAR CLUB: 155br.

BROWN THOMAS: Kieran Harnett 34t; TIPPERARYPHOTOS.COM: 167cla, 167clb; TRINITY COLLEGE, DUBLIN:, 39cr, 40c, 40b, 40crb, 40cra; *The Marriage of Princess Aoite and the Earl of Pembroke*, Daniel Maclise 14t; TRIP ART DIRECTORS: 110c; ROD TUACH: www.photographersdirect.com 93bl.

VIKING SPLASH TOURS: 156bl.

WHELANS: 135bl.

Front Endpaper: DUBLIN TOURISM IMAGE LIBRARY: DRTA Lcl.

Pull-out Map Cover: ALAMY IMAGES: STOCKFOLIO 672

JACKET
Front – ALAMY IMAGES: STOCKFOLIO 672; Back – ALAMY IMAGES: Peter Titmuss clb, Ian Townsley tl; DORLING KINDERSLEY: Alan Williams cla; SUPERSTOCK: 1812197 bl. Spine – ALAMY IMAGES: STOCKFOLIO 672t.

All other images are © Dorling Kindersley. For further information see www.dkimages.com

---

SPECIAL EDITIONS OF DK TRAVEL GUIDES

DK Travel Guides can be purchased in bulk quantities at discounted prices for use in promotions or as premiums. We are also able to offer special editions and personalized jackets, corporate imprints, and excerpts from all of our books, tailored specifically to meet your own needs.

To find out more, please contact:
(in the United States) **SpecialSales@dk.com**
(in the UK) **TravelSpecialSales@uk.dk.com**
(in Canada) DK Special Sales at **general@tourmaline.ca**
(in Australia) **business.development@pearson.com.au**

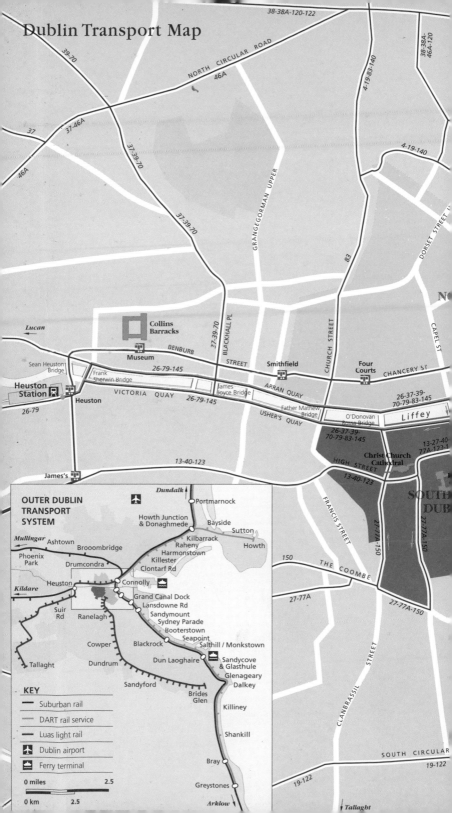

Dublin Transport Map

38-38A-120-122

NORTH CIRCULAR ROAD
46A

39-70

37

37-46A

37-39-70

38-38A-46A-120

4-19-83-140

4-19-140

46A

GRANGEGORMAN UPPER

83

DORSET STREET

CAPEL ST

N

Collins Barracks
Museum
BENBURB
37-39-70
BLACKHALL PL.
STREET
Smithfield
CHURCH STREET
Four Courts
CHANCERY ST

Sean Heuston Bridge
Frank Sherwin Bridge
26-79-145
James Joyce Bridge
ARRAN QUAY
26-37-39-70-79-83-145

Lucan

Heuston Station
Heuston
26-79
VICTORIA QUAY
26-79-145
Father Mathew Bridge
USHER'S QUAY
O'Donovan Rossa Bridge
Liffey
26-37-39-70-79-83-145

13-27-40-77A-122-1

13-40-123
Christ Church Cathedral
HIGH STREET
13-40-123
27-77A-150

James's

SOUTH DUB

OUTER DUBLIN TRANSPORT SYSTEM

Dundalk
Portmarnock

Mullingar Ashtown
Brooombridge
Howth Junction & Donaghmede
Bayside
Sutton
Kilbarrack
Raheny
Howth
Harmonstown
Killester
Clontarf Rd

Phoenix Park
Drumcondra

FRANCIS STREET

150

THE COOMBE

27-77A

27-77A-150

Kildare
Heuston
Connolly
Suir Rd
Ranelagh
Grand Canal Dock
Lansdowne Rd
Sandymount
Sydney Parade
Booterstown
Seapoint
Salthill / Monkstown
Cowper
Blackrock
Dundrum
Dun Laoghaire
Sandycove & Glasthule
Glenageary
Dalkey
Sandyford
Brides Glen
Killiney
Tallaght

CLANBRASSIL STREET

Shankill

SOUTH CIRCULAR

KEY

— Suburban rail
— DART rail service
— Luas light rail
✈ Dublin airport
⛴ Ferry terminal

Bray
19-122

0 miles   2.5
0 km   2.5

Greystones
Arklow
Tallaght
19-122